# IN DEFENSE OF THE FAITH

"I will confess you forever, for all that you have done; and I will endure for your name, for it is good before your saints" (Psalm 51.9).

*Moscow, Russian Historical Museum 129, MS Chludov Psalter (ninth cent.) fol. 51 v.*

# IN DEFENSE OF THE FAITH

## The Theology of Patriarch Nikephoros of Constantinople

**By**

**John Travis**

HELLENIC COLLEGE PRESS
Brookline, Massachusetts
1984

Financial assistance for the publication
of this book was generously provided by
the Taylor Foundation.


Published by HELLENIC COLLEGE PRESS
50 Goddard Avenue
Brookline, Massachusetts 02146


Printed in the United States of America

Cover design by Mary C. Vaporis

Library of Congress Cataloging in Publication Data

Travis, John.
In defense of the faith.

Bibliography: p.
Includes index.
1. Nicephorus, Saint, Patriarch of Constantinople.
I. Title.
BX395.N415T73 1984 230'.14'0924 84-504
ISBN 0-916586-96-0
ISBN 0-916586-97-9 (pbk.)

*To*
*my Parents*

# Contents

# *Foreword*

Very few scholars engaged in the study of Byzantine intellectual history have sufficient patience and dedication to undertake a systematic description of the entire theological worldview of an individual author. John Travis is presenting such a study on Patriarch Nikephoros, an eminent representative of the Byzantine Orthodox theological tradition during the latter episodes of the iconoclastic controversy.

The specific contribution of Nikephoros to the defense of images and their veneration has already been studied by the late Paul Alexander and, earlier, by A. J. Visser, and there is a third specialized monograph on his ecclesiology by O'Connell. What Travis adds to the achievements of his predecessors is the entire theological context of traditional Byzantine religious outlook, which allows us to understand the learned patriarch both as a man of his age and as a witness to tradition.

Future research on Nikephoros will have to concentrate on his still unpublished and, therefore, unutilized *Refutation* (*Ἔλεγχος καὶ ἀνατροπή*) of the iconoclastic synodal decree of 815, but the scholar, or scholars who will engage in this task will have the advantage of using the present comprehensive monograph, as a companion of their research. Fr. Travis should be highly commended for having achieved such a comprehensive compendium of information on an important theological personality of Orthodox Byzantium.

John Meyendorff

# *Acknowledgments*

The publication of this book is made possible by the faculty authorship grant of the Taylor Foundation, Greek Orthodox Archdiocese of North and South America.

I am grateful to these eminent scholars who contributed in a most important and generous way toward the completion of this work: the Right Reverend Dr. Demetrios Trakatellis, bishop of Vresthena, University of Athens; Professor Panagiotes Chrestou, Patriarchal Institute for Patristic Studies, Thessalonike; Professor Stephen Gero, Orientalisches Seminar, University of Tübingen; the late Reverend Professor Georges Florovsky, Princeton University; and Reverend Professor John Meyendorff, St. Vladimir's Theological Seminary. The latter's foreword is sincerely appreciated.

In particular, I wish to thank the Reverend Dr. N. Michael Vaporis, Dean of Hellenic College, for his editorial erudition and complete devotion since 1979 in improving my text and for making available the resources and facilities of the Hellenic College Press. The assistance given to me by my students, Elias Bouboutsis and Savas Zembillas, is also acknowledged.

Special appreciation must also be expressed to my parents and friends, as well as the president, dean, faculty, and students of Hellenic College/Holy Cross Greek Orthodox School of Theology for their prayers and encouragement. I am especially indebted to His Eminence Archbishop Iakovos, the great Orthodox leader of the Americas and spiritual father, who has paternally blessed my humble efforts to grow as a priest and theologian.

# Selected Bibliography With a List of Abbreviations

## NIKEPHOROS' WORKS

### Unpublished

*Elengchos* — *Ἔλεγχος καὶ ἀνατροπὴ τοῦ ἀθέσμου καὶ ἀορίστου καὶ ὄντως ψευδωνύμου ὅρου τοῦ ἐκτεθέντος παρὰ τῶν ἀποστατησάντων τῆς καθολικῆς καὶ ἀποστολικῆς ἐκκλησίας καὶ ἀλλοτρίῳ προσθεμένων φρονήματι ἐπ᾽ἀναιρέσει τῆς τοῦ Θεοῦ σωτηρίου οἰκονομίας*, Paris, Bibliothèque nationale, MS Coislinianus 93, fols. 1-185; MS Parisinus Graecus 1250, fols. 173-332.

### Published

*Antir.* 1,2,3 — *Ἀντίρρησις καὶ ἀνατροπὴ τῶν παρὰ τοῦ δυσσεβοῦς Μαμωνᾶ κατὰ τῆς σωτηρίου τοῦ Θεοῦ Λόγου σαρκώσεως ἀμαθῶς καὶ ἀθέως κενολογηθέντων ληρημάτων*, PG 100.205-534 (*Antir.* 1.205-328; 2.329-74; 3.375-534); the conclusion of *Antir.* 3, the patristic *florilegium*, is found in SS 1.336-70.

*Antir. Epiph.* — *Ἀντίρρησις καὶ ἀνασκευὴ τῶν Εὐσεβίου καὶ Ἐπιφανίδου λόγων τῶν κατὰ τῆς τοῦ Σωτῆρος ἡμῶν Χριστοῦ σαρκώσεως ληρωδηθέντων*, SS 1.371-503.

*Antir. Eus.* — Ibidem SS 4.292-380.

*Apol.* — *Τοῦ ὁσίου πατρὸς ἡμῶν Νικηφόρου πατριάρχου Κωνσταντινουπόλεως Ἀπολογητικὸς πρὸς τὴν καθολικὴν ἐκκλησίαν περὶ τοῦ κατὰ τῶν σεπτῶν εἰκόνων πάλιν νέου σχίσματος*, PG 100.833-50.

*Chaps. 12-Mai* — *Κεφάλαια ΙΒ. δι᾽ὧν ἐλέγχονται οἱ τῆς ἀποστασίας ἔξαρχοι, προσκόψαντες εἰς τὴν ἱερὰν ἡμῶν καὶ ἀμώμητον πίστιν, ἀνατρέποντες τὴν ἔνσαρκον καὶ σωτήριον οἰκονομίαν τοῦ δεσπότου Χριστοῦ καὶ Θεοῦ ἡμῶν· ὅθεν κατὰ τοὺς θείους κανόνας καὶ φιλευσεβεῖς νόμους, ἀλλότριοι τῆς ἁγίας τοῦ Θεοῦ καθολικῆς καὶ ἀποστολικῆς ἐκκλησίας τυγχάνουσι· καὶ ὡς οὐκ ἔξεστιν αὐτοῖς λαλεῖν οὔτε ἐπὶ ἐκκλησίας οὔτε ἐπὶ κοινοῦ καὶ δημώδους δικαστηρίου*, SR 152-56.

| | |
|---|---|
| *Chaps. 12-PK* | Ibidem, Papadopoulos-Kerameus, eds., *Ἀνάλεκτα ἱεροσολυμητικῆς σταχυολογίας* 1 (1891) 454-60. |
| *Epikr.* | *Ἐπίκρισις, ἤτοι διασάφησις τῶν οὐκ εὐαγῶς ἐκληφθεισῶν κατὰ τῶν ἱερῶν εἰκόνων χρήσεων, γενομένη παρὰ τῶν προεστώτων τοῦ ὀρθοῦ τῆς ἐκκλησίας δόγματος*, SS 1.302-35. |
| *Histor. syntomos* | *Ἱστορία σύντομος ἀπὸ τῆς Μαυρικίου Βασιλείας*, NOH 3-77. |
| *Letter* | *Letter to Pope Leo III*, PG 100.169-200. |
| *Logos* | *Λόγος ὑπὲρ τῆς ἀμωμήτου καὶ καθαρᾶς καὶ εἰλικρινοῦς ἡμῶν τῶν Χριστιανῶν πίστεως καὶ κατὰ τῶν δοξαζόντων εἰδώλοις προσκεκυνηκέναι*, PG 100.533-831. |
| *Prol.* | *Κατὰ τῶν ἀσεβῶς τετολμηκότων εἴδωλον ὀνομάσαι τὸ θεῖον ὁμοίωμα, καὶ ὅτι δεῖ ἕπεσθαι ταῖς πατρικαῖς παραδόσεσιν, ἔτι δὲ καὶ τὶ ἔστι γραπτὸν καὶ περιγραπτόν, καὶ πῶς νοητέον τὸ οὐ ποιήσεις πᾶν ὁμοίωμα, ἀνασκευή τε τῶν δησσεβῶς εἰσληφθεισῶν πατρικῶν ῥήσεων παρὰ τῶν τῆς ἐκκλησίας ἐχθρῶν*, SS 233-91; an alternative title is given under MS Coislinianus 93 and MS Parisinus Graecus 1250: *Πρόλογος καὶ ἀνατροπὴ τῶν δι'ἐναντίας χρήσεων*. |

## OTHER SOURCES, WORKS, AND PERIODICALS

| | |
|---|---|
| Alexander, "Council" | Paul J. Alexander, "The Iconoclastic Council of St. Sophia (815) and its Definition (Horos)," DOP 7 (1953) 37-65. |
| Alexander, *Nikephoros* | _________ *The Patriarch Nicephorus of Constantinople:* Ecclesiastical Policy and Image Worship in the Byzantine Empire (Oxford, 1958). |
| Anastos, "Ethical Theory" | Milton V. Anastos, "The Ethical Theory of Images Formulated by the Iconoclasts in 754 and 815," DOP 8 (1954) 151-60. |
| Anastos, Argument" | _________ "The Argument for Iconoclasm as Presented by the Iconoclastic Council of 754," Late Classical and Medieval Studies in Honor of A. M. Friend, Jr., ed. Weitzmann and Kurt (Princeton, 1955) 177-88. |
| Anastos, "Iconoclasm" | _________ "Iconoclasm and Imperial Rule 717-842," CMH 4.1.61-104. |
| Androutsos, *Dogmatike* | Christos Androutsos, *Δογματικὴ τῆς Ὀρθοδόξου Ἀνατολικῆς ἐκκλησίας* (Athens, 1907). |

| | |
|---|---|
| Beck, "Church" | Hans-Georg Beck, "The Greek Church in the Epoch of Iconoclasm," *Handbook of Church History*, eds. Hubert Jedin and John Dolan, 12 vols. (New York, 1965–), vol. 3: *The Church in the Age of Feudalism*, ed. Friedrich Kempf et al., trans. Anselm Biggs, pp. 26-53. |
| Blake, "Note" | Robert P. Blake, "Note sur l'activité littéraire de Nicéphore Ier Patriarche de Constantinople," *Byzantion. Revue Internationale des Études Byzantines* 14 (1939) 1-15. |
| Bonis, *Eisagoge* | Konstantinos G. Bonis, *Εἰσαγωγὴ εἰς τὴν Ἑλληνικὴν Χριστιανικὴν γραμματείαν μέχρι τοῦ θ. αἰῶνος: Κατὰ τὰς παραδόσεις τοῦ τακτικοῦ καθηγητοῦ τῆς Θεολογικῆς Σχολῆς τοῦ Πανεπιστημίου Ἀθηνῶν Κωνστ. Γ. Μπόνη* (Athens, 1968). |
| BZ | *Byzantinische Zeitschrift* (1892–). |
| CMH | J. B. Bury, gen. ed., *The Cambridge Medieval History*, 5 vols., 2d ed. (Cambridge, 1957-67), vol. 4: *The Byzantine Empire*, pt. 1: "Byzantium and Its Neighbours"; pt. 2: "Government, Church and Civilization," edited by J. M. Hussey, D. M. Nicol, and G. Cowan. |
| Constantelos, *Philanthropy* | Demetrios J. Constantelos, *Byzantine Philanthropy and Social Welfare*, Rutgers Byzantine Series (New Brunswick, N.J., 1968). |
| Crafer, *Apokritikos* | T. W. Crafer, trans. *The Apocriticus of Macarius Magnes* in Translations of Christian Literature, ser. 1: Greek texts, gen. eds. W. J. Sparrow Simpson and W. K. Lowther Clarke (London, 1919). |
| de Boor, NOH | Carolus de Boor ed., *Nicephori Archiepiscopi Constantinopolitani Opuscula Historica, accedit Ignatii Diaconi Vita Nicephori*, Bibliotheca Scriptorum Graecorum et Romanorum (Leipzig, 1880). |
| DOP | *Dumbarton Oaks Papers* (Cambridge, Mass., 1941–). |
| FC | Roy Defarrari, gen. ed., *The Fathers of the Church: A New Translation*, 67 vols. (New York, 1947-74). |
| Florovsky, "Origin" | Georges Florovsky, "Origen, Eusebius, and the Iconoclastic Controversy," *Church History* 19 (1950) 77-96. |
| Florovsky, *Review* | __________ Review of *The Patriarch Nicephorus of Constantinople: Ecclesiastical Policy and Image Worship in the Byzantine Empire*, by Paul J. Alexander *Church History* 28 (1959) 205. |

| | |
|---|---|
| Florovsky, "Function" | _________ "The Function of Tradition in the Ancient Church," GOTR 9 (1963); repr., *Bible*, pp. 74-85. |
| Florovsky, *Bible* | _________ *Bible, Church, Tradition: An Eastern Orthodox View*, 1 (Belmont, Mass., 1972). |
| Gero, *Leo III* | Stephen Gero, *Byzantine Iconoclasm During the Reign of Leo III: With particular attention to the oriental sources*, Corpus Scriptorum Christianorum Orientalium, vol. 346; subsidia 41 (Louvain, 1973). |
| Gero, "Notes" | _________ "Notes on Byzantine Iconoclasm in the Eighth Century," *Byzantion* 44 (1974) 23-42. |
| Gero, "Doctrine" | _________ "The Eucharistic Doctrine of the Byzantine Iconoclasts and its Sources," BZ 68 (March 1975) 4-22. |
| Gero, *Constantine V* | _________*Byzantine Iconoclasm During the Reign of Constantine V: With particular attention to the oriental sources*, Corpus Scriptorum Christiana Analecta, vol. 384; subsidia 52 (Louvain, 1977). |
| Giannopoulos, "Didaskalia" | B. N. Giannopoulos, «Ἡ περὶ ἀγγέλων διδασκαλία τοῦ πατριάρχου καὶ ὁμολογητοῦ Νικηφόρου Α. (†829),» *Theologia* 44 (1973) 312-38. |
| GOTR | *The Greek Orthodox Theological Review* (Brookline, Mass., 1954–). |
| Grumel, "Douze Chapitres" | V. Grumel, "Les 'Douze Chapitres contre les Iconomaques' de Saint Nicéphore de Constantinople," *Revue des Études Byzantines* 17 (1959) 127-35. |
| Hardy, *Christology* | Edward Rochie Hardy and Cyril C. Richardson, eds., *Christology of the Later Fathers*, vol. 3 in LCC (Philadelphia, 1954). |
| Hennephof, *Textus* | Herman Hennephof, ed., *Textus Byzantinos ad Iconomachiam Pertinentes, in usum academicum*, Byzantina Neerlandica, ser. A: *Textus*, fasc. 1 (Leiden, 1969). |
| Ignatios, *Life* | Ignatios Diakonos, *Βίος τοῦ ἐν ἁγίοις πατρὸς ἡμῶν Νικηφόρου, ἀρχιεπισκόπου Κωνσταντινουπόλεως καὶ νέας Ῥώμης* in de Boor, NOH 139-217. |
| Jaeger, *Theology* | Werner Jaeger, *The Theology of the Early Greek Philosophers: The Gifford Lectures 1936*, trans. Edward S. Robinson (1947; Oxford paperbacks, London, 1967). |
| Jenkins, "Social Life" | R. J. H. Jenkins, "Social Life in the Byzantine Empire," in CMH 4.2.78-103. |
| John Damascene, *Ekd. pisteos* | John Damascene, *Ἔκδοσις ἀκριβὴς τῆς ὀρθοδόξου πίστεως*, PG 94.789-1228. |

| | |
|---|---|
| Karmiris, *Synopsis* | John Karmiris, *Σύνοψις τῆς δογματικῆς διδασκαλίας τῆς Ὀρθοδόξου Καθολικῆς Ἐκκλησίας* (Athens, 1960); trans. by George Dimopoulos (Scranton, Pa., 1973). |
| Karmiris, *Ekklesia* | ________ *Ἡ περὶ Ἐκκλησίας Ὀρθόδοξος δογματικὴ διδασκαλία* (Athens, 1964; repr. in THE, 1964 ed. s.v. "Ἐκκλησία"). |
| Karmiris, *Mnemeia* | ________ *Τὰ δογματικὰ καὶ συμβολικὰ μνημεῖα τῆς Ὀρθοδόξου Καθολικῆς Ἐκκλησίας* (*Dogmatica et Symbolica Monumenta Orthodoxae Catholicae Ecclesiae*), 2 vols., 2d ed. rev. and enl., vol. 1 (Athens, 1960), vol. 2 (Graz, 1968). |
| Kitzinger, "Cult" | Ernst Kitzinger, "The Cult of Images in the Age Before Iconoclasm," DOP 8 (1954) 83-150. |
| Koch, "Christusikone" | Lukas P. Koch, "Zur Theologie der Christusikone," *Benediktinische Monatschrift: Zur Pflege Religiösen und Geistigen Lebens* 19 (1937) 375-87; 20 (1938) 32-47,168-75,281-88,437-52. |
| Ladner, "Image" | Gerhart B. Ladner, "The Concept of the Image in the Greek Fathers and the Byzantine Iconoclastic Controversy," DOP 7 (1953) 1-34. |
| LCC | John Baillie; John T. McNeill; Henry P. Van Dusen, gen. eds., *The Library of Christian Classics*, 26 vols. (Philadelphia, 1953-66). |
| LCL | *Loeb Classical Library*, vols. 1– (Cambridge, Mass., 1912.). |
| Mai, SR | A. Mai, *Spicilegium Romanum*, vol. 10: *Synodus Cpolitana, Constantius Diaconus, Severus Ant., Leontius, Nicephorus Patr., Nicolaus I. Patr., Photius ad Armenius, et Minora Alia. Poggii Epistolarum Centuria et Oratio* (Rome, 1844). |
| Martin, *Controversy* | Edward James Martin, *A History of the Iconoclastic Controversy* (London [1930]). |
| MEE | *Μεγάλη Ἑλληνικὴ Ἐγκυκλοπαιδεία*, 24 vols., 4 vols. supps., 2d ed. (Athens, 1926-57). |
| Meyendorff, *Theology* | John Meyendorff, *Byzantine Theology: Historical Trends and Doctrinal Themes* (New York, 1974). |
| Meyendorff, *Christ* | ________ *Christ in Eastern Christian Thought*, 2d ed. (New York, 1975). |
| *Mikron Euchologion* | *Μικρὸν Εὐχολόγιον ἢ Ἁγιασματάριον* (Athens, 1956). |

Nissiotis, "Doctrine" — Nikos A. Nissiotis, "The Importance of the Doctrine of the Trinity for Church Life and Theology," in *Orthodox Ethos*, pp. 32-69.

NPNF — Philip Schaff and Henry Wace eds., *A Select Library of Nicene and Post-Nicene Fathers of the Christian Church*, 2d ser., 14 vols. (New York, 1890-1900).

O'Connell, *Ecclesiology* — Patrick O'Connell, *The Ecclesiology of St. Nicephoros I (758-828) Patriarch of Constantinople: Pentarchy and Primacy*, Orientalia Christiana Analecta, 194 (Rome, 1972).

*Orthodox Ethos* — Angelo J. Philippou, ed., *The Orthodox Ethos: Essays in honour of the centenary of the Greek Orthodox Archdiocese of North and South America*, Studies in Orthodoxy, vol. 1 (Oxford, 1964).

OS — *Ostkirchliche Studien* (1952–).

Ostrogorsky, "Epistemological Foundations" — George Ostrogorsky, "Gnoseologičeskija osnovy vizantijskago spora o sv. ikonad" [The epistemological foundations of the Byzantine controversy on the holy images], *Seminarium Kondakovianum* 2 (1928) 47-52.

Ostrogorsky, *Studien* — _________ *Studien zur Geschichte des byzantinischen Bilderstreites*, Historische Untersuchungen, pt. 5 (Breslau, 1929; repr., Amsterdam, 1964).

Ostrogorsky, *History* — _________ *History of the Byzantine State*, trans. Joan Hussey with a forward by Peter Charanis, Rutgers Byzantine Series, new rev. ed. (New Brunswick, N.J., 1969).

Oulton, *Eusebios* — J. E. L. Oulton, trans., *Eusebius, The Ecclesiastical History*, 2 vols., LCC (London, 1932; repr., Cambridge, Mass., 1964-65).

Ouspensky, *Theology* — Leonide Ouspensky, *Theology of the Icon*, trans. Elizabeth Meyendorff (Crestwood, N.Y., 1978).

Ouspensky-Lossky, *Icons* — Leonid Ouspensky and Vladimir Lossky, *The Meaning of Icons*, trans. G. E. H. Palmer and E. Kadloubovsky, forward by Titus Burckhardt (Boston, 1952).

G. Papadopoulos, *Symbolai* — Georgios I. Papadopoulos, *Συμβολαὶ εἰς τὴν ἱστορίαν τῆς παρ'ἡμῖν ἐκκλησιαστικῆς μουσικῆς: Καὶ οἱ ἀπὸ τῶν ἀποστολικῶν χρόνων ἄχρι τῶν ἡμερῶν ἡμῶν ἀκμάσαντες ἐπιφανέστεροι μελῳδοί, ὑμνογράφοι, μουσικοὶ καὶ μουσικολόγοι* (Athens, 1890).

N. Papadopoulos, *Leitourgia* — Nikolaos P. Papadopoulos, ed., *Ἡ Θεία Λειτουργία: Περιέχουσα τὸν ἑσπερινόν, τὸν ὄρθρον, τὴν προσκομιδήν, τὰς τρεῖς λειτουργίας Ἰωάννου τοῦ Χρυσοστόμου,*

| | |
|---|---|
| | *Βασιλείου τοῦ Μεγάλου καὶ τῶν προηγιασμένων, ὡς καὶ πολλὰ ἄλλα χρήσιμα εἰς τοὺς ἱερεῖς καὶ διακόνους*, new ed. G. Kariophilli (Athens, n.d.). |
| *Papers and Minutes* | John S. Romanides, Paul Verghese, and Nick A. Nissiotis, eds., *Unofficial Consultation between Theologians of Eastern Orthodox and Oriental Churches (August 11-15, 1964): Papers and Minutes* in GOTR 10 (Winter, 1964-65). |
| *Pedalion* | *Πηδάλιον τῆς νοητῆς νηὸς τῆς μιᾶς ἁγίας καθολικῆς καὶ ἀποστολικῆς τῶν Ὀρθοδόξων ἐκκλησίας: Ἤτοι ἅπαντες οἱ ἱεροὶ καὶ θεῖοι κανόνες τῶν ἁγίων πανευφήμων ἀποστόλων τῶν ἁγίων οἰκουμενικῶν τε καὶ τοπικῶν συνόδων καὶ τῶν κατὰ μέρος θείων πατέρων, κτλ.*, ed. Agapios Hieromonk and Nicodemos the Monk, 3d ed. of Sergius H. Raftanis (Zante, 1864; 7th repr., Athens, 1970). |
| Percival, *Councils* | Henry R. Percival, ed., *The Seven Ecumenical Councils of the Undivided Church: Their canons and dogmatic decrees, together with the canons of all the local synods which have received ecumenical acceptance*, vol. 14 in NPNF (1899; repr., Grand Rapids, Mich., 1977). |
| PG | J. P. Migne, ed., *Patrologia cursus completus*, ser. graeca, 161 vols. (Paris, 1857-66). |
| Philippou, "Mystery" | Angelo Philippou, "The Mystery of Pentecost," in *Orthodox Ethos*, pp. 70-97. |
| Pitra, SS | J. B. Pitra, ed., *Spicilegium Solesmense complectens Sanctorum Patrum Scriptorumque Ecclesiasticorum Anecdota hactenus Opera, etc.* 4 vols. (Paris, 1852-58). |
| Romanides, "Cyril" | John S. Romanides, "St. Cyril's 'One Physis or Hypostasis of God the Logos Incarnate' and Chalcedon," *Papers and Minutes*, pp. 82-102. |
| Schmemann, "Byzantium" | Alexander Schmemann, "Byzantium, Iconoclasm and the Monks," SVSQ 3 (Fall, 1959) 18-34. |
| Schönborn, *L'Icône* | Christoph von Schönborn, *L'Icône du Christ: Fondements théologiques élaborés entres le Ier et le IIer Concile de Nicée (325-787)* (Fribourg, 1976). |
| Sideris, "Position" | Theodore Sideris, "The Theological Position of the Iconophiles during the Iconoclastic Controversy," SVSQ 17 (1973) 210-26. |
| Siotis, "Eucharistia" | Markos A. Siotis, «Θεία Εὐχαριστία: Αἱ περὶ τῆς θείας εὐχαριστίας πληροφορίαι τῆς Καινῆς Διαθήκης ὑπὸ τὸ |

| | |
|---|---|
| | φῶς τῆς ἐκκλησιαστικῆς ἑρμηνείας,» *Ἐπιστημονικὴ Ἐπετηρὶς τῆς Θεολογικῆς Σχολῆς Ἀριστοτέλειον Πανεπιστήμιον Θεσσαλονίκης* 2 (1957) 153-223. |
| Stephanides, *Historia* | Basileios K. Stephanides, *Ἐκκλησιαστικὴ Ἱστορία: Ἀπ' ἀρχῆς μέχρι σήμερον*, 2d ed., rev. and enl. (Athens, 1959). |
| SVSQ | *St. Vladimir's Seminary Quarterly* (Crestwood, N.Y., 1952–). |
| *Synaxarion* | *Συναξάριον τῆς Ἐκκλησίας Κωνσταντινουπόλεως* in *Propylaeum ad AA. SS. Novembris*, ed. H. Delehaye (Brussels, 1902). |
| THE | *Θρησκευτικὴ καὶ Ἠθικὴ Ἐγκυκλοπαιδεία*, 12 vols. (Athens, 1962-68). |
| Theodorou, *Theologia* | Andreas Theodorou, *Ἡ Θεολογία τοῦ Ἰουστίνου, φιλοσόφου καὶ μάρτυρος, καὶ αἱ σχέσεις αὐτῆς πρὸς τὴν ἑλληνικὴν φιλοσοφίαν* (Athens, 1960). |
| Travis, "Nikephoros" | John Travis, "The Role of Patriarch Nicephorus (A.D. 758-828), Archbishop of Constantinople, in the Iconoclastic Controversy," (Th.D. dissertation, The Iliff School of Theology, 1977). |
| Travis, "Art Object" | ________ "The Art Object: An Image in Plato's Philosophy," (Ph.D. dissertation, University of Colorado, 1981). |
| Trembelas, *Dogmatike* | Panagiotes N. Trembelas, *Δογματικὴ τῆς Ὀρθοδόξου Καθολικῆς Ἐκκλησίας*, 3 vols. (Athens, 1959-61). |
| Visser, *Nikephoros* | A. J. Visser, *Nikephoros und der Bilderstreit: Eine Untersuchung über die Stellung des Konstantinopeler Patriarchen Nikephoros innerhalb der ikonoklastischen Wirren* (The Hague, 1952). |

# *Introduction*

Past historians tended to describe the iconoclastic controversy negatively as "perhaps the darkest age of Europe within historical times."[1] Particularly misleading were statements superficially describing iconoclasm as "in itself of little importance intellectually," and claiming that "intellectual curiosity was practically dead. On the orthodox side there is scarcely a sign of it."[2] These generalizations were based upon the uncritical premise that "Byzantium was supposed to have been spiritually dead and exhausted long before the Iconoclastic Controversy arose, and the conflict itself was merely a symptom of sterility of the Byzantine Church."[3]

With renewed interest in this historical period these 'absolute' statements fortunately have been abandoned. The truth of the matter is that the iconoclastic controversy raging for more than a century (726-843)

> was undoubtedly one of the major conflicts in the history of the Christian Church. It was not just a Byzantine conflict; the West was also involved in the dispute.... In the history of the Christian East it was...a turning point. All levels of life were affected by the struggle. The fight was violent, bitter, and desparate.[4]

Iconoclasm was a complex phenomenon. Events based upon social, political, economic, cultural, and religious factors often interacted in such a way as to form a matrix of conflicting determinants even within the same group of consenting individuals. The antinomies of each personality were frightfully real: the victor against Islam, Leo III, was the pioneer of iconoclasm; the orthodox Studite monk, Theodore, was also the war hawk; the military genius, Constantine V, was at the same time the iconoclastic theologian.

Recognizing that the complexity of the crisis also must include an understanding of the ecclesiastical forces at work, recent scholars have attempted to recover the theological setting of the controversy. As a doctrinal issue, the religious question of whether to retain images became the dominant theme which characterized the age of crisis. Their research of this period has been directed increasingly toward examining the historical personages whose literary achievements cannot be overlooked.[5] Concerned with Byzantine intellectual thought after the seventh century, recent publications have dispelled as anachronistic the assumption that the last puff of orthodox vitality was consummated with John Damascene, considered as the last Greek father of the Church.

This study acknowledges the direction taken by modern scholarship, and emphasizes that a recovery of the theology of the period through its historical personalities is needed before an inclusive historical synthesis is seriously attempted.[6] One such personage who has left a rich literary legacy is Patriarch Nikephoros, archbishop of Constantinople (A.D. 758-828). His importance as a theologian and polemicist in the iconoclastic controversy has only recently been recognized.[7] Unfortunately, he has been little read; there are no reliable translations of the edited texts, themselves sorely uncritical, into any modern European language; "there is no real advance in the interpretation of the documentary evidence";[8] and, finally, to our knowledge, there is no monograph on the theology of Nikephoros which includes his teachings on issues other than the veneration of icons.[9] This work attempts to fill this need by working from Nikephoros' own texts.

With the exception of the *Letter*, *Apology* (*Apologetikos*), and *Verification* (*Epikrisis*) all of the patriarch's known theological works fall within the period of his exile. His literary legacy has bequethed to its modern readers problems not uncommon in other Byzantine sources: sheer bulk of material, repetitious expression, a concentration of corollary postulates interwoven within dependent clauses which obfuscate the main argument, and grammatical corrections of an editorial nature. These problems, compounded by Nikephoros' own method of presentation which defies a 'scientific' taxonomy of topics, have made it difficult to sort out the particulars of Nikephorian theology.

A theological basis representative of his acumen as a theological polemicist, however, can be presented from the following published texts: *Letter*, *Apologetikos*, *Epikrisis*, *Logos*, *Refutation* (*Antirresis*) *1*, *2*, *3*, *Refutation against Eusebios* (*Antirresis Eusebiou*), *Refutation against Epiphanides* (*Antirresis Epihanidou*), and *Chapters 12*.[10] In addition to the patriarch's main concern, the theology of icons, other theological topics appear, making their inclusion for study equally justifiable and essential. All these, as presented by Nikephoros, comprise an articulation of theological truths, namely, a defense of the faith.

Complying with the freedom afforded by orthodox tradition concerning theological methodology, which in no way intends to assume finality, we can consider Nikephoros' theology under these chapter headings: God, world: creation and creator, angels, aesthetics, man, Christ, mission and salvation, church, sacraments, tradition: its place, role, and twofold expression; written tradition, unwritten tradition, the individual, and eschatology. Before a reconstruction of his theology is possible, it will be helpful to see the iconophile within the historical context of the iconoclastic controversy.

## NOTES

1. J. B. Bury, *History of the Later Roman Empire*, 2 vols. (London, 1889), 1,337.
2. Martin, *Controversy*, pp. 3,4.
3. Florovsky, "Origen," p. 78.
4. Ibid., p. 77.
5. Of mention are Alexander, *Nikephoros*; Visser, *Nikephoros*; O'Connell, *Ecclesiology*; Travis, "Nikephoros"; Gero, *Leo III*; idem, *Constantine V*; and Paul Speck, *Kaiser Konstantine VI: Die Legitimation einer fremden und der Versuch einer eigenen Herrschaft. Quellenkritische Darstellung von 25 Jahren byzantinischer Geschichte nach dem ersten Ikonoklasmus,* vol. 1: *Untersuchung;* vol. 2: *Anmerkungen und Register* (Munich, 1978).
6. See Florovsky, "Origen," p. 80.
7. That Nikephoros is "a mighty exponent of the Greek genius" is a characterization given early in this century by I. Andreev, as a "Notation," in the *Russian Historical Journal* 7 (1921) 215-18, and later cited by Florovsky, "Origen," p. 79. Correspondence with Florovsky reiterated that an examination of Nikephoros' theology is "utterly important" (31 August 1973).
8. Florovsky, *Review*, p. 205.
9. Alexander, *Nikephoros*, p. 157. Nikephoros' ecclesiology and christology is examined summarily in only eleven pages without substantive documentary evidence by Visser, *Nikephoros*, pp. 97-108. Schönborn in *L'Icône*, pp. 203-17, drawing from Nikephoros' writings, reconstructs the patriarch's notion of image.
10. See list of abbreviations for the complete Greek titles and bibliographical entries. The works, as listed, follow the chronological order as examined by Alexander, *Nikephoros*, pp. 162-88, with the exception of *Chaps. 12* which, according to Grumel's investigations, belongs to the winter or spring of 821; "Douze Chapitres," pp. 127-35. The latter was not studied by either Alexander or his mentor, Blake. The *Prologue and refutation* (*Prologos kai anatrope*) chronologically preceeds *Chaps. 12*. Even though scholars have consulted this work, they agree that when published it could make an even greater contribution toward understanding the second period of iconoclasm.

# 1

# *Patriarch Nikephoros*

The paucity of biographical data makes any assessment of a historical personage less than conclusive. The following account is no exception. While there is no separate autobiographical account, which undoubtedly would serve as a valuable source, biographical facts can be derived from Nikephoros' biographer, Ignatios; Nikephoros' own writings; and scattered references of the period.[1]

Ignatios was a contemporary of both Tarasios and Nikephoros. According to Suidas' entry, Ignatios was a deacon and *skeuophylax* of the Cathedral of Hagia Sophia, in charge of everything pertaining to the divine service, before becoming metropolitan of Nikaia.[2] Despite excessive rhetoric, a characteristic of Byzantine hagiographers, and the consonant iconophilism between biographer and his subject, Ignatios has presented a surprisingly objective narrative of Nikephoros' life. The *Life* is an important source of biographical information.[3]

The other biographical source, Nikephoros' writings, does not contain additional data; rather, it provides more or less reflective information. In his account there emerges an introspective personal profile derived from his own reflection as he addresses various theological problems. Based on these two sources, Nikephoros' life may be divided into three periods, as: a layman, a patriarch, and a martyr in exile.

## NIKEPHOROS THE LAYMAN

Nikephoros was born in Constantinople during the reign of Constantine V.[4] He came from an aristocratic family which was attached to the service of the imperial government. The date of his birth is not mentioned by Ignatios. Based on Alexander's research of the *Collection* (*Synaxarion tes Ekklesias Konstantinoupoleos*), however, there is no reason for not placing Nikephoros' birth around 758.[5]

The birth of Nikephoros coincided with a brewing storm of persecution which began soon after the iconoclastic Synod of Hieria (754). It reached its climax with the martyrdom of Stephen the Younger (November 765), abbot of the monastery of Mount Auxentios in Chalkedon, and included Nikephoros' father, Theodore. Serving as imperial secretary, Theodore was removed from office and banished to distant Pontos. In spite of threats and tortures, and even promptings from Constantine V, Nikephoros' father remained true to iconophilism. After a second exile Theodore died under the greatest physical hardships.[6]

His father's martyrdom and his mother's constant vigilance left a permanent impression upon the young Nikephoros which was to remain with him the rest of his life.[7] The descriptions found in his theological writings repeatedly mention the cruel persecution of those earlier days. Even though written near the end of his life, the narrative is frightfully vivid.

Ignatios provides no additional information concerning Nikephoros' personal experiences as a child and student before the year 775. He does present, however, a brief outline of the educational curriculum of the day, which, as Alexander characterizes, "reads like the ἀνακεφαλαίωσις (or list of chapter headings) of an elementary handbook of logic and physics."[8]

The first mention of general education was when Nikephoros assumed the post of imperial secretary around 775. It can also be assumed that he continued his education at the imperial court under the tutelage of an elementary schoolmaster (*grammatistes*). His training during these early years must have been heavily secular. This included the study of grammar, poetry, and rhetoric, advancing to astronomy, geometry, music, and arithmetic with the completion of philosophy.[9]

At what point Nikephoros learned his theology remains unclear. Even though the religious part of his general education emphasized singing the psalms,[10] reciting from the lives of the saints, and memorizing biblical and patristic passages, it can be assumed that Nikephoros' theological training must have occurred later during his years at the monastery.[11] Also, it is most likely that his theological knowledge increased during his patriarchate and exile, especially after he assumed the role of a dogmatically-competent polemicist. As his writings indicate, he was familiar with the theological arguments of John Damascene.[12]

Another unresolved issue is Nikephoros' rise to the office of the imperial secretariate. This is especially problematic since his appointment in 775 was sanctioned by either Constantine V or Leo IV, both iconoclasts. The mild tone displayed toward these iconoclastic rulers—a far cry from what a fiery iconophile's description might contain—found in Nikephoros' first known work, *Brief History* (*Historia syntomos*),[13] substantiates the view held by Alexander, that from 775 to the Seventh Ecumenical Synod "Nicephorus adopted an attitude more diplomatic than bold."[14]

His boldness appeared at the Synod of Nikaia in 787. Ignatios' description of Nikephoros' activities and the account recorded in the acts of the synod, which identifies him as the imperial spokesman (*basilikos mandator*), indicates the scope of Nikephoros' responsibilities at Nikaia.[15] His duties included reading a letter from Pope Hadrian, but most important, reading a declaration of orthodoxy which represented the views of his imperial masters, Constantine VI and Irene.

Nikephoros recorded his impressions as a participant of the synod later in his theological writings. He insisted, for example, that the correctness of patristic teaching as found in the writings of the church fathers, and the sanctity of the synod be preserved by both dissident factions, iconophiles and iconoclasts, alike.[16] From 787, then, Nikephoros appeared openly as a spokesman of orthodoxy, of the conciliatory brand represented by Patriarch Tarasios. It is difficult to define the hierarch's influence upon the young Nikephoros. That there was an influence cannot be disputed. Nikephoros served under Tarasios when the latter was secretary, and after 784, patriarch.

A complete turn occurred in Nikephoros' life when he abandoned his secular career of twenty years (775-97) to retreat into monasticism. Likening him to Elijah, prophet of the wilderness, Ignatios writes that Nikephoros retired to an isolated mountain, establishing his eremitic habitation. Eventually he turned to cenobitic life and founded the monastery of Ta Agathou.[17]

His reasons for espousing monasticism cannot be explained with absolute certitude. Alexander's comment that "Nicephorus' departure was not a flight into monastic life, but either a retreat which was meant to be temporary, or the consequence of political disgrace"[18] needs clarification. Many supporters of imperial-male succession were dissatisfied with the ascension of Irene as 'emperor' of Byzantium in 797, considering her involvement in the blinding of her son. It is during this transitional shift of power that Nikephoros retired from court life. There is, however, no evidence showing that Nikephoros was forced to depart, even if he supported Constantine VI. In fact, his writings give no indication of any political overtones suggesting political disgrace. To be sure, Nikephoros' departure was not because of politics. The second point made by Alexander must also be dismissed. That the retreat into monastic life was meant to be temporary, simply is not in keeping with the assumptions of monasticism: the path to salvation is not temporary, or—to state it affirmatively—it is forever.

What is more plausible is that Nikephoros' departure, indeed, was a flight into monastic life. Ignatios' account repeats a familiar metaphor in orthodox thought. The retreat into monasticism and the monk's struggle to gain the eternal prize of salvation is similiar in duration and intensity to the physical training of a good athlete.[19] The importance of this metaphor is missed by Alexander who advises his readers "to look through the curtain of holiness with which Nikephorus himself and the hagiographer have surrounded the events."[20] On the contrary, Ignatios' biographical panoply of 'holiness' is consonant with the traditional practice of many fathers of the Church. They felt the need to renew themselves spiritually through sustained asceticism, which only monasticism could offer. Without denying political considerations, one must also recognize the spiritual value that a Byzantine placed upon his soul. The gaining of eternal gifts was for him a most basic and intensely personal commitment. It follows that the flight into monastic solitude was for Nikephoros a narrow path which he felt religiously and personally bound to assume.

It was not much later, between 802-06, under the insistence of Nikephoros I and probably the influence of Patriarch Tarasios, that Nikephoros accepted the administrative responsibility of the largest poorhouse in Constantinople.[21] His social task, as described by Ignatios, assumed an ecclesiastical character.[22]

Trying to identify which office Nikephoros held is difficult because Ignatios does not specify it. A distinction exists between the *orphanotrophos*, who was in charge of the orphanage, and the *ptochotrophos*, director of the poorhouse.[23] In Byzantium, even though the poorhouses, hospitals, and orphanages were left to the care of the Church, they still remained under the financial control of the State and were often richly endowed by the emperors. The *orphanotrophos*, moreover, was an imperial appointee.[24] Whichever office he held, this was to be Nikephoros' stepping-stone for his election to the patriarchate in 806, immediately following the death of his predecessor, Tarasios.

## NIKEPHOROS THE PATRIARCH

The election to the patriarchate normally was accomplished in two steps: the election, where the emperor often effectively intervened, and the ordination. The activity of the emperor at any given time depended upon the balance of interests between Church and State, and this was no exception in Nikephoros' case. Since the Studites refused to consider a layman as a candidate, they naturally did not nominate Nikephoros. In fact, no one could agree on a choice.[25] The emperor, finally, resolved the dilemma by naming his namesake to the patriarchal throne. On 5 April 806 the candidate was tonsured a monk,[26] on the ninth ordained a deacon, followed by the tenth, Good Friday, a presbyter, and as bishop on Easter Sunday.[27] So, in spite of Studite non-support, the former imperial secretary and ascetic, by becoming patriarch of Constantinople, stood between the strongly-independent emperor and the equally powerful monastic Studite faction.

Nikephoros' nine year tenure (806-15) as patriarch witnessed the political vicissitudes of three imperial masters: Nikephoros I (802-11); Michael I Rangabe (811-13); and Leo V (813-20). His reaction to the issues was dictated by the wider politics of imperial policy toward the Church and ecclesiastical, particularly monastic, reaction against it. At stake was the testing of the delicate interdependence (*synallelia*) between Church and State. In background and temperament Nikephoros was Tarasios' disciple, and consequently, an advocate of moderate policy. His experience as imperial secretary naturally must have brought him closer to the emperor. This cannot be interpreted as a weakness, but rather as a conciliatory effort. What is true—and this is essential—is that as intense partisan politics receded into the background to surrender to the theological issue of images, especially with the new outbreak of iconoclasm under Leo V, the moderate Nikephoros assumed more initiative and turned to a committed radical position.

During the reign of Emperor Nikephoros I (802-11), the patriarch had little influence on political affairs. The prohibition by the emperor of the customary enthronement letter (*synodikon*) attests to this.[28] It was a prevailing hierarchal custom for a newly-elected patriarch to write letters of enthronement to the pope and to the three other patriarchs. The reason for this prohibition lies in the hostile attitude of Nikephoros I toward the West which was directed not only at the Carolingian Empire but also at the papacy. This hostility was probably further aggravated by the Studites. Already displeased with the emperor's cancellation of tax remissions to the monasteries and his revival of the 'moechian' (adultery) controversy in January 809, these extremists would use the pope as an irritant, mocking imperial authority by overriding emperor and even patriarch, claiming that the pope alone represented the authority of the Church, knowing, nonetheless, that he was too far to impose limitations upon them, even if he wished to do so.

All this changed after 811 when the political status of the patriarch greatly increased as imperial policy changed also. In 812, under Michael Rangabe, Nikephoros sent the letter to Pope Leo III. The patriarch now was free to state that Emperor Nikephoros prevented him from sending it any sooner: "Let it rather be known...that the authority's harsh and implacable policy prevailed, [thus] hindering us to do what was traditionally proper."[29] With Michael easily controlled by the Studites, the isolationist policy which the empire experienced earlier was completely reversed. More importantly, by taking the position that the coronation was imposed on the pope by Charlemagne, Nikephoros espoused a policy whereby the Byzantines could renew their relations with the papacy once again.

There is no doubt that Nikephoros sided with the group which favored Michael Rangabe. His refusal to support the legitimate heir, Staurakios, while insisting upon an affirmation of orthodoxy at the coronation ceremony of Michael and promising protection of all monastic orders, should be understood as consistent with his policy to reconcile extremists of both factions. The patriarch now becomes the protector of both secular clergy and monastic orders, while at the same time overriding court intrigue between Staurakios and his wife, Theophano. This reversal of loyalty has yet to be examined by specialists of iconoclasm.

During Michael Rangabe's reign (811-13), the patriarch had greater freedom than under Nikephoros I, but this was gradually undermined by the Studites. The excommunication of Joseph, abbot of the monastery Ta Kathara, the re-establishment of peaceful relations with the papacy, and the offensive in the Balkans, illustrate Michael's acceptance of the Studites' advice.

The Studites' interference with State policy-making decisions, however, divided the empire along partisan political lines and led to disastrous consequences. Against Michael I and Nikephoros, who together sued for peace and urged the acceptance of negotiations with Krum, Theodore Studites and his zealous followers insisted upon a vigorous prosecution of war. The Studite policy toward Byzantium's bitter enemy to the North prevailed, but the consequence was the ignominious defeat of the imperial army at Versinicia near Adrianople in June 813. What complicated the incident was that half of the Byzantine army, assembled for battle, refused to fight. This was the Anatolikon theme, the old bulwark of iconoclastic support. By July of the same year, Michael had abdicated. His short reign of two years prepared the way for a change of policy and the end of Studite supremacy.

The patriarch once again assumed the role of kingmaker. In view of his earlier involvement with Michael, this comes as no surprise. The patriarch openly accepted Michael's abdication and supported the ascendancy of Leo V Armenian (813-20), the general of the Anatolikon. The extent of Nikephoros' role and Theodore Studites' cooperation, has not been adequately established.[30]

Leo V, an otherwise administratively competent ruler, soon thereafter revealed his iconoclastic colors.[31] The new emperor, modeling himself after Leo III and Constantine V, pursued an intense program of iconoclastic revival. A justification for this reversal of policy, as stated by Anastos, could be that Leo V "was convinced that the iconoclastic policy of Leo and Constantine was pleasing in the sight of God and accounted for their success in warfare, and that the military failures of the 'orthodox' Emperors like Irene, Constantine VI, Nikephorus I and Michael I were proof of divine disapproval of the images."[32]

The empire, in fact, under Leo V enjoyed peace from the Bulgars as well as the Arabs. With Krum's sudden death in April 814, the offensive against Constantinople was averted by a thirty-year peace treaty between Omurtag, his son, and the imperial government. With internal dissension experienced in the caliphate after the death of Harun ar Rashid (809), the Arabs also proved no threat to Byzantium. Consequently, the years between 813-15 witnessed a deterioration of the patriarch's power. As imperial pressure intensified, so the breach between emperor and patriarch increased.

What contributed to the radical change in the patriarch's activity? As the revival once again assumed a character of harsh religious reform, political allegiances, which had churchmen on opposing political sides regardless of doctrinal agreement—a phenomenon characteristic under the iconophile emperors—receded. The struggle, as in the time of Constantine V, assumed the character of a theological war of nerves. What had divided the Studites and the secular clergy before was quickly forgotten. Once again the principle of Church autonomy concerning ecclesiastical matters was at stake. Supporting this principle, the Studites allied themselves with Patriarch Nikephoros in common cause against the emperor. Each exerted pressure to gain supremacy over the other. Attempts of Leo V to persuade the secular clergy to endorse the *florilegium*, a list of patristic quotations which favored iconoclasm, met with increased resistance from orthodox circles.[33] In turn, the patriarch not only organized resistance—and here the Studites united with him— but, also, launched a literary barrage. Nikephoros' two earliest theological works, *Apologetikos* and *Epikrisis,* appeared during this period.[34]

By taking the initiative in appointing members to his committee, among them an Armenian compatriot, John Grammatikos, Leo from the beginning had isolated Nikephoros. What is recorded in the *Life* as a theological debate between the emperor and patriarch on Christmas Day 814, gives the impression that neither party was ready to concede, and, in fact, reconciliation was out of the question. It was again a test of imperial assertion, understood as increased prerogatives to the disgrace of the Church.[35]

This time there was an irreparable open breach. The emperor moved to influence his court to accept his iconoclastic views. Despite the patriarch's appeal to Empress Theodosia, and to several other officials including the imperial secretary Eutychianos, an iconoclast, Leo forcefully pursued his iconoclastic policy.

Events quickly worsened for the hierarch. He had become completely isolated, even from his clergy, who either had been persecuted by Leo or had joined the ranks of the iconoclasts. Serious illness became the catalyst for his enemies to remove him from office. The prospect of remaining in office, only if he too accepted iconoclasm, was inacceptable to Nikephoros. The illicit resident synod read the accusations. Arousing an angry mob, the iconoclasts even attempted murder. On the first day of Lent, 1 April 815, Patriarch Nikephoros resigned. The sick hierarch was carried upon a cot across the Bosphoros, never to return to Constantinople.[36]

## NIKEPHOROS THE MARTYR IN EXILE

Soon after Nikephoros' resignation, Leo convened the iconoclastic Synod of Hagia Sophia in 815. Under the emperor's puppet, Patriarch Theodotos, the synod repudiated the decisions of the Seventh Ecumenical Synod of 787 and recognized as valid the acts of the previous Synod of Hieria (754).[37] A cruel persecution of iconophiles followed. As the persecution raged outside of the confines of Constantinople, many of the 'secular' clergy became confessors of the faith, but many abbots became iconoclasts. The latter brought down upon themselves the wrath of both Theodore and Nikephoros.

Because of his activity as a vigorous proponent of icon veneration, Theodore Studites also suffered imprisonment and, finally, exile. A common allegiance was shared now between these two former political adversaries. One fact remained certain. The Studites under Theodore, as well as the pope and other patriarchs, still considered Nikephoros the legitimate patriarch of Constantinople. Toward the end of Theodore's life (d. 826), a belated conciliatory attitude was cemented between Studites and secular iconophile clergy, as described by Theodore himself: "Now is the time for concord, now is the time for mutual suffering."[38]

From the monastery of Ta Agathou, Nikephoros was deported to the monastery of the martyr Theodore. His plight was no better under Michael II, the founder of the Amorian Dynasty (820-29). Seizing power after the murder of Leo V on Christmas Day 820, Michael II continued the iconoclastic policy of the Isaurians. Less fanatic than his predecessor, he stopped the persecution. But his insensitivity to the theological question of the images resulted in neither recognizing the Seventh Ecumenical Synod nor the iconoclastic synod. His inflexibility was clearly evident in approving the nomination of Antony, bishop of Sylaion, who had collaborated earlier with John Grammatikos in drafting the acts of 815, to succeed Theodotos, instead of recalling Nikephoros to the patriarchate.

Under these circumstances, Nikephoros, refusing offers from the emperor to return to Constantinople provided that he kept silent concerning the problem of images, remained in exile, suffering all its bitterness. Unlike Theodore, whose correspondence extended even to the pope, the martyr in exile refrained from becoming involved in ecclesiastical matters, which could have entailed potentially explosive, political repercussions.

Nikephoros, instead, turned to a literary refutation of iconoclasm. His works indicate a program governed by sustained argumentation against the heterodoxy of Constantine V and the definition with its appended *florilegium* of the Synod of Hagia Sophia. Nikephoros, as Alexander suggests,

> seems to have felt that his enforced abdication had delivered him from responsibilities which he had always loathed and that he could be of greater help to his cause by laying the theological and philosophical foundations for the future restoration of image-worship for which he hoped and prayed.[39]

Indeed, the patriarch might have entertained the notion that his work would serve as the groundwork for a future orthodox synod. If this is the case, Nikephoros' significance lies more within this period of exile, rather than in the preceding period as a hierarch actively in office. For the history of Byzantine intellectual thought, then, his contribution cannot be underestimated.

With his untimely death on Easter Sunday 828, Nikephoros' dream for the restoration of the images was not yet realized.[40] The iconophiles had to endure another fifteen years of persecution under Theophilos until, finally, on 11 March 843, the issue of icon veneration was resolved.

Not until the restoration of the icons became a reality did attention turn toward the iconophile martyrs of the past generation. Under the initiative of Patriarch Methodios (843-47), the body of Patriarch Nikephoros, martyr in exile, was taken to Constantinople, and on 13 March 847 in solemn rites was placed in the Church of the Holy Apostles. A final tribute is preserved by the *synaxaristes*, who eulogized this event in a characteristic Byzantine play on names: "As the city [of Constantinople] accepts your saintly body which was lead in victorious entry, O Nikephoros, so it celebrates this holiday of victory."[41]

## AN ASSESSMENT

An examination of Nikephoros within the historical context of the iconoclastic crisis has shown him to have been a vibrant personality whose struggle was just as much within himself as with the circumstances surrounding his life. The experiences which Nikephoros had as a layman, patriarch, and a martyr in exile markedly influenced his theological writings.

Character is always difficult to define. It has been stated by Aristotle that "to what point and to what extent a man must deviate before he becomes blameworthy it is not easy to determine by reasoning, any more than anything else that is perceived by the senses; such things depend on particular facts, and the decision rests with perception."[42] Whether Nikephoros is to be criticized for acting one way, instead of another, relevant to the circumstances surrounding his office (were they beyond his control?), is an assessment which should not imply a position of neutrality on his part. Rather, a fair critique must rest upon a principle of involvement. For Nikephoros, this meant a policy of moderation where concessions could be made to extremists of both imperial and ecclesiastical factions, and which, when principles of faith were involved, included resistance.

A successful statesman, defined as one who significantly 'moves' history, often tends to be less moderate than innovative and dramatic in his moves. Patriarch Nikephoros was neither of the latter. Whether he should be censured for not resembling a Photios, in view of the circumstances surrounding his tenure in office, is perhaps arbitrarily uncritical.

Neither should his policy of moderation be evaluated as a weakness. Alexander harshly characterizes the moderation of the patriarch:

> During his conduct in the patriarchal office, these positive sides of his personality [faith, education, scholarly inclinations, experience in the imperial and ecclesiastical administration] were offset by a flaw, the weakness of his character. If Nicephorus' career is reviewed, it is found that only rarely did he act on his own initiative.[43]

As noted, it is difficult to describe a moderate, like Nikephoros, in terms of a leader with innovative and self-determinate qualities. Moderation, certainly, does not imply no position at all, for this would be an absence of character. Moderation—to draw from Aristotelian ethics—is a position which calls for an equilibrium between excess and deficiency. The merit of character lies not in judgments of weakness or strength, but rather, in the aiming of a relative mean which is easy to miss and difficult to hit. The 'moechian' scandal, as it was called, suffices to illustrate that moderation is not necessarily a weakness in character.

The patriarch is seen as a moderate choosing the lesser of two evils: an assertive Emperor Nikephoros I or Studite discontent. The scandal began in September 795. By divorcing his wife and marrying his mistress, Theodote, Constantine VI was bitterly criticized for committing adultery by Plato, abbot of the monastery of Sakkoudion, and his nephew Theodore Studites. The controversy reached its peak when Tarasios consented to the emperor's wishes and allowed a priest named Joseph to bless the marriage. This consent alienated the 'secular' clergy, who were under the leadership of the patriarch, from the monks.

In January 809, Emperor Nikephoros called a synod to recognize the marriage of Constantine VI with Theodote. Whether or not the emperor was interested in clarifying the finer distinctions of marriage as prescribed by canon law was really not the point. Rather, the controversy became an excuse to test the legal boundaries of imperial authority. Ostrogorsky's appraisal of Nikephoros' action in reviving "the moechian controversy in order to demonstrate that the Emperor was not bound by canons,"[44] clearly confirms that he was, as Anastos states, "a strong ruler and zealous exponent of Byzantine absolutism."[45]

The incident prompted open criticism from the Studite monks, who accused Patriarch Nikephoros, as they did earlier his predecessor Tarasios, of not using stronger measures of opposition. This action could be interpreted as a weakness in character especially when contrasted to the patriarch's confirmation of the excommunication of Joseph later in 809 under Michael, a decision which favored the Studites and placated the extremists.

In the former situation the patriarch was not acting of his own free will, but was obeying orders. The political situation under Nikephoros I could have proved to be more than delicate. Joseph's reinstatement perhaps was a reward from the emperor for the abbot's role in liquidating a bloodless coup of Bardanes Tourkos (803), in which case the problem was decided above the patriarch's authority.[46] If the hierarch's stance appears to be, as Bonis suggests, "very lenient toward Emperor Nikephoros I,"[47] this hardly proves that he was weak in character.

The patriarch defends his inability to act more positively under Nikephoros by recalling in his *synodikon* to Pope Leo III many years later (812) that "it is not easy to oppose the reigning powers [who are in office], who are carried away by their own wishes and strive to fulfill all their desires."[48] Unlike Theodore Studites, Nikephoros could not afford to act with complete disregard of these factors.

Patriarch Nikephoros' lot, then, was in many ways typical of a Byzantine prelate, as described by Alexander, "highly educated, passionately interested in theological issues, obedient to the wishes of his imperial masters, yet determined to suffer martyrdom rather than condone attacks on Christian faith and dogma."[49] A moderate patriarch who is not afraid to commit himself when the orthodox faith is at stake is an example of strong character. It is precisely these moments of life which count. This degree of involvement, exemplified throughout his life and crystallized during his years of exile, is the standard by which Nikephoros' actions can be measured by the Church. Because of his contribution both as an orthodox polemicist and as a martyr in exile, Nikephoros continues to remind and inspire the faithful, who in turn honor him as a saint. His memory is celebrated on 2 June, and also, 13 March; the latter is the commemoration of the transfer of his relics to Constantinople.

## NOTES

1. Ignatios, *Life*, pp. 139-217. Two contemporary scholars have utilized this work as a primary source for the life of Nikephoros: the more complete account by Alexander, *Nikephoros*, and the other by Visser, *Nikephoros*. For the patriarch's writings, see above,

pp. i-ii. Other biographical data is found in Theodore Studites, *Letters* 1-2, PG 99.903-1679; *Synaxarion*; and Photios, *Letters* 1-3, PG 102.585-990. Biographical essays not listed by Alexander in *Nikephoros*, p. 54, are MEE, s.v. "Νικηφόρος, Πατριάρχης Κωνσταντινουπόλεως," by Philaretos Vapheides; THE, s.v. "Νικηφόρος ὁ Α.' Πατριάρχης Κωνσταντινουπόλεως"; and Bonis, *Eisagoge*, pp. 96-98.

2. DeBoor in NOH, p. 138, records that Suidas also mentions that Ignatios was a *grammatikos*, which Visser, *Nikephoros*, p. 50, interprets to mean a position synonymous with "a professor of philology."

3. The 'golden age' of hagiography extended from the iconoclastic period to the tenth century. Not only the *Life*, but also, other *Lives* of Tarasios, Theodore Studites, Stephen the Younger, and Gregory Dekapolites were circulating; see Franz Dölger, "Byzantine Literature" in CMH 4, pt. 2,224-25. Visser, *Nikephoros*, p. 49, describes the *Life* as "a typical Byzantine biography of a saint."

4. Ignatios, *Life*, p. 142.

5. Alexander, *Nikephoros*, p. 54; cf. *Synaxarion* 725.12.

6. The second banishment is mentioned in *Synaxarion* 723, as well as in *Life*, p. 143.

7. Nikephoros' mother, Eudokia, witnessed her son's career in court as well as in the Church. Accordingly, Nikephoros "paid her due respect throughout her life"; Alexander, *Nikephoros*, p. 56. Cf. Theodore Studites, *Letters* 2.18.1174. Nikephoros' brothers also are mentioned by Theodore, ibid. 1173.

8. Alexander, *Nikephoros*, p. 57, n. 3.

9. Ignatios, *Life*, p. 144. The difference between a *grammatistes* and a *grammatikos* is analogous to our distinction between an elementary school teacher and a scholar; see above, n. 2; also Alexander, *Nikephoros*, pp. 149-50.

10. "He tuned the musical lyre, but not that of Pythagoras of Samos, or the impostor Aristoxenos, but rather the one with one hundred and fifty strings (i.e. the psalter)"; Ignatios, *Life*, p. 150, trans. Alexander, *Nikephoros*, p. 57.

11. Ignatios, *Life*, p. 148. Steven Runciman in *Byzantine Civilization* (London, 1933), p. 180, incorrectly suggests that Nikephoros "went to a Church seminary" to continue his education.

12. Alexander, *Nikephoros*, p. 59; Visser, *Nikephoros*, p. 99.

13. *Histor. syntomos*, covering the years 602-769, i.e. from the murder of Emperor Maurikios to the marriage of Leo Khazar to Irene, was written soon after the death of Constantine V. A. Ehrhard places the dates between 775-97; *Kirchenlexikon*, 2d ed., s.v. "'Nikephoros,' Wetzer und Welte." For other arguments of dating and manuscript tradition, see Alexander, *Nikephoros*, pp. 157-62.

14. Alexander, *Nikephoros*, p. 59.

15. "He was entrusted with the imperial heraldship over that holy assembly by virtue of which he delivered the purity of the faith as a message to all; he cried out and made plain the ancient representation and worship of the holy images as if speaking from a place commanding a wide view; thereby he became the colleague of the holy assembly even before (he donned) the sacred garment"; Ignatios, *Life*, p. 146, trans. Alexander, *Nikephoros*, p. 60.

16. *Apol.* 846-48.

17. Ignatios, *Life*, pp. 144,147,201. It is incorrect to assume that he was tonsured a monk at this time, rather than before his elevation to the patriarchate; see below, p. 16, n. 26.

18. Alexander, *Nikephoros*, p. 63.

19. Ignatios, *Life*, p. 144.

20. Alexander, *Nikephoros*, p. 63.

21. Constantelos in *Philanthropy*, p. 265, reflects an opposite view; namely, that Nikephoros "had been forced by the iconoclastic party to administer the 'very great *pto-*

*cheion*' before he was elected to patriarch."

22. Ignatios, *Life*, p. 152. According to Canon 8 of the Synod of Chalkedon, *ptochotrophos* was an ecclesiastical office.

23. Constantelos' comment in *Philanthropy*, p. 265: "there is no reason to identify this *ptocheion* with the Great Orphanage," fails to do justice to Alexander's distinction in *Nikephoros*, p. 64: "but an orphanage is different from a poorhouse." Alexander does not attempt to identify Nikephoros with either office. On the other hand, Constantelos' account (pp. 265-66) of the second known poorhouse in Byzantium, located near the Church of SS. Archippos and Philemon in the Galata section of the capital, probably can be identified with "the great poorhouse (*tou megistou ptocheiou*)," as described by Ignatios, *Life*, p. 152.

24. W. Ensslin, "The Government and Administration of the Byzantine Empire," in CMH 4, pt. 2,26. For the origins and foundations of the *ptocheia*, see Constantelos, *Philanthropy*, pp. 257-69.

25. The Studites preferred one from their own circle, possibly Theodore. Theodore's ignorance as to who was a proper candidate, as he himself expressed in *Ἐπιτάφιος εἰς Πλάτωνα τὸν ἑαυτοῦ πνευματικὸν πατέρα* 34, PG 99.837, substantiates the view in *Life*, p. 154, which characterized the impasse felt by the synod in choosing a candidate who would be acceptable to all.

26. "Τῆς οὖν θείας ἐπ'αὐτῷ τελετῆς τοῦ μοναχοῦ προβάσης"; *Life*, p. 157.

27. For a detailed description of the enthronment service, see ibid., pp. 157-58.

28. One such letter has survived, *Letter to Pope Leo III*. The term *synodikon* is often applied to it, because like a creedal document ratified by members of a synod, it is "a chancery document rather than a literary work"; Alexander, *Nikephoros*, p. 163. It contains biographical information, customary formulas of hierarchical protocol, and ends with a long creed; the format follows what any other patriarch would have written.

29. *Letter* 197.

30. For the period between the defeat at Versinicia to Michael's abdication, see an interesting account based upon a report found in a letter of Pope Leo III to Charlemagne dated 25 November 813, in *Monumenta Germaniae Historica Epistolae Karolini Aevi* 5.8.99, quoted in Alexander, *Nikephoros*, pp. 78-80.

31. Ignatios, *Life*, p. 164, states that as Nikephoros was placing the coronation crown upon Leo, it seemed as if the patriarch was touching thorns, and as a result, confessed that he felt a fierce pain.

32. Anastos, "Iconoclasm," p. 99.

33. Alexander is cautious in identifying the *florilegium* compiled by the committee with the *florilegium* attached after the definition of the Synod of Hagia Sophia. With some omissions and additions the latter, however, is representative of the labors of Leo's committee; see Alexander, *Nikephoros*, pp. 127-28.

34. *Apol.* 833-50; and *Epikr.* 302-35.

35. *Life*, p. 167. An intense debate between two iconophile bishops and Leo is preserved in the *Life of Niketas* cited by Alexander in *Nikephoros*, p. 131, which illustrates this battle between Church and State: "Emilianos, bishop of Kyzikos said: 'If as you said this is a Church inquiry, O emperor, let it be inquired into in the Church as is the custom, for from old and from the beginning Church inquiries are inquired into in Church, and not in the imperial palace.' 'But I too,' says the emperor, 'am a son of the Church, and as a mediator I shall listen to both parties and after a comparison of the two I shall determine the truth.' To this there answered Michael bishop of Synnada, 'If you are a mediator, why do you not do the job of a mediator? (I say this) because the one side you shelter in the palace and even assemble and encourage, even giving them permission to teach their impious doctrines; whereas the other side does not dare to utter a sound even on the streets and crouches down

everywhere before your decrees. This is characteristic not of mediation but of dictation.'"

36. Ignatios, *Life*, pp. 190-97.

37. For a fuller discussion of this synod, see Alexander "Council," pp. 37-65; for a conflicting viewpoint, see Anastos, "Ethical Theory," pp. 153-60.

38. *Letter* 2.127.1412.

39. *Nikephoros*, p. 228.

40. Ignatios, *Life*, p. 213. According to *Synaxarion* 725, after completing his seventieth year, Nikephoros died. Thus, nine years of his life were spent in the capital as patriarch and another thirteen years in exile.

41. This literary device is lost in translation: "Νίκης ἑορτὴν ἡ πόλις Νικηφόρε, δοχὴν ἄγει σου λειψάνου νικηφόρου"; Georgios G. Gegle, ed., *Μηναῖα. Περιέχον: Ἅπασαν τὴν ἀνήκουσαν αὐτῷ ἀκολουθίαν μετὰ τῆς προσθήκης τοῦ τυπικοῦ κατ'ἀρχαίαν μὲν νεωστὶ δὲ τυπωθεῖσαν διάταξιν τῆς Ἁγίας τοῦ Χριστοῦ Μεγάλης Ἐκκλησίας*, 12 vols. (Athens, n.d.), vol. 3: *Μηναῖον τοῦ Μαρτίου*, p. 78 (hereafter *Menaia* cited by particular month).

42. *Nicomachean Ethics* 2.9.19-23. Hereafter translated Aristotelian passages will be cited from Richard McKeon ed., *The Basic Works of Aristotle* (New York, 1941), and will follow the standard pagination in Bekker's edition of Aristotle's Greek text.

43. *Nikephoros*, p. 225.

44. *History*, p. 187.

45. "Iconoclasm," p. 91.

46. See Alexander, *Nikephoros*, p. 87.

47. *Eisagoge*, p. 96.

48. *Letter* 197.

49. *Nikephoros*, pp. 229-30.

# 2

# *God*

Three themes constitute Nikephoros' treatment of God: the trinitarian dogma, the existence of God and knowledge of God's essence, and the divine attributes.

## THE TRINITARIAN DOGMA

As other fathers before him had done, Patriarch Nikephoros theologizes about God in trinitarian terms. Even though his discussion of the Trinity is tempered by the cause of his day, namely, icon veneration which only with the iconoclastic controversy had become a doctrinal issue,[1] it remains an example of orthodox patristic formulation. When considering the existence of God, the knowledge of God's essence, and the divine attributes, as understood within the hypostatic union of the Trinity, Nikephoros works from a basis which accepts that the question of God is the basic theological question, and ontology is neither static nor unapproachable. It follows that essence (God's being *qua* being) is seen in light of existence, of God's self-revelation in the reality of life. As Nissiotis states, "The grace of God in His revelation...is given directly by God Himself, through His life acting in three Persons, as an immediate reality without any human limitation. Man cannot know God unless God has known him."[2] Underlying Nikephoros' statements is the irrefutable truth that the reality of the Triune God is revealed in scripture and tradition, formulated in the Nicene-Constantinopolitan Creed (325-81), expounded by the fathers of the Church, and intimately experienced by the faithful community in its liturgical worship. The teaching of the one Triune God is a continuous assertion which expresses itself within the common conscience of the Church.

Nikephoros presents two professions of faith in *Letter* and *Logos* which deal specifically with the doctrine of the Trinity. In expression and style they are consonant with earlier formulations, particularly those of Gregory of Nyssa and Gregory the Theologian (Nazianzos). Like those of John Damascene and Tarasios, the patriarch's account is directly and patently expressed. He says only as much as is necessary concerning the Trinity, and then proceeds to christological concerns, wherein the second person is more elaborately described. This sense of urgency is seen especially in *Logos* where creedal pronouncements of the Trinity are expressed in a liturgical style reminiscent of the *anaphora* of Basil's liturgy. These creedal affirmations introduce what is really to occupy Nikephoros' attention, the incarnation of the Logos.

## THE EXISTENCE OF GOD AND KNOWLEDGE OF GOD'S ESSENCE

The existence of God for Nikephoros is an irrefutable fact: "I confess to believe in one God Father almighty, creator of all [things], ruler and lord."[3] "Concerning the great, most divine and sublime mystery of God's wisdom," God's essence remains a deep and unfathomable mystery.[4] Man's knowledge of God is relative and partial. Reason, moreover, prefers to remain speechless and silent before the Triune God.[5] The patriarch cites Romans 11.33: "O the depth of the riches both of the wisdom and knowledge of God! How unsearchable are his judgments, and his ways past finding out!"[6]

## THE DIVINE ATTRIBUTES

Using the language of divine attributes, Nikephoros asserts something about God's nature. As John Damascene states, these "declare not His nature, but attributes of that nature."[7] Undoubtedly, the patriarch considered the limitation of speaking about God in terms of divine attributes. They are neither essential nor real distinctions. If they were, they would differentiate the nature of God, which is simple. Neither are they subjective and universal concepts having no objective reference to God.[8]

Nikephoros presents two classes of attributes: concerning God's essence and God in relation to the world. The latter will be discussed under "world: creation and creator." The first class is divided into "essential attributes (*ousiode idiomata*)" and "personal attributes (*prosopika idiomata*)."[9] The latter pertains to each person of the Trinity. The former is common to the three persons viewed as one divine essence and nature.

This twofold distinction of attributes referring to God's essence is important for an orthodox understanding of the hypostatic union of the Trinity. Borrowing Gregory the Theologian's phraseology: "One, therefore, in three is the godhead, and the three are one," Nikephoros' distinction, "one godhead [divinity] in the three [persons]," establishes the unity and sameness of the divine essence. Because of this unity, all three persons have the same essential attributes. It follows that they act with one will and in cooperation. The Trinity "is recognized in identical-purpose and will, singular power and operation."[10]

The second distinction, "three hypostases in the one godhead," is as fundamental as the former. The Trinity refers to the three persons, Father, Son, and Holy Spirit, and their specific activities. The difference between the hypostases is characterized by their personal attributes: "The unbegottenness and cause of all things which pertain to the Father, the birth to the Son, and the procession to the Holy Spirit."[11]

It follows that Nikephoros accepts the difference between the hypostases, and at the same time their unity of essence in the one Triune God. He rejects the monarchianism of Arianism, which distinguishes the divine essence into "greater or smaller," and Sabellianism, which blurs the real distinctions between the three persons.[12] Nikephoros does not attempt to theologize further on the nature of *perichoresis*; namely, how each person is in the other without being combined or co-mingled, united without confusion in the one Triune nature.

Two lists of essential attributes are found in his writings which characterize the unity (oneness) of God's essence. *Logos* states: "Having no beginning, unseen, incomprehensible, unalterable, without end."[13] The second, more comprehensive and earlier, list is in *Letter*:

> Trinity consubstantial, super-essential, unseen, incomprehensible, indivisible, unalterable, simple and without parts and uncompounded, without dimension, always the same, incorporeal, without quality, unquantitative, equal in honor, glory and divinity; non-tactual and non-palpable, without shape, infinitely good, light eternally shining, thrice-shining, absolute light, always in that manner and having those attributes.[14]

Unlike John Damascene, the patriarch does not discuss these attributes further. Nor do his lists compare in all respects with Damascene's.[15] Nikephoros' polemical intent to relate these attributes with his discussion on circumscription could explain the listing of these but not other attributes.[16] These essential attributes prove that God is uncircumscribable, inasmuch as he cannot be defined in the dimensional categories of time, place, or quality.

As to the personal attributes of each hypostasis which characterize its respective activity, Nikephoros presents the following. God the Father is understood as the cause of creation and the power which brought all things from nothingness into being. Our knowledge of the Father is through the Son, and by his grace we are knowledgeable of the Trinity.[17]

God the Son is often referred to in relation to the first person of the Trinity. The Son's activity specifically concerns the salvation of the world.[18] There is one divine will, and "the will [of the Son] is not different from that of the Father." This also applies to "knowledge, power and similar things." Reference is made to John 10.15 and 16.15 to support this unity of persons, as being the same in will, power and authority.[19] By excluding any division or separation of essence, the patriarch unequivocally denies the subordination of any hypostasis in the Triune God.

Nikephoros' description of Christ in *Logos* 584 could be interpreted as an argument for subordination. A careful reading proves otherwise. Christ is "the reflection (*apaugasma*) of the Father's glory, the light from light, the identical image of the Father, the character of his hypostasis." The locutions "the identical image of the Father (*ten aparallakton tou patros eikona*)," and "the character of his person (*ton charaktera tes hypostaseos autou*)" both refer to the identity of essence with the Father.[20] The personal attribute of Christ "begotten of the Father before all ages,"[21] which implies that the birth of the Son is an eternal activity in the same essence of God to be distinguished from generation or creation, defines this non-relational identity between Father and Son.

A similar description of Christ "as the icon of God the Father" appears in *Antirresis*.[22] Nikephoros employs the relation between God the Father and God the Son to convince his readers that whatever honor is given to an image, this in turn refers to the archetype. In no way does this comparison imply that Christ is causally subordinate to the Father. The patriarch does not confuse the essential difference between the hypostatic relations in the Triune God and the relation which exists between an image and its prototype.[23]

His position concerning the former remains clear. Christ is not a "toward some one thing (*pros hen*)" relation to the Father.[24] The Son in the truest sense is the same in essence with the Father, and consequently, equal in glory, honor, and worship. Referring to John 14.7; 9-10, Nikephoros never wavers from the fact that the Son is "equally honored" with the Father. The patriarch only intends to make an analogy in order to justify the honor due to an image. As the honor given to the Son goes to the Father, so the honor given to the icon is intended for its archetype which it represents.[25]

God the Holy Spirit is co-existent and co-eternal, and therefore, worthy of the same honor and glorification as the Father and the Son. Its procession (*ekporeusis*) is understood by Nikephoros as formulated by the Second Ecumenical Synod of Constantinople in 381: "And in the Holy Spirit, the Lord, [and] the life-giver, who proceeds from the Father, who with Father and Son is worshiped and glorified together; who spoke through the prophets."[26]

Nikephoros regards the procession as non-temporal and eternal. In other words, the Spirit proceeds from the Father alone. As the Father and Son, it exists eternally (*synaidion*): "In one Holy Spirit which proceeds from God the Father, and with the Father and Son is that which is asserted to be divine and glorified together, as co-existent and co-eternal."[27] The difference between the eternal procession of the

Spirit and the begottenness of the Son from the Father remains a mystery. Nikephoros emphasizes that these personal properties remain unconfused, immovable, and, in fact, distinct for each hypostasis.[28]

The phrase "through the Son (*di' Hyiou*)" most often refers to the eternal life of the Trinity, the *homoousios* of the hypostases. It appears in the writings of Gregory of Neokaisareia, Cyril of Alexandria, and John Damascene. The locution is also used by these fathers when speaking of the chronological procession of the Spirit, namely, its temporal appearance in the world through the Son. Chronological procession, being an instrumental cause, refers to the mission of the Spirit. This procession is different from eternal procession which refers to the third person's origin of being and action.

The sending of the Spirit "through the Son" in either usage does not imply, moreover, that the third person proceeds from the Son as well as from the Father. This latter usage, known as the Latin *filioque*, destroys the unity (*monarchia*) of the one Triune God. The personal attribute of "without beginning and uncaused," applicable to God the Father only, is common to the Son also.[29]

The patriarch does not purposely employ the locution "through the Son" to make these distinctions. There is no reason to suppose, however, that he was unaware of the difference between the eternal procession of the Spirit from the Father alone, and its chronological procession "through the Son." A reference to temporality is made in *Letter* which might suggest chronological procession. Here Nikephoros wants to establish the relationship between the third person and the Trinity by differentiating the Spirit as a hypostasis, while uniting it without confusion within the Trinity:

> The Holy Spirit which has its existence from the Father, and which is not begotten, but proceeding [from the Father], is eternally visible together with the Father and Son, and is not without beginning on account of the procession from the Father; for according to the causal account, the Father is the principle (*arche*) of it [Spirit] as well, but temporally speaking, it too is without beginning.[30]

The absence of even the hint of a *filioque* debate in the patriarch's writings—one would have expected to find it in the *Letter*—substantiates Karmiris' observation that "until the ninth century, the Eastern Church, viewing the Latin *filioque* as a *theologoumenon* [an opinion not having the force of dogma] did not attack it officially, inasmuch as the Church of Rome herself, in the person of Pope Leo III, repulsed it."[31]

The patriarch's interest is also directed to understanding the Spirit's 'experiential' mission in the world. Its activity comes to fruition within the worshiping congregation. It is the saving grace for the individual as seen in the sacramental life (baptism, eucharist). It is also the strength and comforter (*parakletos*) of the persecuted members of the Church. Most importantly, the Spirit, "the giver of life," acts as the principle of sanctification directing and perfecting a state of peace and harmony within the life of the Church. The Holy Spirit is the peace of the Church. This can be realized only when the Church "moves and does all things from the divine Spirit."[32]

The patriarch never loses sight of the special task of the Spirit. Its dynamism reveals the personalism of the Triune God. The third person is not reduced to a functionary and dependent element in the Trinity. The phrase "in that which all things are"[33] implies, rather, that the Spirit is the Triune God whose dynamic and personal love makes all creation fruitful and directs it toward its final eschatological realization.

## NOTES

1. Kitzinger in "Cult," p. 121, states that before the period of iconoclasm "theology cannot be considered as being more than a contributing cause of the expanding cult of images. Had it been a primary cause one might well expect that expansion to have taken place in the fifth and early sixth centuries when the struggle with monophysitism was at its height and the need to demonstrate the reality of the Incarnation was particularly great.... Still less could it be maintained that the image was as yet a vital part of doctrinal strife."

2. "Doctrine," p. 34.

3. *Letter* 181.

4. *Logos* 584.

5. Ibid. 724.

6. Ibid. Translated scriptural passages hereafter are cited from the following editions: *The Septuagint Version of the Old Testament and Apocrypha: With an English Translation and with various readings and Critical Notes* (London, n.d.); and *The New Testament of Our Lord and Saviour Jesus Christ: According to the Received Greek Text, together with the English Authorized Version* (New York, 1961). Any differences with Nikephoros' scriptural citations will be noted in note references.

7. *Ekd. pisteos* 800.

8. *Letter* 181: "And that [Trinity] which is recognized not by mere names [predication]."

9. Nikephoros also refers to the personal attributes as *aphoristikai idiotetes* in *Logos* 580. Both descriptions are used in *Letter* 184.

10. *Logos* 581.

11. Ibid.

12. Ibid.

13. Ibid. 580.

14. 181.

15. See *Ekd. pisteos* 808-09.

16. See below, pp. 174,205.

17. *Logos* 724.

18. Ibid. 581: "Through [the Son] all [things] were made and are preserved toward essential sustenance."

19. Ibid. 800.

20. A similar account is given by Theodoretos (430) in *Αἱρετικῆς Κακομυθίας Ἐπιτομή*, PG 83.452-53: "The reflection of glory [of the Logos] teaches the co-sameness [of Father and Son]. The character of the hypostasis and the preciseness of the similarity shows and teaches the difference of the hypostases."

21. For the Greek text, see Karmiris, *Mnemeia*, 1,77.

22. 3.405,485.

23. See below, pp. 50,68,70-83.

24. *Antir.* 3.405.

25. Ibid.

26. Karmiris, *Mnemeia*, 1,77.

27. *Logos* 580.

28. Ibid. 580-81.

29. *Letter* 184.

30. Ibid.

31. Karmiris, *Synopsis*, p. 20, n. 29.

32. *Logos* 509,564,712.

33. *Letter* 184.

# 3

# *World: Creation and Creator*

The reality of the one Triune God is also seen through his creation. The dominant theme of Nikephoros' cosmology is the interaction between creation and creator. The patriarch defines this close and inseparable relationship through God's divine attributes as they relate to the world. These refer to God's will and his knowledge.

## ATTRIBUTES REFERRING TO GOD'S WILL

Of the divine attributes concerning God's will the most fundamental, for Nikephoros, is the omnipotence (*pantodynamia*) of God. This attribute is dramatically manifested in the act of creation. The creator's power (*dynamis*) toward creation is stated forcefully by the patriarch: "We believe in one God Father almighty, creator and lord of all things seen and unseen."[1] The will of the Father is eternally the same as and indivisible from that of the other hypostases. The Trinity "is recognized in identical-purpose and desire, singular power, and operation."[2] By this singular power God "brings forth all from that which is not toward existence." The world came into existence out of non-existence and this was because of his sovereign will. He is "the creator of all creation."[3]

An added dimension of omnipotence is God's rulership over all. The name 'king' (*basileus*) in its fullest sense refers only to God. He is "the great and magnificent king." There is a magnificence of sheer power and vastness which is beyond comparison. God is "the Lord of the angels, the ruler of the celestial, terrestrial, and infernal regions."[4] Kingship also applies to Christ, but not in any diminished sense of authority. Christ "reigns with the Father through the ages."[5]

God's rule is unique and is contrasted to that of the tyrant. Nikephoros cites Makarios Magnes' fourth book of his *Responses* (*Apokritika*), which contains an interesting debate between Makarios Magnes, a fourth century Christian, and his (imaginary?) interlocutor, a Greek peripatetic, concerning God's rule.[6] The Greek philosopher views "God's single rule (*monarchia*) with the manifold rule (*polyarchia*) of those who are worshipped as gods."[7] The interlocutor contends that a monarch "is not one who is alone in his existence, but alone in his rule, and rules over his own race, namely, his own kind." Consequently, there is no difference between Emperor Hadrian and God. Both are monarchs. The former rules over men "of the same race who share the same nature"; the latter "likewise would not properly be called a monarch, unless he ruled over other gods; because this would pertain to his divine greatness and his heavenly and abundant honor."[8]

Makarios Magnes' objection completely demolishes his interlocutor's argument. A homonym does not imply identity of essence. "We find that the thing [its nature] is not derived from the name, but that the name bears the truth from the thing."[9] An example of this distinction is when the name 'warm' is applied both to the fire and to one who approaches the fire. The fire is 'warm' because its nature is to be warm (*physei thermon*), while the man is 'warm' relatively, by virtue of his position of being close to the fire (*thesei thermon*).[10]

Citing 1 Corinthians 8.5-6 Makarios maintains that God rules "not as having the same name [as the other gods] as being one of them, but as one, who is uncreated, and rules over created things."[11] So, his rule is singularly unique because it is based upon his nature.

Not being forceful and crude over those who are like him, and, therefore, tyrannical, God rules with love and prudence over his inferiors. Metaphorically depicted, God is like "a teacher who imparts lessons to his students, makes his students wise, and still retains his wisdom"; he is "like the sun, which illuminates things, shines upon them so they themselves partake of the light, yet he is never illuminated by them."[12]

Makarios argues, then, that God's rule is the only monarchy. This contention is based upon his nature and upon his way of rule, the aim of which is to sanctify all things.[13]

Impressed by this debate, Nikephoros utilizes the same theme of contrasting God's rule to tyrannical despotism. With the second supposition in mind, that God's rule aims toward the good end of its subjects, the patriarch boldly contrasts God's rule to Constantine V's reign. The tyrant is described as a ruthless conqueror drunk with battle fever and set on wanton destruction.[14] The former's rule, on the other hand, is the only legitimate monarchy, desiring not our destruction but our salvation: "He is called the God of salvation and God of our healings."[15]

God's rule also implies that he is eternal. The divine attribute of eternity is seen through his power to govern. Both power and influence are all-encompassing and have no temporal end. God's eternity is realized by people of every generation and of every age.[16]

God's ruling activity is directly related to providence (*pronoia*). References to Plato's demiurge or Aristotle's unmoved movers, which as efficient causes relate only to the initial act of the world's generation, are foreign to Nikephoros' cosmological thought. According to him, providence is that activity which preserves and allows creation's development. It is God's synergy with creation which demonstrates that he is the unique creator.[17] This care extends to all creatures individually and collectively. Nikephoros emphasizes that God is the preserver and caretaker of all existent things: "God is the creator and ruler of those things, the giver of the breath of life to them, the guardian, the preserver of all, the benefactor, who governs and brings forth all things in his wisdom, who grants to all their being and ability to live well."[18]

The last phrase, "who grants to all their being and ability to live well," suggests that Nikephoros acknowledges a sense of order inherent in the nature of phenomena. This orderly preservation granted by God manifests itself in each species by the "ability to live well." Propositions, such as 'the sun shines', 'it is raining', 'the earth produces food', are statements of fact. These refer to events which necessarily conform to the physical laws of nature. By mentioning such events—at least these are uncomplicated examples of conformity to physical laws—Nikephoros, in fact, recognizes that the world preserves itself not by chance or accident, but under laws of nature which God himself established. All things, then, are under his care and providence.[19]

The patriarch argues that divine providence is ultimately connected to man's salvation. God's mercy and benevolence, having reached all parts of the world through his gift of salvation to us, confirm that his rule is good. The cooperation between the three persons is seen more clearly in the Triune Godhead within the special activity of providence.[20]

A corollary of omnipotence, rulership, eternity, and providence is God's love and peace as directed to his creation. As "creator and initiator of all," God has established "the gift of peace" in the world: "I will make with them a covenant of peace; it shall be an everlasting covenant with them (Ezekiel 37.26)."[21]

## ATTRIBUTES REFERRING TO GOD'S KNOWLEDGE

Of the divine attributes referring to God's knowledge,Nikephoros considers only the wisdom of God. His wisdom is inexpressibly manifested in the mystery of creation and salvation: "Who is able to proclaim his mercy and wonders?" The patriarch describes God's wisdom as "the abyss of wisdom or, rather, self-wisdom" which, pertaining to his essence, remains a mystery. God's mind can only be seen as absolute and complete. Even from the perspective of natural revelation through creation, God's wisdom cannot be completely understood. "He created all things in wisdom" and in inexpressible beauty.[22]

By regarding creation as an activity of God, Nikephoros focuses upon God's divine attributes as they relate to the world. Omnipotence, rulership, eternity, providence, love and peace, as well as wisdom point to the work of a knowing and volitional God. What externalizes the dynamism and personalism of the one Triune God is the movement from eternity to temporality (*anarchos en chrono*), from creator to creation, from absolute thought to natural revelation.

According to Nikephoros, God is revealed indirectly through the mystery of creation. Natural revelation is an indirect, but legitimate way of knowing about him. Of course, it is propaedeutic to the reality of supernatural revelation. The latter is the most perfect revelation of God to the world through Jesus Christ. Even though the mystery of creation does not reveal "the essence [of God's] being," it "shows us the greatness of his goodness."[23]

## NOTES

1. *Logos* 580.

2. Ibid. 581.

3. Ibid. 636,700.

4. Ibid. 700. It is ironic that this threefold imagery of power would apply centuries later during the Avignon captivity to papal power, symbolized by the wearing of the tiara by Clement V (1305-14); see Stephanides, *Historia*, p. 525.

5. *Logos* 709.

6. *Epikr.* 309-17.

7. Crafer, *Apokritikos*, p. 143; cf. *Epikr.* 309.

8. *Epikr.* 309.

9. Ibid. 312.

10. Ibid. The *thesis-physis* distinction was used also by the stoics in their account of natural theology; see Werner Jaeger, *The Theology of the Early Greek Philosophers: The Gifford Lectures 1936*, trans. Edward S. Robinson (London, 1967), p. 3.

11. *Epikr.* 312.

12. Ibid. 315,314.

13. Ibid. 314: "God, who makes things godlike, sanctifies those who approach him, and the blissful state is given to them by him."

14. *Logos* 701.

15. Ibid. 700.

16. Ibid. 628.

17. Ibid. 720-21.
18. Ibid. 720.
19. Ibid. 700.
20. Ibid. 709,700; cf. John 5.17.
21. Ibid. 733.
22. Ibid. 724,701.
23. *Antir. Eus.* 469.

# 4

# *Angels*

The patriarch maintains that God's creation consists "of all things seen and unseen."[1] In contrast to John Damascene, whose account of the perceptible world is comprehensive,[2] Nikephoros is interested primarily in the incorporeal world. Angelology, a perennial topic for all Eastern fathers,[3] assumes an even more exalted position for Nikephoros because it justifies the pictorial represntation of angels.[4] An examination of these incorporeal creatures or angelic powers, angels and devil, may be discussed under seven headings: the existence, creation, nature, ministry, orders, representation of angels, and the devil.[5]

## THE EXISTENCE OF ANGELS

The patriarch unequivocally affirms the existence of angels. Their existence is supported by the experience of both Moses and Paul, representatives of the Old and New Testaments,[6] and by the history of tradition.[7]

In addition to appealing to tradition, Nikephoros presents a philosophical demonstration of their existence based upon a distinction between circumscription (*perigrapton*) and uncircumscription (*aperigrapton*).[8] He supposes that the iconoclasts claim that angels are not circumscribed because they are supersensible entities. The patriarch, instead, accepts that angels are circumscribable in a qualified sense.[9] First, being in time, they have a beginning, therefore, they are circumscribable in time. Second, since they are creatures, they are definable by their creator, and so, their nature can be circumscribed. Third, they are circumscribable by human apprehension "for inasmuch as they are intellects (*noes*), they share in each other's thoughts and know to some extent each other's nature; for one form of circumscription is apprehension."[10] The proof demonstrates that besides the "familiar and ordinary" sensible things, there are other entities which do in fact exist. It makes sense to give an account about them intelligibly.

## THE CREATION OF ANGELS

That angels are created beings is accepted by Nikephoros. As to the moment of their creation, he is not explicit. Phrases, such as "the first shining from God"; "second lights, reflections of the first light [God]," suggest that the incorporeal world was created in time before the visible world.[11]

## THE NATURE OF ANGELS

The nature of angels remains incomprehensible to us.[12] In other words, their essential nature is beyond our sensible descriptions.[13] Nikephoros does give a general description of angels. They are "simple and completely incomposite beings" who have no sensible bodies. Their being is incorruptible and eternal "by the grace received from their creator." More precisely, they are "beings which are intellectual as well as intelligible."[14]

Assuming that the angel's form (*morphe*) is its essence (*ousia*), it follows that the angel is an "intellectual being (*noera ousia*)." It is also intelligible (*noeton*) and can be comprehended by us, because we have the capacity to perceive the mentally-perceptible. The reason for this lies in the nature of man's soul; it is also intellectual and intelligible. Nikephoros insists, however, that man is not "intellectual nature." His essence is a composite "of intellectual soul and body."[15]

The patriarch also describes the holy angels as "heavenly powers." This characterization refers to their eternal service and vigilance before God. They are in "constant motion" moved by their divine longing as free-willed beings to serve him and to receive "directly and uniquely [without precedence] the splendor of God's divine ray."[16]

## THE MINISTRY OF ANGELS

The angelic nature is inextricably related to the angel's function. Referring to Psalm 103.4: "Who makes his angels spirits, and his ministers a flaming fire,"[17] Nikephoros concludes that angels serve a double function: as liturgists to God (*leitourgoi*); and ministers to man (*diakonoi*).

First, their service is to minister to God as "liturgists of the first light [God]" in a permanent and unchangeable way. The most perfect and complete service is rendered by those powers closest to God's throne, called brigade (*taxiarchia*). These angelic powers are in constant service to the Triune God and are the first to be "in communion (*en metousia*)" with his glory.[18] They are "forever filled by the divine and most beautiful light [of God]." The mystery of their ministry is illustrated when the angels "sing unceasingly and resoundingly concerning the divine goodness."[19]

Second, the ministry of angels includes the protection of humankind and the natural world. This guardianship (*epistasia*) is directed by God.

Through his providence and beneficence, the incorporeal powers are able to provide a ministry specifically directed toward our salvation.[20] This is accomplished by their visual appearance to man. Even though angels perform their ministry on earth, Nikephoros claims that their nature remains "unknown to us." Their appearance is simply a symbolic figuration.[21]

Angelic appearances have been numerous and unique throughout history. Examples of such appearances, as witnessed by Abraham, Jacob, Tobias, Isaiah, the myrrh bearing women, even the angelic revelations recorded in the apocalyptic literature of Zechariah, confirm that the degree and the way angels appear to men is dependent upon God's command. In each case, angels have appeared in relation to their particular ministry. This justifies their being pictorially represented "until today by Christians."[22]

Nikephoros understands that the intercessory role of angels is an important dimension of their service to man:

> Since [the angels] are holy and divine-like, liturgists of the divine splendor, second lights, and reflections of the first light, and ministers of our salvation, it follows, indeed, that their images are honorable and holy. We offer the proper honor to them and entreat their sacred intercessions because we know and believe that our doxologies and thanksgivings, petitions and supplications are offered to God through them.... Our petitions are led to the ears of the Lord of Sabaoth...[the angels] intercede for our salvation.[23]

## THE ORDERS OF ANGELS

According to Nikephoros, the hierarchical order of angels is seven. Not citing a particular scriptural text, he uses the number 'seven' without suggesting that there are only these and no other orders.[24] Seven is "a noble number," which "solemnly" proclaims the completeness of the angelic world-order.[25]

On this point, Nikephoros differs from other church fathers. Gregory of Nyssa, for instance, claims eight, and elsewhere six orders, while John Damascene, following the pseudo-dionysian writings, asserts nine.[26] The fathers are not in agreement concerning the number of angelic orders, the kinds of orders, as well as their hierarchical classification. Nevertheless, they, including Nikephoros, agree that there must be a myriad of powers unnamed.[27]

The discussion of the cherubim, members of the first celestial triad, proves that the patriarch similarly had in mind the idea of angelic order. The name 'brigade' probably is a synonymous term which denotes this first celestial triad: "The highest of all the super-mundane intelligible beings, which are the most God-like, are called brigade."[28]

Two questions must be raised. Does the hierarchical order commit Nikephoros to the thesis that there is a corresponding degree of perfection revelant to each order? If this is accepted, does it follow that the higher orders are excluded from their ministry to man?

As to the first question, the patriarch's description of the cherubim affirms the view of the fathers that there is a real difference in perfection between higher and lower orders. This does not imply a difference in nature. By experiencing "neither desire, drive or volition," as understood in terms of the sensible world, angels remain as they are with respect to their perfection as it refers to their common nature.[29] Nikephoros does not accept graduation to other orders. The difference lies in the perfection of wisdom and knowledge appropriate to intelligible beings.

To summarize, the degree of perfection in the hierarchical order rests with each order's approximate relation to God as defined in the way through which each becomes a communicant of the divine wisdom and beneficence. The first member of the highest order, the cherubim as "most godlike (*theoeidestatoi*)" in form, in contrast to the other "inferior (*katadeesteroi*)" orders, have the most 'direct' relation to God.[30] The first thesis, then, would be accepted by the patriarch.

It does not follow, however, that he adopts the second question. He rejects the view found in the pseudo-dionysian writings that only the lower orders serve man.[31] Referring to the appearance of the seraphim, the second member of the highest order, to Isaiah, Nikephoros concludes that all angels, when commanded by God, serve as his ministers for man's salvation. The patriarch agrees with scriptural and patristic tradition, specifically with the Cappadocian fathers and Paul: "Are they not all ministering spirits, sent forth to minister for them who shall be heirs of salvation?" (Hebrews 1.14).[32]

## THE REPRESENTATION OF ANGELS

Nikephoros' discussion of angels ultimately is directed to the justification of pictorially representing the spiritual world. The claim to be proved is that angels, by nature incorporeal and spiritual, can be represented in art.[33] The issue of whether it is possible to venerate angels since they are also pictorially represented, is also set within a personal and intense debate between the orthodox Nikephoros and his interlocutor, Epiphanides.[34] A reconstruction of the patriarch's most important arguments validating angelic representation is possible.

The initial demonstration is an appeal to traditional practice. By simply looking around, one will find pictorial motifs of angels in all Christian churches.[35] Angelic representation has continued in practice since Old Testament times (e.g. the ark, Solomon's temple).[36] Epiphanides attacks the validity of this practice: "I say that not even those [Israelites] wanted to worship [the cherubim]."[37] Nikephoros retorts that Epiphanides misjudges the piety of the Israelites, whose petitions are sincerely directed to the cherubim. Moreover, there is the certitude that through these petitions the Israelites will be helped by their "beneficient lord and God."

In another argument Epiphanides appeals to canon 35 of the Laodikian Synod (364) to argue against the traditional practice of venerating angelic icons.[38] The canon strictly forbids Christians "to name the angels."Giving them names, instead of calling upon them by name, is tantamount to falling into idolatry. The reason for implementing this canon was to curb the exaggerated idea of certain Christians concerning angelic powers.[39] Called *Angelikoi*, they believed that intercessions should not be directed to Christ, but rather, to the angels whom they considered as lesser gods.

Nikephoros insists that Epiphanides has refused to make a crucial distinction between reverence and honor (*time*) given to angels, who as servants of God intercede in our behalf, and worship (*proskynesis*) which belongs only to the living and true God. Supported with biblical examples, Nikephoros argues that the reverence shown to angelic beings and their icons need not be idolatrous. Epiphanides' use of canon 35 is inapplicable to the justification of angelic icons, and furthermore, it is an example of misrepresenting traditional practice.[40] The patriarch considers the appeal to traditional practice to be an irrefutable demonstration.

A stronger argument for angelic representation is based upon the nature of angels. That they are created beings, and as such can be circumscribed, proves that angels can be represented. The patriarch does not deny that angelic nature remains "unknown to us."[41] What we see is a symbolic figuration representative of their particular ministry; this is what can be pictorially depicted:

> If one, therefore, was to hear that the holy angels were seen sometimes in bodily form, one should not presume anything else, other than that those [angels] which we recognize by their assigned ministries, who look after us upon the earth, whose being is unknown to us, indeed, appear symbolically figured (*symbolikos schematizomenous phainesthai*).[42]

Nikephoros' demonstration, based upon the nature of angels, is significant to the history of the problem of angelic representation because it offers a sharper and different perspective from what had been that of his predecessors. Angelic representation had already been affirmed in the fifth session of the Seventh Ecumenical Synod. Under the presidency of Tarasios, the orthodox patriarch of Constantinople, the synod agreed with John, archbishop of Thessalonike, that only God can be named 'incorporeal.' Angels and all other beings of the spiritual world have a kind of aerial nature (*somata lepta, aeria, aerodes ousia*). Because of this nature, they are able to assume a corporeal form visible to the human senses. It is this corporeal form that can be pictorially represented.[43]

Nikephoros' formulation, based upon what most of the Eastern fathers had already written,[44] however, presupposes two pairs of distinctions. The first pair is between beings "by nature (*physei*)" and "by adoption (*thesei*)". An example of the former is Jesus Christ who by nature (*physei Theos*) is the same as the other persons of the Trinity. Angels are beings by adoption, related to God as created spiritual beings. The second pair is between beings which are circumscribable or describable (*perigraptos*), and therefore, can be iconographically represented, and beings which are not circumscribable (*aperigraptos*), and thus, cannot be depicted, for example, God the Father.

By utilizing these two pairs of distinctions, Nikephoros was not forced to introduce the rather embarrassing notion of an aerial nature, a quasi-corporeality, in order to justify angelic representation. Whatever 'corporeality' angels assume is not derived from their nature (which is not an aerial nature). Rather, their unique, visually sensible appearances are due to God's command.[45] One way to understand the argument is to utilize Aristotle's distinction between accident and substance. Corporeality is a kind of co-incidental predication having nothing to do with the essential nature of an angel. Corporeality is related accidentally to its subject only in so far as it symbolizes the angel's particular ministry.[46]

Nikephoros' strongest argument of justifying angelic representation is by an appeal to God's authority. Because of man's incapacity to see intelligible beings as angels directly, God has commanded "that the blessed heavenly powers appear in symbolic impressions (*entypotikois symbolois*)." This directive is due to God's "divine goodness and fatherly care for us."[47] The patriarch believes that the Old Testament commandment given to Moses: "See, thou shalt make them according to the pattern shewed thee in the mount" (Exodus 25.40),[48] is just one of many acts of providence directed toward man's salvation: "The beneficient progressions of divine providence are revealed by those [angelic powers], and consequently, their [pictorial] representations, which are terrestrial imitations of them, are allowed due to divine condescension."[49]

Nikephoros repeatedly asserts that to deny iconographic angelic representation is a blasphemous act against God's authority.[50] "No one in his right mind would doubt that the making of representations here is commanded by God."[51] The irreconcilability between a tactual image and its incorporeal subject, "and rightly the forms of those that are free from form, and the figures of the unfigured are presented," is resolved 'theologically' by an appeal to God's authority: "Indeed, first the commandment of God; and whatever God says and does is venerable; therefore, nothing is by chance or done by him in vain."[52]

The disparity between an image and its subject is also resolved 'philosophically'. This third argument is based upon the relation between the image and its incorporeal subject. Two claims are made by Nikephoros: there is an 'ontological' distinction between angels and their holy representations (*hiera apeikonismata*);[53] and they are related to each other in some real sense.

As to the first claim, there is no question that a pictorial representation is different (*anomion*) from its real subject because it is a different kind of existent. Nikephoros states the obvious in reminding his readers that the cherubim of the ark are only images of the real cherubim who surround God's throne. The subtlety is seen when he describes these representations as "made of hands (*cheirokmeta*)" and "made of golden material (*chrysokmeta*)." These representations have no substantiality of their own: "As images of images, they are less distinct and less similar, and very much apart from their exemplary cause [the real cherubim]." Furthermore, they are "dim imitations and representations presented as shadowy figures."[54] This characterization seems to exclude the possibility of any relation existing between an image and its subject. This is not Nikephoros' intention. The 'ontological' distinction only establishes what is obvious. The pictorial representations are not only numerically different, but, more importantly, essentially different in kind to their archetypes.

Concerning the second claim, the patriarch sees the relation between an image and its angelic subject as a relation of similitude. Borrowing from the *Categories* of Aristotle, he defines this similitude in two ways. The angelic representation is similar to its subject because both have a common name; and it is similar to its subject because of its "toward something (*pros ti*)" relation.[55]

The pictorial representation is a 'true' representation because it shares the same name with its subject. They are named equivocally. Therefore, both should be honored and respected: "These divine images are named equivocally as those [incorporeal powers], share in the apellation, and become worthy of the glory and grace [of their archetypes]."[56] The connection between equivocity and honor is supported by apostolic tradition which considers angelic icons equally to other icons of saints "and having with those the same rights of worship."[57] For Nikephoros, even though an angelic icon is similar with its archetype by sharing a common name, it does not follow that the 'ontological' difference can be erased.[58] Similitude and equivocity, then, do not imply that the nature (or essence) of an image *qua* image is the same as its subject.[59]

Nikephoros defines the 'toward something' relation: "The similar is similar by being similar." With this definition in mind, he states that the cherubim of the ark are "copies of those [cherubim], that is, equal images (*isotypa*) [of the real cherubim]."[60] His argument, however, is hopelessly condensed and ambiguous. What the patriarch means by a 'toward something' relation is not made clear in his angelology. While not citing the specific Aristotelian reference, Pitra's note leads us to suppose that a reconstruction of the argument via Aristotle might be intelligibly made in favor of the patriarch.[61]

The angelic representation is related to its subject by "being explained with reference to that other thing." The minimum condition of similitude is a comparison with something else, or what Aristotle calls "external reference."[62] Nikephoros' 'toward something' relation, however, goes beyond a simple comparison of two existents. His angelology hints at an internal, substantive relation existing between an angelic icon and its subject. The reference to an exemplary cause; the issue of equivocity, equal honor and veneration; and the assertion that the angelic icons are "equal images" direct us to conclude that there is a kind of partial 'identity' relation suggested by the 'toward something' distinction.[63] It makes sense to say that the image and its subject are identical in similarity, but also, dissimilar (*anomion*) with respect to their separate natures. It is within this interpretation that the following statement should be understood: "Not icons of cherubim, nor similitudes, nor figures, but the commanding God who used the same name, with a clear and great voice, named [the representations] cherubim."[64] The tension between ontological separateness and relational similitude, therefore, justifies angelic representation philosophically, and also opens the way for the justification of Christ's iconographic representation.[65]

Nikephoros regards the pictorial depiction of angelic form as a product which manifests a cooperation between God, creation, and man. The cherubim of the ark are made of the finest material elements and by the best craftsmen, thus imitating the glory of their archetypes.[66] The material representation of angelic beings enables man to visualize their particular ministry symbolically.[67] This harmonious synergy between God and his creation cannot be considered an abstraction.

> These holy representations, which are made from the purest and most splendid material,...composed by men's hands as commanded by God—the inanimate, the unmovable, the unconscious, have the same name as those [incorporeal powers], share in the apellation, and become worthy of the glory and grace [of their archetypes].[68]

The patriarch's demonstrations appeal to tradition, angelic nature, God's authority, and the philosophical relation between an image and its subject. Each justifies the representation of angels iconographically. For this reason they are propaedeutic to an understanding of what an icon is. The finished product is what makes the spiritual world actually visible to us. Angelic pictorial representation is one example of cooperation between God and creation: "The craftsmanship is human; its end is the product of our art; it is God who commands and directs [us to that end]."[69]

## THE DEVIL

The patriarch does not specifically discuss the existence, creation, incorporeal nature, role, and iconographic representation of demons. This does not imply that the proofs and conclusions relevant to angelology are not also the same for the fallen angels.[70] Demonology is a part of Nikephoros' discussion of angels.

The patriarch presents information which was already common knowledge to his ninth century readers. The importance of his account lies in its dual purpose. First, a didactic reason for discussing the devil serves to sensitize his readers to the power and dangerous reality of this spiritual being. Second, a moral purpose is directed to encourage the orthodox not to despair in their struggle against the devil's followers, the iconoclasts; and also, it is intended to condemn an alliance between the devil and the iconoclasts.

There are two strands in the patriarch's narrative: a biblical perspective and a medieval Byzantine outlook concerning the reality of satan's power and influence. Most of his descriptions of the devil are derived from the apocalyptic literature of the Old and New Testaments. His attention is directed not to the legions of demons, but rather, exclusively to the archdemon, satan. The devil is graphically described as the dragon who has received authority to rule over the proud spirits (demons), and "to bait" men toward evil.[71] Characterized as the "invisible tyrant," "the common enemy and hostile devil of our nature," he is the angel who fell from the grace of God. The patriarch attaches the worst sin, pride, to the devil. "He breathes evil, and the swirling hurricane of impiety greatly rises and becomes inflamed." Moreover, the devil is "the father of the lie," and his methods are filled with deceit.[72]

Satan is present from the beginning of creation. He is responsible for heresies, especially idolatry. His presence is felt particularly in the iconoclastic controversy. The patriarch does not miss an opportunity to emphasize that a deceitful alliance has been established between the devil and the iconoclasts. The fallen angel is loose from his liar and leads his followers in sacrilege and blasphemy against God's people. Turning away from Christ and his Church, the iconoclasts, "moved voluntarily by their pride to have power," anxiously have freed the devil to lead them.[73]

Nikephoros unequivocally believes that there exists a powerful being called the devil, who is the originator of all that is evil, blasphemous and antithetical to God. Neither does the patriarch minimize the reality of the devil's influence in the world. Psychological or physical explanations, which dismiss that the devil is a separate existent, are foreign to the patriarch's thought. He is a child of the Medieval Byzantine world whose understanding of satan's power and influence was a very serious one.

Two factors united to create and sustain the conservatism of the Byzantine Empire: orthodoxy and hellenism. Expressed within the artistic and literary products of homeric and classical Hellas is a side of hellenism which reveals a conglomeration of all the primitive and superstitious drives which were imprinted in the daily lives and needs of those who were called Hellenes.[74] The real spirit of hellenism, brought out by Homer, Hesiod, Plato, Aristotle, the tragedians, and sculptors, is a composite of genius and superstition, logic and divinations, beauty and sorcery, moderation and witchcraft.[75] Scholars often have underestimated the importance of this other side of hellenism which even affected the 'intellectualism' of official Byzantine theology. The fusion of hellenism with orthodoxy defines the Byzantine world. Jenkins describes this dual climate:

> The pride and pomp of religion, which filled the capital and the large towns, and which was more spiritually interpreted in a thousand seminaries, awoke only a feeble echo in the remote hamlets of Anatolia and Hellas, where the bear-leader peddled his tufts of prophylactic fur, the venerable 'centurion' assumed a divine wisdom and almost a divine status, the magician foretold from the shapes of the sunset clouds the future of those who resorted to his skill, and the very monks themselves, dedicated to the worship of a higher creed, were not ashamed to invite old witches to prophesy according to the patterns formed by barley-grains. All these impostors were denounced by the Church,[76] but the very fact that such denunciations were repeated century after century is striking proof of their inefficacy.[77]

According to Nikephoros, witchcraft, sorcery, and similar pagan rites were the work of the devil. The characterization of the devil as "the charmer of the evil eye and the contrary of good things" strongly suggests that the 'evil eye' or "the spell of the evil eye (*baskania*)" was taken very seriously by the patriarch.[78] The phenomenon is not a Byzantine fabrication. It is a primitive belief found in both biblical and pagan traditions.[79] Nikephoros, in agreement with Basil, attributes the 'evil eye' directly to satan.[80]

The duality between hellenism and orthodoxy is nowhere more readily seen than in Byzantine hagiography. The hagiographer delights in leaving no detail unnoticed in his description of satan's power. At the same time, he is ready to affirm the saint's victory over the devil. This victory is the Byzantine's resolution of the moral struggle between good and evil. Even though the demon's power is great and formidable "seemingly bent to undermine the kingdom of Christ, to drown our faith, and to dislodge our holy dogmas," the devil, as Nikephoros believes, has no real power. What remains for him and his followers is the "eternal fire." Satan already "is stripped naked of [true] rule...he is crowned with shabby and infamous glory." Citing Isaiah 32.6, the patriarch, finally, scorns the devil as the worst fool who vainly continues to fight against God: "For the fool shall speak foolish words, and his heart shall meditate vanities."[81]

## NOTES

1. *Logos* 580.

2. *Ekd. pisteos* 881-917. The reader of astronomy is referred to Damascene's interesting discussion of the heavenly planets at 881-900.

3. For a comparison between classical and Christian accounts of angels in light of early Christian apologetics, see Theodorou, *Theologia*, pp. 146-54.

4. See Giannopoulos, "Didaskalia," pp. 312-38.

5. *Logos* 768-81 is the earliest and fundamental account of Nikephoros' theology of angels. *Antir.* 2.345-53; 3.480-81; and *Antir. Epiph.* 318-25 are latter passages which deal with the justification of angelic representation, and either repeat or appeal to the theological exposition of *Logos*. Both *Antir. Eus.* 454-55 and *Prol.* 248-49 are incidental to the argument. Finally, *Epikr.* is not representative of the patriarch's angelology, since only Makarios Magnes' views are examined by him.

6. *Logos* 768-69.

7. *Antir.* 2.348.

8. Ibid. 345. This distinction is discussed fully by Nikephoros when considering the nature of an icon; see below, pp. 54-57.

9. *Antir.* 2.345: "For if someone might say that they are uncircumscribable, but they are not completely so."

10. Ibid.

11. *Logos* 769; *Antir.* 2.353. Nikephoros' position is consonant with that of most fathers, particularly Gregory the Theologian and John Damascene; see *Ekd. pisteos* 873: "Some say, therefore, that [the angels] became [were created] before all creation, as Gregory the Theologian says: 'First [God] conceives the angelic and heavenly powers, and the conception was made actual! Others, on the other hand, say that [they were created] after the creation of the first heaven; and all confess before the creation of man.' I concure with the Theologian. First, the intelligible substance should be created, and therefore, the sensible, and then, from both man himself."

12. *Logos* 781.

13. *Antir.* 2.345; *Logos* 769.

14. *Antir.* 2.349; *Logos* 769.

15. *Antir. Eus.* 435.

16. *Logos* 769,772.

17. Ibid. 769. Nikephoros' use of the metaphor that angels are flame, also appears in other patristic writings. It illustrates their natural tendency to serve God, and in no way refers to their incorporeal nature; see Trembelas, *Dogmatike*, 1,415 and n. 24.

18. *Logos* 769,772,773. *En metousia* does not suppose that the angelic essence is identical with God's, who is characterized as "divine supersubstantial [being] (*thearchikes hyperousiotetos*)."

19. Ibid. 773.

20. *Antir.* 2.349.

21. *Logos* 781.

22. *Antir.* 2.349-53.

23. Ibid. 353. Giannopoulos in "Didaskalia," p. 329, asserts that Nikephoros' angelology is not necessarily connected to christology. Unlike the Shepherd of Hermas, Origen, Ambrose et al., the patriarch does not explicitly state that angels intercede for us through Christ, as the saints do, but to God directly. "Most likely, Nikephoros is of the opinion that the God-man is not an intercessor of God and angels, but only of God and man."

24. Eph. 1.21 would have supported this deduction.

25. *Logos* 777. The sanctity of the number 'seven' appears in one of the earliest of Greek philosophies, Pythagoreanism.

26. In *Ekd. pisteos* 872-73 the nine orders are divided into three celestial types (*triadikai diakosmeseis*). The first is the highest and consists of the seraphim, cherubim, and thrones. These angelic powers are in direct communion with God's glory because of their unceasing vigilance before God; cf. *Logos* 772. The middle triad is composed of the dominions, powers, and mights. These receive God's glory through the first celestial order; cf. ibid. 772. The third includes the principalities, archangels, and angels.

27. Commenting on Eph 1.21, Origen remarks that "from him [Paul] it is seen, that besides those principalities, powers and mights enumerated in the passage, there are others named in this world, which the apostle did not enumerate, nor are they comprehensible by someone else; and others exist, which in this world are not named, but in that one which is to come will be named"; Origen Περὶ 'Αρχῶν 1.5.1, ed. Prussian Academy, p. 69, quoted in Trembelas, *Dogmatike*, 1,427.

28. *Logos* 773.

29. Ibid. 772.

30. Ibid.

31. *Antir.* 2.352.

32. Ibid. For a general discussion, see Trembelas, *Dogmatike*, 1,429-31.

33. *Antir.* 2.348.

34. According to Nikephoros, the iconoclasts have confused Epiphanides with Epiphanios, an orthodox bishop of Cyprus (380). They mistakenly have used Epiphanides to support their iconoclastic views; *Antir. Epiph.* 318-25.

35. *Antir.* 2.348.

36. *Antir. Eus.* 454.

37. *Antir. Epiph.* 319. Nikephoros reminds his readers that the orthodox Epiphanios would have never spoken against what God had commanded to Moses; ibid. 318.

38. Ibid. 320.

39. *Pedalion*, pp. 433-34.

40. *Antir. Epiph.* 321,322.

41. *Logos* 781.

42. Ibid.

43. See *Pedalion*, p. 316, n. 1, and Trembelas, *Dogmatike*, 1,416.

44. For references to Basil, Athanasios, Origen, Tertullian, Cyprian, and Augustine, see *Pedalion*, p. 316, n. 1.

45. *Antir.* 2.352.

46. In orthodox churches, for example, the archangel Michael, depicted on the north door of the *iconostasion*, appears in the regalia of a soldier armed with sword and shield. Gabriel (on the south door), though, is described iconographically as a bearer of glad tidings holding a staff. Each is "symbolically figured" with respect to his particular ministry; *Logos* 781.

47. *Logos* 777.

48. Both editors of Nikephoros have mistaken the reference: Pitra in SS 4.249, n. 2, as Exod 25.60, and Migne in PG 100.347, n. 95, as 25.22.

49. *Logos* 776.

50. *Antir.* 2.348-49.

51. *Prol.* 249.

52. *Logos* 777.

53. *Antir.* 2.348.

54. *Logos* 773-76.

55. *Prol.* 249.

56. *Antir.* 2.348.

57. Ibid. 3.480. In *Antir. Epiph.* 319-20, Epiphanides contends that neither angels nor apostles want to be worshiped. Worship belongs only to the savior Christ. He supports this claim by citing Rev 19.10 (Pitra in SS 4.319, n. 4, has misidentified the quotation as 21.8), and Acts 10.25-26. The first passage refers to when John fell before the angel in order to worship him. The angel responded: "See thou do it not: I am thy fellow-servant, and of thy brethren that have the testimony of Jesus; worship God." The second passage concerns Peter's response to Cornelius who "fell down at his feet, and worshipped him. But Peter took him up, saying, Stand up; I myself also am a man." Epiphanides' argument implies that since the angels themselves declare that they should not be worshiped, they do not want to be represented iconographically either. The patriarch accuses Epiphanides of applying the term 'worship' indiscriminately to God, angels, and holy men. The fact that the angelic powers and the saints show such humility and goodness by not demanding reverence justifies "that they must be honored; therefore, they are worthy of much respect"; ibid. 325-26.

58. "A real man and a figure in a picture can both lay claim to the name 'animal'; yet these are equivocally so named, for, though they have a common name, the definition corresponding with the name differs for each"; Aristotle *Categories* 1.1a3-4.

59. *Logos* 777.

60. *Prol.* 249.

61. Pitra, SS 4.249, n. 3.

62. *Categories* 7.6a36-37; 6b11.

63. *Logos* 773; *Antir.* 2.348; *Prol.* 249.

64. *Logos* 776.

65. *Antir.* 3.481.

66. *Logos* 772.

67. *Antir.* 2.353.

68. Ibid. 348.

69. *Logos* 776.

70. An example of iconographic representation is found in icons of St. George. Mounted on a horse, the saint is shown slaying the devil, who is personified as the dragon. The motif which depicts a saint slaying a dragon or barbarian symbolically represents victory over evil. It was well known as early as the fifth and sixth centuries particularly in the frescos (wall-paintings) of Egyptian monasteries; see THE, s.v. "Γεώργιος. Ὁ Τροπαιοφόρος. Μεγαλομάρτυς: Εἰκονογραφία," by Maria G. Soteriou.

71. *Logos* 705.

72. Ibid. 704,544,745.

73. Ibid. 745,708-09.

74. See Jenkins, "Social Life," pp. 102-03. Jenkins is too restrictive in his identification of paganism only with the rural community. It found its way into the cities, too.

75. "It has often been remarked that the content of modern Greek folklore is decidedly pagan, and that much of it derives, directly or indirectly, from the pre-Christian age"; ibid. p. 103.

76. Cf. canon 61 of the Sixth Ecumenical Synod (680) in *Pedalion*, pp. 272-75.

77. Jenkins, "Social Life," p. 102.

78. *Logos* 544.

79. See Prov 23.6; 28.22; Gal 3.1. It is believed that a person who has the evil eye is governed by malice against someone and directs the charm usually against physical beauty. "From a Christian point of view, the evil eye can be considered as superstition which indirectly rejects or blunts the belief in Divine Providence"; see THE, s.v. "Βασκανία," by Demetrios N. Moraitis. There are liturgical prayers read by the orthodox priest specifically for someone afflicted with another's sorcery; see "Εὐχὴ ἐπὶ βασκανίαν" in *Mikron Euchologion*, pp. 264-65. This prayer asks the Lord "to send away every diabolical activity...cunning curiosity, harm, evil eye of criminal and wicked men from your servant (name). [If] the sorcery happened either against beauty, courage, success, or zeal and malice,...send to him [your servant] an angel of peace...a guardian of soul and body...and protect him from every evil...through the intercessions of the Theotokos,...the light-shining archangels, and all your saints. Amen." It is worth noting that an angel of peace is sent to reside where demons earlier had occupied. Other prayers are by Basil the Great (pp. 250-55); and John Chrysostom (pp. 256-61).

80. *Logos* 544,704.

81. Ibid. 704.

# 5

# *Aesthetics*

Nikephoros bases his notion of aesthetics on the suppositon that creation, being circumscribable, can be iconographically represented. Beauty in creation is expressible through art. He regards artistic representation as the product of harmony between God, creation, and man. A relationship exists between art and creation understood as a cooperation between God the creator, man the artisan, and created matter. Placing art in its proper 'ontological' order, the patriarch accentuates the similitude as well as the natural difference between the art object and creation:

> God, the creator and craftsman of all things, brought forth created nature from non-being into being. While art imitates nature [created matter], it is not the same in essence as it; but it is that which taking the natural form [creation] as its exemplar and prototype, consists of a certain thing like and similar (*eoikos ti kai homoion*) [to creation] which can be seen in many artists' artifacts.[1]

For Nikephoros, then, art is imitative of creation in all respects. The craftsman is like the creator in the process of making an artifact; "the painters through [their] art imitate nature."[2] The artistic product is 'really' similar to creation without being its 'real' exemplar. Matter, such as wood or pigment, which are products of creation, become the means by which the artifact assumes its material form, that which is manufactured. With this inseparable relationship in mind, the patriarch's aesthetics may be discussed under these headings: the painter, his craft, and the product (icon).

## THE PAINTER

Like the musician and poet, the artist's goal is to present the highest good (archetype) in the truest and most expressive way that is permitted by his craft. Reflecting a strikingly refined artistic sensitivity, the patriarch explains that "the most experienced of the artisans" use "the brighter materials and the clearer colors, which flower the appearance [of the archetype] to the utmost, and are artistically appealing and give glory to it, inasmuch as the image (*to empheres*) can be preserved to the truer [archetype]."[3] The artisan, then, must be skilled in his craft.

The importance of his experience is found in the older liturgical books. Both the calligrapher and the painter of miniatures have a common function: to present vividly to the reader's memory the teaching of Christ's salvation for man. "On the one hand, through calligraphic genius the teachings of divine history appear to us; on the other hand, by the excellence of painting, those same things are shown to us." The painter's skill in the use of lines and color variations enables the beholder of the icon to envision "the meeting of historical events."[4]

In addition to being knowledgeable as a skilled craftsman, the iconographer must have the esoteric inspiration and mystical openness in order to capture the essence of his subject. That iconography has been closely tied to the monastic ethos is no historical accident.[5] The conclusion drawn from Nikephoros' account is that the persecution against iconophile monks was directed also to the eradication of iconography itself.[6] In a play on words, the patriarch sardonically accuses the iconoclasts of being "the persecutors of color (*chromatomachoi*), rather, persecutors of Christ (*christomachoi*)."[7]

The painter's spiritual character is beautifully described by Nikephoros. The iconographer is taken up to the heavens to become a witness "of the divine and paradoxical spectrum, a percipient and initiate of the heavenly powers." According to his talent and aptitude, the iconographer preserves this divine spectacle through his art. Through the Spirit, God's mysteries are revealed to the artist. As a recipient of these revelations, the artist in turn presents the archetype in visual imagery. "So that he does not forsake this holy gathering [of saints], he echoes as the key sounded by the holy Spirit."[8] The orthodox iconographer is an example of a mystical harmony between creation and God, craftsmanship and divine inspiration, piety of character and knowledge of divine things.

## THE CRAFT

A basic supposition in Nikephoros' aesthetics is that a craft must be functional. The claim 'art for art's sake' is foreign to his thought. In defining iconography as a craft, the patriarch supports his remarks by citing two fourth century fathers, John Chrysostom (398), and Basil the Great (370), bishop of Kaisareia in Asia Minor.

The reference to Chrysostom is not accidental.[9] Both Nikephoros and Chrysostom had a common background. They were ascetics before becoming patriarchs. They decried the debauchery and corruption found in the high levels of Byzantine aristocracy. Both, finally, suffered martyrdom in exile.

According to Chrysostom, true art consists "of those crafts which must sustain and be constructive for our needs and the continuation of life."[10] The ability to distinguish the useful from the useless lies within man's reasoning which is illuminated by God's wisdom: "God has given us wisdom too, so that we can find methods[11] by which we will be able to shape our life."[12]

Chrysostom distinguishes between those useful crafts which apply to the temporal life and iconography (*zographike*) which is useful "toward the future life." The fourth century father does not scorn any useful art, such as medicine or architecture. Rather, what is "superfluous" cannot be called art. Examples of the latter are cooking and baking "which are severely useless and detrimental, ruining body and soul."[13]

Functionalism is the standard of all craft and this is defined by ethical utility. "Deforming the usefulness [of life] by mixing crude art in the art, they lead this [craft] at most toward the vulgar." "Crude art (*kakotechnia*)" is fraudulent because it pampers all the hedonistic desires of man, and leads "to the mother of all disease and sufferings, luxury." Chrysostom considers that any craft which falls short of its true function of usefulness should not be called art. For example, if the art of building "is to build homes and not theaters, working for the necessary things and not the superfluous things of life, then, I call it art."[14]

Nikephoros accepts Chrysostom's premise that anything which does not express necessity is superfluous. The patriarch, however, makes an important clarification. The functionalism of art is not contained in the art itself, but rather, lies in its beneficial effect upon its recipients. Medical art, for instance, cannot be defined as either beneficial or harmful on the basis of its tools, which consist of both elixirs and poisonous concoctions mixed as medicine. It is a beneficial craft because of its effect upon a patient. The purpose of medical art is to heal the sick: "The doctor, above all, is concerned with what is beneficial (*pros to ophelimon*)."[15]

Nikephoros cites Basil's sermon, "Against those who indulge in riches,"[16] which places ornamental decoration in its proper perspective. The iconoclasts perceive the more decorative icons as decadent art and are scandalized by the use of many colors and lines. The patriarch accuses them of not distinguishing between decoration and the content (subject-matter) of the icon, namely, its archetype.[17] As a response to social excesses, Basil's apostolic and ascetic moralizing reveals something of the everyday life in Byzantium. That Nikephoros would cite this sermon further suggests that these problems had not diminished, but rather, had remained virtually unaltered.

Basil's criticism is directed to those women whose primary concern is to make themselves pleasing to the world. "A million flatterers run to do their wishes; the same women gather around themselves the dyers of flowers, the goldsmiths, the perfume dealers, the weavers, the embroiderers. They do not give the husband one moment to breathe by their constant demands." The husband's fortune, no matter how great, will be no match for the woman's insatiable desires, not even for her bath oil. Basil scorns the abuses made of some of creation's finest products:

> Flowers from the sea, oyster or clam, are preferred in place of the wool of sheep; and she is shackled with gold, the heaviest of metals. One of these [precious stones] becomes an ornament used as a headband for them and another is placed around the neck, another in belts and another shackles hands and feet.[18]

The effect of this kind of decorative vanity is an increase in ethical degeneration.

An important distinction, for Nikephoros, concerning ornamental decoration can be established by comparing this quotation with Basil's discussion on building the tabernacle.[19] The best of creation's materials were used for the tabernacle. None of these materials were condemned by God. These same materials are often used in the ornamentation of women. The patriarch sees that both situations are not the same. The ornamentation applied to women results in the superfluous and leads to spiritual corruption. The decoration of the tabernacle raises man to the worship of God. The materials of the physical world receive an exalted value because they are used for the glory of God.[20]

The importance of these fourth century views for Nikephoros cannot be overestimated. The patriarch strongly accuses the iconoclasts of not differentiating functionalism from ornamentation as both Chrysostom and Basil had done. A refutation of the iconoclastic position enables the patriarch to define clearly the legitimacy of iconography as a craft.

First, Nikephoros respects any craft whose purpose is 'toward something' useful and necessary. A goldsmith's work is "empty and futile" when it is directed to satisfying worldly desires. His craft is worthy of praise when directed to making holy things. In this sense, there is nothing superfluous about the goldsmith's craft.[21]

Second, Nikephoros subordinates all decorative aspects to the functional purpose of the craft. The icon's value does not lie in its ornamentation nor in its material base (wood, pigments), but rather, in "the radiant remembrance and grace of the archetypes." Its worth is in the vision of its archetype. This does not suggest that ornamentation has no place in the craft. The represented subject comes to life for the beholder because of the painter's attention to decoration in his craft. Referring to chariot races, a favorite subject-matter for fresco-painters, Nikephoros concedes that these motifs are acceptable insofar as they represent something useful, respectable and honorable, such as historical events.[22] He takes a more moderate position than Chrysostom concerning those motifs which were in popular use on walls and even on clothing. Readers of Chrysostom are familiar with the father's denunciation of chariot races in the hippodrome.

We might use the following example to elucidate the patriarch's view. If the subject-matter of an icon depicts a chariot running over a martyr, it is visually depicted for a useful purpose. The beholder is not only instructed concerning the incidents of martyrdom, but also, is a witness of the saint's courage. On the other hand, if the chariot is an element in a motif whose subject-matter is only to delight and excite, then that visual representation is "toward delight...and deceit of the eyes [of the beholder]."[23]

Third, iconography as a craft has a divine purpose, our salvation and future blessedness. Orthodox iconography, for Nikephoros, has a sense of purposeful urgency and immediacy whose end concerns our immediate salvation. At the same time, it bears the fruits of our piety. Its standard is that it "leads us to the evangelical vision and memory of those things characterized as honorable and venerable."[24]

Fourth, iconography is functionally instructive. Nikephoros repeatedly emphasizes the importance of pictorial representation as an educational visual aid.[25] In a discussion of perception, which links him to the natural philosophy of the ancients, the patriarch extols the superiority of visual imagery. Drawing from Aristotle's theory of perception, which places vision above all other physical senses,[26] he acknowledges the advantages of visual perception. Compared to auditory sense, vision's perceptual field and intake is more inclusive and quickly comprehensible. Also, things learned through visual perception are not as easily forgotten. These impresssions "are marked in [our] souls," and thus, remain with us longer.[27] The advantage of visual impressions, as opposed to auditory reception, becomes more noticeably true among the illiterate peasants.

Moreover, the patriarch considers visual representation superior to oral communication. The spoken word as a communication medium is characterized by its rapidity for the hearer. A visual representation, however, is clearer and more distinct. The weakness of speech, an oral impression, is that it can be distorted and debated. This does not happen with a visual impression, whether it is presented either in written form or in a pictorial representation. The advantage of visual perception, then, is that its impressions are trustworthy (*to axiopiston*). The scriptural written account and pictorial impressions represent "what is faithfully true."[28]

Iconography, a functionally instructive craft, is justified by a demonstration of the advantages of visual perception. The patriarch sees an inseparableness between the craft and perception. The requirements of clarity, vividness in the representation, directness, and likeness to the represented subject are conditions also of perceptual knowledge. In meeting these conditions, the craft instructs the Christian to see the meaning of its spiritual subject. The result of this vision, iconographically represented, is beneficial to the spiritual life of the Christian. The perceptual conditions of the craft, as understood by Nikephoros, have justified his claim: "Through the icons, the knowledge of the archetypes draws near to us."[29] It would be impossible, therefore, to know the archetype if the craft itself could not first present its subject authentically, having met the requirements of perception.

## THE PRODUCT (ICON)

Nikephoros characterizes the icon as "the result of the craft."[30] The icon is the finished product within which all elements of the craft and the 'ethos' of the craftsman meet. But what is the 'nature' of the icon? To answer this, Nikephoros utilizes an aesthetic-philosophical basis which becomes an original addition to the iconophiles' arsenal of image justification.[31] He understands the icon in two important ways: its relation to its archetype, and the distinction between art (*graphe*) and circumscription (*perigraphe*).

### The Relation of the Image to its Archetype

The iconoclastic position, represented by Nikephoros' interlocutor, Constantine V, is an attempt to dismiss the nature of the icon by refusing to accept the 'essential' difference between the image and its archetype, and at the same time, holding that both are identical in nature. These two iconoclastic premises initiate an important examination by the patriarch which defines the nature of the icon by its relation to its archetype.[32] This relation clarifies what constitutes the difference as well as the similitude between image and archetype.

The patriarch presents a definition of the nature of an image:

> The archetype [pattern, model] is an existing principle and exemplar (*paradeigma*) of a form (*eidous*) shaped after it, and the cause of the likeness of the similitude. Of the image, however, the following definition says what one might say about objects produced by art: an image is a likeness (*homoioma*) of an archetype which reproduces in itself by way of resemblance the entire form of what is impressed upon it, and which differs from it [archetype] merely by the difference of essence (*ousias*) with respect to matter (*hylen*); or an imitation (*mimesis*) and similitude ( *apeikasma*) of a pattern which differs in essence and substratum (*to hypokeimeno*); or an artifact (*technes apotelesma*) shaped in imitation of a pattern but differing in essence and subject (*to hypokeimeno*); for if it does not differ in some respect, it is not an image, nor an object different from the

> model. Thus, an image is a likeness and a figuration (*ektypoma*) of things being and existing.[33]

The definition with its philosophical terminology superiorly demonstrates the patriarch's link to the classical thought of both Plato and Aristotle. Concerning the nature of an image, the definition presents three alternative ways of defining the relation of the image to its archetype. Each way identifies the difference and similarity between the two.

An image is different from its archetype because of its material essence. To make this distinction between icon and archetype seems elementary and unduly trivial. Nikephoros, though, thought that this was not self-evident to the iconoclasts. Addressing himself to Constantine V, he argues that the archetype, Christ, is a different existent from his iconographically represented image even in a material sense: "You should not be intimidated to represent Christ in a simple way because of the difference in the essence (*to heteroousion*) of the image. For Christ is one and that which is iconographically presented in a material sense is another [thing]."[34]

An image is different from its archetype with respect to its matter and form as well.[35] As an existent consisting of matter and form, an image is 'ontologically distinct' from its archetype. "How, then, can it still be called icon and similitude, if whatever is represented does not differ in nature [from its archetype]?" Whereas the iconoclasts claim that the icon must be consubstantial (*homoousion*) with the prototype, Nikephoros' view is much more refined. The difference lies not only in matter, but in the 'complete' substantiality of the icon as an existent. The icon *qua* substantial existent (matter and form) is other (*heteroousion*) than its archetype.[36]

Finally, an image is what it is, an artifact, because it either is a likeness, or an imitation and similitude.[37] The patriarch appears to be using synonymous terms in his definition. Likeness implies the notion of figuration, something being impressed upon it. Resemblance and imitation also suggest similitude. What is otherwise the case is that each term, defines a certain relation between image and archetype, and is connected to one, and no other, descriptive difference. "The difference of essence with respect to matter" can be seen more clearly if it is contrasted to the locution "an image is a likeness of an archetype." Or, the substantiality of an image, "differing in essence and subject," is understood when an image is seen as an existent; namely, "an artifact shaped in imitation of a pattern," or "an imitation and similitude of a pattern." Even if the terms are synonymous, their descriptions show unique facets of the icon's 'real' nature. All these converge to define the image as "a likeness and a figuration of things being and existing." In other words, a true image reproduces its model faithfully.[38]

Nikephoros' definition also elucidates the meaning of an archetype. Paradigm, form, pattern, model, and prototype are terms which categorically distinguish the archetype from its image, and at the same time, relate it to its pictorical representation (likeness, imitation, resemblance): "The archetype is an existing principle and exemplar of a form shaped after it, and the cause of the likeness of the similitude."[39] The proof of reality rests with the archetype. True images can only be true if they represent something which is truly real.

The parallel to Plato's forms as standards or paradigms is not to be overlooked. The forms are the immutable principles which define all aspects of the citizen's life. The same metaphysical criteria which apply to the 'good life' also refer to the art object. The judge of an artistic image, according to Plato, "must know, first of all, what is the nature of the object; next, how correct is the imitation; and third, how well the given images have been fashioned both with words, music and rhythms."[40]

Consequently, when Nikephoros refutes the iconoclastic claim that images are idols, these premises concerning the nature of an archetype are presupposed. What makes an idol not an image is the fact that there is no archetype of the idol. The patriarch regards its archetype as fraudulent, illusory, and therefore, not real.[41]

These philosophical distinctions are the building blocks for other clarifications concerning the nature of an image. There is a causal connection between the image and its archetype. The image is the effect (*to aitiaton*) of the archetype. It is, therefore, derivative of the archetype because the latter is the image's cause (*to aition*). The connection is described as a 'toward something' relation.[42]

The relation between image and archetype is such that when thinking of one, the other is also acknowledged.

> As, indeed, a father is called the son's father, and in turn, the son is called the father's son; and in the same way [a friend is] a friend's friend,...likewise, the master is the slave's master, and in turn [the slave is the master's slave]...it follows, therefore, that the archetype is the archetype of an image, and an image is the image of its archetype.[43]

Nikephoros is describing a relation identical to Aristotle's mutual correlative. He acknowledges Aristotle's condition of having a reciprocity of correlation. One important prerequisite is that the correlated terms should be defined by only that name which expresses the correlative notion. Aristotle elucidates this:

> The term 'slave', if defined as related, not to a master, but to a man, or a biped, or anything of that sort, is not reciprocally connected with that in relation to which it is defined, for the statement is not

exact.... If the correlative of 'the slave' is said to be 'the master', then, though all irrelevant attributes of the said 'master', such as 'biped', 'receptive of knowledge', 'human', should be removed, and the attribute 'master' alone left, the stated correlation existing between him and the slave will remain the same, for it is of a master that a slave is said to be the slave.[44]

So it is between the image and its archetype. Again along Aristotelian lines, the patriarch is correct in supposing that even if the archetype should disappear, the mutual correlation between it and icon does not also end, as maintained by the iconoclasts.

Insofar as an image is similar to its archetype, it is 'identical' with the original. Identity with its archetype does not mean ontological sameness.[45] Nikephoros understands this special kind of partial identity as likeness or similitude.

> Now likeness, which is something of an intermediate relation, mediates between the extremes—I mean, the person represented and the representation, uniting and connecting [the image and its archetype] through the form [of the archetype], even though they differ in nature. For although they are different objects (*allo kai allo*) according to their nature, they are not different subjects (*allos kai allos*); and the image is another self. For the knowledge of the primary form [archetype] is obtained through the figure [image], and in it the hypostasis of the person represented can be discerned.[46]

The passage is significant because of the direction which Nikephoros' reasoning takes in defining partial identity. The duality between ontological separateness and relational similitude, even though awkwardly expressed, is very much in the foreground. An image and its prototype are different objects, but they are not different subjects. To illustrate this, the patriarch presents the relatives of 'father-son' where the reverse from an image-archetype model is true. Moving beyond Aristotle's discussion of mutual correlatives, he maintains that each component of the 'father-son' relation "is not a different object, since they participate in the same essence, but they are a different subject, differing in otherness of the hypostases." In other words, father and son are different subjects because they are two different selves, or hypostases.[47]

In contrast, image and archetype are identical, not because they are different objects, namely, not being of the same essence or nature. Rather, they are identical because they are not different subjects. To regard the image as an identical subject to its archetype leads to a metaphysical position of talking in terms of a synergy between image and archetype. The knowledge of the archetype is obtained through its image by being represented iconographically. The image, in turn, is an imitation of that primary form.[48] That the archetype's hypostasis is 'within' and 'of' the image is the dramatic claim which Nikephoros ultimately makes.

Other clarifications follow from this identity-similitude premise which are just as important for understanding the nature of an image. Equivocation inextricably is connected to likeness. The naming applies to both image and archetype. For example, the term 'king' refers both to the 'king', one object, and to 'the king's image', another object.[49] Nikephoros' explication parallels Athanasios' (d. 373) reasoning, who argues:

> There is the idea and the form of the king in the image; and the idea [which is] in the image is in the king [archetype]. The king's likeness is unchanged in the image. Thus, he who beholds the image, sees the king in it, and again, he who beholds the king recognizes that he is the one who is in the image.... The image might say: 'I and the king are one. Therefore, I am in him, and he is in me.'[50]

Once equivocation is granted, the next step can easily be taken: "The honor rendered to the image passes to the prototype."[51] Nikephoros regards the identity-similitude between the image and its archetype as an inseparable relationship. It is within this context that mutual glorification is understood: "Since the icon is related [to the archetype], for this reason, it is glorified together with the glorified prototype, and again it is honored together with the honored [prototype]." The iconophiles claim that by destroying the images, which are the likenesses of their prototypes, the archetypes in turn are dishonored.[52]

Participation in a simultaneous identity and difference also becomes part of the iconophiles' arsenal in defining the relation of image and archetype.[53] Nikephoros acknowledges the duality of this relation: "Both are not the same [identical], but somehow, on the one hand, they resemble each other in form (*to eidei*), and somehow, on the other hand, they do not resemble in essence (*te ousia*)."[54] He resolves this dual relation not by the identity of essence, but rather, by the identity of form.

The reason why the first alternative is inapplicable is because an image is not 'an essential image': "It does not have identity of essence, nor can we in all respects predicate what is predicated of the pattern, as pattern also of the image derived from it."[55]

The difference between image and archetype, then, must lie in the identity of form: "Since pictorial representation is an external factor, and not sharing the definition of the essence, why do our opponents stir in vain and contend that now what is naturally united will be separated?" The patriarch maintains that the identity of form defines the nature of an image as a relation to its archetype. The iconoclasts' mistake is to regard sameness (*to tauton*) and otherness (*to heteron)* under the category of substance (*ousia*), when in fact, it should be considered under the categories of relation, such as quality (*poion*). In considering the identity and difference of an image 'essentially' (under the category of substance), Constantine fails to distinguish "the difference of object which distinguishes natures, but introduces the difference of subjects; inasmuch as he determines hypostases which change the identity of subjects, and by necessity posits many hypostases and as many Christs as there are images."[56]

Alexander's unsupportive statement that "Constantine had never claimed identity of archetype and image but merely consubstantiality,"[57] fails to appreciate Nikephoros' devastating refutation of his interlocutor. The reason why Alexander made such a distinction remains unclear. It is precisely because Constantine claims 'essential' identity between archetype and image that his position supports consubstantiality.[58] The iconoclastic position leads to a tautology between an archetype and its image. This impasse can be expressed by using the propositional model 'A = A'. By considering identity relationally in terms of similarity and difference, Nikephoros is not logically inconsistent.[59] He claims identity, 'A = A' for the image and archetype because both have the same referent, the archetype. At the same time, he presupposes their non-identity, 'A ≠ A', or their non-consubstantiality. The image is 'essentially' different because its nature is not the same as its archetype. The absurdity of Constantine's reasoning is to identify all things as the same in essence: "He advances here the notion of sameness, to which otherness is conjoined, and these are considered in terms of essentiality."[60]

## The Distinction between Art and Circumscription

The second way by which the patriarch understands the nature of the icon is to distinguish art from circumscription. His efforts in making this technical distinction appear obscurely trivial. Once again, his argumentation is directed against his opponents, the iconoclasts, who utterly obfuscate the issue. The latter use the terms 'writing' (*graphein*) and 'painting' (*eikonizein*) interchangeably with 'circumscribing' (*perigraphein*). By confusing the distinction, they ignore ordinary language usage as well as ecclesiastical teaching.[61]

Nikephoros' distinction, more importantly, becomes the presupposition for his christological premise that the iconographic representation of Christ does not imply his circumscription. This was just what the iconoclasts denied. According to them, it is impossible to present the uncircumscribable in any material form. They accused the iconophiles of establishing by pictorial representation a new person of Christ according to the flesh, separated from his divine essence. So, the patriarch's formulations are conclusive because they create a basis for justifying Christ's representation. Alexander acknowledges the importance of making this distinction between art and circumscription as the patriarch's "own contribution to the doctrine of images."[62]

Nikephoros distinguishes between two kinds of art (*graphe*).[63] The first, writing, consists of symbols which form characters of letters and syllables. These flow in a certain order to form the literary meaning of a written composition. The second kind of art is painting. It imitates by being like its archetype. Each kind has its own unique manner of presentation. The former presents itself through oral declamation, while the latter represents the archetype by means of color and line.[64]

Circumscription describes how something is. It is a description of the definition of an existent. According to the patriarch, "the thing circumscribed either is circumscribed by place, time and beginning, or by apprehension."[65] Angels and souls are examples of circumscribable things.

> [Circumscription] is produced by place, as bodies are, for they are enclosed by place, inasmuch as place is 'the limiting surface of the body continent at which it contains the thing contained.' What did not exist before and began its existence in time is circumscribed by time and beginning; in this way, angels and souls are said to be circumscribed.... And what is apprehended by thought and knowledge is circumscribed by apprehension.[66]

If an existent cannot be determined within these dimensions of space, time, and apprehension, it is uncircumscribable. Insofar as his humanity is concerned, Christ is circumscribable in all three ways: "The noncorporeal was circumscribed in place; the non-temporal who had taken on temporality, was circumscribed in time; and the incomprehensible [God], who vested himself with human corporeality, was understood [by us]."[67]

The distinction between art and circumscription is further developed by Nikephoros. The limit of the artist's craft is dependent upon the existence of the circumscribed object. The archetype to be apprehended must have spatial reality so that the artist might then be inspired to represent it iconographically.[68]

By representing the archetype on a wall or panel, it does not follow that the portraitist is circumscribing his subject. The patriarch's use of "limiting (*periorizesthai*)" implies the notion of enclosing the person portrayed. The portrait's spatiality is not the same as that of the circumscribed subject. The latter's spatiality is a feature of the archetype's definition or essence.

The method of presentation by painting is also different from circumscription. Pictorial representation is attained by colors and other artificial means, while the circumscription of a subject is accomplished by the categories of place, time and apprehension. Nikephoros concludes that only circumscription presents us with the true essence of the subject because circumscription is the limit of the thing-in-itself. Consisting of those attributes of *definienda*, i.e. place, time and apprehension, circumscription is the basis of the thing's definition.

The form by which the content-matter is presented differs between painting and circumscription. Painting is 'representational' because it "presents the bodily form of the person to be painted by impressing his outline, form, and resemblance." Circumscription, on the other hand, is 'definitional' because it "defines the enclosed" in the three ways mentioned above.[69]

Both circumscription and painting are different in their nature. The former is not related to anything else. It is "an inseparable" composition of the archetype. To be 'a man' means to be "always in place, in time, and in apprehension, it follows that his nature is circumscribed." Painting, a relational entity, however, is related to its circumscribed archetype by its likeness or similitude to the prototype. Still, "it is separate from it [archetype] and exists on its own [ground]." Consequently, painting can be performed in the absence of the subject in many places. This is not the case for circumscription which defines its object. By enclosing its object "simply and indefinitely" in the dimensional categories, circumscription is an inseparable condition of the archetype.[70]

Since painting exists wholly "in perception and ostensible observation," it will not be identical to circumscription. The inclusion of dimensional categories, such as time, apprehension, and place, widens the apprehension of the sensible object. Circumscription offers a definitionally fuller notion of the archetype's essence than that of painting.[71]

Painting and circumscription are not reciprocal terms. "Painting is contained in circumscription, but circumscription is not contained in it, but contains it [painting]. Therefore, they are not reciprocal, for circumscription is the more general term.... Conversely, it is not the case that if a thing is circumscript, it is likewise painted."[72] The distinction is made against the iconoclasts who viewed the two terms as synonymous. When referring to circumscription, they really meant pictorial representation. According to Nikephoros, "neither does painting circumscribe the man even if he is circumscribable, nor does circumscription represent him pictorially even if he is capable of pictorical representation, for each one will have its own function."[73]

The patriarch presents a long litany of examples, such as "the year, the law of Moses, idolatry, sovereignty and power over a people, human life, diseases (especially one day fevers), flowers, Jacob's descent into Egypt and the return of his progeny, the Babylonian exile, the aerial breeze, speech," to prove that these fall under circumscription and not painting.[74] Somewhat exaggerated, these are supposed to illustrate the premise that painting and circumscription are not reciprocal terms.[75] The patriarch's distinctions provide the basis, then, for the christological thesis that the painting of Christ does not imply his circumscription.

## NOTES

1. *Antir.* 1.225.

2. *Prol.* 279.

3. *Logos* 725.

4. Ibid. 748.

5. The contributions of orthodox monasticism are not limited only to iconography, but include the arts of hymnology and hymnography as well. A golden age of Byzantine hymnology, in fact, occurred during the two centuries of iconoclastic strife.

6. As "the taking down or destroying (*kathairesis*)" of the icons began, "the elevation, placing up (*anairesis*)" of a profane imperial art was encouraged to take the place of religious art in the churches and other public edifices; see Nikephoros, *Histor. syntomos*, pp. 57-77; also his use of "scrap [off the walls] or take down (*apoxeomen e kathairoumen*)" in *Prol.* 289.

7. *Prol.* 282.

8. *Logos* 725.

9. *Prol.* 259-65. The passages are found in Chrysostom's commentary on Matthew; see *Homily* 49.4-5, PG 58.500[509]-01[10]. The patriarch condemns the iconoclasts for not presenting the complete passage, resulting in blatant misrepresentations of Chrysostom's views on aesthetics; ibid. 259-60; 261.

10. Ibid. 260; cf. 259.

11. This phrase was omitted by the iconoclasts in their quotation of Chrysostom; see Pitra, SS 4.260, n. 6.

12. *Prol.* 260; cf. 259.

13. Ibid. 260.

14. Ibid. 261,263,260.

15. Ibid. 262.

16. Ibid. 265: *Τὸν κατὰ πλουτούντων...λόγον*; see PG 31.3.277-304, esp. 288-89.

17. *Logos* 784-85.

18. *Prol. 266.*

19. *Basil's Sermon on the holy book of Exodus* is quoted in *Prol.* 267-68.

20. Along the same line, Damascene maintains that our nature is glorified and becomes transformed into incorruptibility; see Hans Frhr. von Campenhausen, "Die Bilderfrage als theologisches Problem der alten Kirche," *Zeitschrift für Theologie und Kirche* 49 (1952) 58.

21. *Prol.* 270.

22. Ibid. 282,268-69; *Logos* 784.

23. *Prol.* 269.

24. Ibid. The theme that icons keep alive men's memory of the archetype occurs repeatedly in earlier patristic thought; see Norman H. Baynes, "The Icons before Iconoclasm," *Harvard Theological Review* 44 (1951) 99, n. 18.

25. See *Logos* 748-49; *Antir.* 3.380; and *Prol.* 272 where Nikephoros quotes Nilos', abbot of Mt. Sinai monastery (420), Epistle to Olympiodoros the eparch. Nilos responds to Olympiodoros' intent to embellish a church, which the latter had built, with decorative paintings and scenes of daily life, as follows: "Let the hand of the artist fill the church on both sides with pictures from the Old and the New Testaments, in order that the illiterate, who cannot read the Divine Scriptures, should, by looking at the painted images, bring to mind the valiant deeds of those who served God with all sincerity and be themselves incited to rival the glorious and ever-memorable exploits, through which they exchanged earth for heaven, preferring the invisible to the visible"; Leonid Ouspensky, trans., "The Meaning and Language of Icons" in Ouspensky-Lossky, *Icons*, p. 28, n. 3.

26. "All men by nature desire to know. An indication of this is the delight we take in our senses; for even apart from their usefulness they are loved for themselves; and above all others the sense of sight. For not only with a view to action, but even when we are not going to do anything, we prefer seeing (one might say) to everything else. The reason is that this, most of all the senses, makes us know and brings to light many differences between things"; *Metaphysics* 1.1.980a22-28.

27. *Logos* 748-49; cf. Plato, *Philebus* 38e-39c.

28. *Antir.* 3.381,384. There is almost a competitive spirit between the writers (*logographoi*) and the painters (*zographoi*) in presenting their respective craft, as seen in the beautifully copied and illustrated scriptural texts of the period; ibid. 380.

29. *Logos* 749,725.

30. *Antir.* 1.277.

31. Ladner in "Image," pp. 4-5, underscores the importance of considering the image not only in relation to patristic formulations, but also, in light of pre-Christian views "which were based in part on the naturalism of classical Hellenistic art and in part on a spiritualization of the naturalistic image concept through Platonism."

32. *Antir.* 1.225-28; 277-80; 281.

33. Ibid. 277. For a comparative translation, see Alexander, *Nikephoros*, p. 199. A major defect in the latter's translation is the interchange of key Aristotelian terms, which could be misleading. I have retained the synonymous terms of archetype, model, and pattern to refer to *to archetypon*. Substratum and subject are synonymous for *to hypokeimeno*. In place of Alexander's 'substance', the term 'essence' has been used as being etymologically closer to the Greek word *ousia*. The reader, however, must keep in mind that Nikephoros' use of *ousia* carries with it all the Aristotelian suggestions of *ousia* (*to ti en einai*); see *Metaphysics* 7.3.33. For a discussion of the difference between platonic and Aristotelian essence-substance see G. E. M. Anscombe, "Aristotle—The Search for Substance," in *Three Philosophers*, G. E. M. Anscombe and P. T. Geach (Ithaca, N.Y., 1961), pp. 19-21.

34. *Antir.* 1.225.

35. Definitions two and three in ibid. 277 express this same idea: "Differing in essence and subject."

36. Ibid. 228,225.

37. Nikephoros ingeniously argues from a philological point in ibid. 280 to support the notion of similitude. The noun *eikon* derives its meaning from the verb *eiko*. The verb's etymological sense is "to liken (*homoio*)." *Eikon*, therefore, means likeness (*homoioma*) to something. For a comparison with Plato, see my study, "Art Object," pp. 40-52.

38. *Antir.* 1.277. "Even though by the fourth century much of Graeco-Roman naturalism had been given up in the practice of art, the theoretical conception of the image was still based, to a large extent, on the matter-of-fact naturalism or even illusionism of Plato's time and on the Platonic view that a true image reproduces its model faithfully"; Ladner, "Image," p. 8.

39. *Antir.* 1.277; cf. Plato, *Timaeus* 29b.

40. *Laws* 669a9-b3; see Travis, "Art Object," pp. 131 passim.

41. *Antir.* 1.277; see below, pp. 140-41.

42. Ibid. 277-80.

43. Ibid. 277.

44. *Categories* 7.7a29-7b1.

45. Florovsky in *Review*, p. 205, correctly states: "The 'icon' is, basically and by design, a portrait, i.e. a presentation of a real person. Now, a portrait is *neither* a 'symbol', *nor* an 'essential image.'"

46. *Antir.* 1.280; cf. trans. in Alexander, *Nikephoros*, p. 200.

47. Ibid.; cf. *Categories* 7.8a16-18: "The individual man or ox is not defined with reference to something external."

48. *Antir.* 1.280; cf. *Categories* 7.8b1-14; esp. 7-14.

49. 1.280. Equivocation used in connection with the emperor's image was known as early as Eusebios; see K. M. Setton, *Christian Attitude towards the Emperor in the Fourth Century* (New York, 1941). Basil is considered the first to contrast the emperor's corruptible image, which is "an imitation of something corruptible," to Christ's image, whose archetype is otherwise; *Homily* 24: *Κατὰ Σαβελλιανῶν καὶ Ἀρείου, καὶ τῶν Ἀνομοίων*, PG 31.607.

50. *Λόγος* 3: *Κατὰ Ἀρειανῶν* 5, PG 26.332; cf. *Antir.* 1.280.

51. Basil, *Περὶ τοῦ ἁγίου πνεύματος* 18.45, PG 32.149.

52. *Antir.* 1.280.

53. See Ostrogorsky, "Epistemological Foundations," p. 52.

54. *Antir.* 1.280.

55. Ibid. Ladner in "Image," pp. 6-7, correctly assesses the duality of Plato's aesthetics. Even if in the scale of true value, art, as an imitation of nature, is found to have only a secondary reality (*Republic* 597e,603b), it does follow that art is connected "through participation in, or imitation of, intellectual and intelligible principles like symmetry, number, and equality" to the world of forms. For Aristotle, too, an image is not really a 'substance', because it does not meet the principle of natural things, i.e. something in virtue of itself (*kath'auto*); see *Metaphysics* 7. Ladner draws the following conclusion for Christian art: "For the Christian East, not only angels and men but also their symbols and images had gradually come to be incomparably more important than mere things of nature—and the victory of the orthodox image doctrine in the Iconoclastic Controversy completed this development"; pp. 9-10.

56. *Antir.* 1.280-81. Aristotle, it must be remembered, holds that substance is prior to quality: "It is impossible and absurd that the 'this', i.e. the substance, if it consists of parts, should not consist of substances nor of what is a 'this', but of quality; for that which is not substance, i.e. the quality, will then be prior to substance and to the 'this'. Which is impossible"; *Metaphysics* 7.13.1038b24-27.

57. *Nikephoros*, p. 203.

58. *Antir.* 1.228.

59. Cf. Aristotle, *Categories* 8.11a16-19: "The fact that likeness and unlikeness can be

predicated with reference to quality only, gives to that category its distinctive feature. One thing is like another only with reference to that in virtue of which it is such and such; thus this forms the peculiar mark of quality."

60. *Antir.* 1.281. Constantine's reasoning surprisingly moves toward the monism of Parmenides. For the pre-Socratics, there is no distinction between the subject and its quality. Parmenides bears the brunt of criticism from both Plato and Aristotle by failing to make the distinction between existential statements (the referential pointing out of a thing) and predicative statements (the predication of the characteristics of an object); see *Sophist* 263c. According to Aristotle, Parmenides' mistake is to consider 'being' univocally, and therefore, as a single referent; see *Physics* 1.2.185a1-3,187a10.

61. *Antir.* 2.364.

62. *Nikephoros*, p. 209.

63. *Graphe* does not refer only to writing as it does today. The patriarch remarks that sculpture (or carving) was called by the ancients also writing; *Antir.* 2.356.

64. Ibid. 356.

65. Ibid.; see above, p. 30.

66. Ibid., trans. Alexander, *Nikephoros*, p. 207.

67. Ibid. 357.

68. The terms 'writing' and 'painting' are used synonymously in ibid.

69. Ibid.

70. Ibid. 357,360.

71. Ibid, 360.

72. Ibid. Anastos in "Argument," p. 180, n. 19, succinctly states the iconophile position: "That which is circumscribable can be seen by the eye and represented in a painting, mosaic, or picture. Uncircumscribable, on the other hand, is practically a synonym for 'invisible'. That which is uncircumscribable cannot be seen and, consequently, cannot be depicted by an artist. A man is circumscribable and can be painted or photographed; his soul, like the plans or purposes which he forms in his mind, cannot."

73. *Antir.* 2.360.

74. Ibid. 360-61. Nikephoros accuses the iconoclasts of misreading Asterios' (fourth century bishop of Amasenos in Pontos) *me graphe ton Christon* with meaning *me perigraphe*"; 364.

75. Two examples are worth noting: time and speech in ibid. 360-64. In the case of time, Nikephoros presents an interesting theory. The problem is to decide whether the year, with its measurement and divisions of seasons, is an example of circumscription or pictorial representation. The dilemma is solved by defining time by the categories of circumscription, especially apprehension. All measurements, including the sun's revolution, are ways of apprehending objective time subjectively. In the case of speech, which is circumscribable, it does not follow that it can be pictorially represented because apprehension is not something which has body or form. Moreover, abstract notions, such as justice and courage are circumscribable. If they are pictorially represented, this does not entail that they can also be circumscribed.

# 6
# *Man*

The patriarch's discussion of man is not lengthy, nor is it radically different from earlier patristic and Byzantine formulations. This is not to suppose that he considers the subject of secondary importance. What he does develop is important, because it contributes to his primary concern, the justification of pictorial representation. The two dominant themes in his understanding of man are man's unique position in creation: divine-human relation; and primordial state, Adam's sin, and the fall of man.

## MAN'S UNIQUE POSITION IN CREATION: DIVINE-HUMAN RELATION

In consonance with other orthodox fathers, Nikephoros acknowledges that man is the highest of all creation. Man's position in creation, without being considered isolated, is singularly unique. That man is defined within the divine-human relation is the dominant theme in Nikephoros' anthropology.[1] He develops this theme under four headings: the act of creation, the reality of God's natural law, the fear of God, and the image-likeness to God.

### The Act of Creation

The divine-human relation is seen first in the act of creation. The Triune God is ever-present and directs the creative act: "Those things pertaining to man's nature were arranged together and composed from the beginning by the creator." Man's makeup includes "the intellectual, the rational, the sensible, the appetitive," but most importantly, "the will."[2] The patriarch does not adhere to the trichotomism of Apollinarios (390), who claimed that man consists of body, corporeal-like soul, and spirit.[3] Man's nature, for Nikephoros, consists of two elements, body and soul, in which rationality, intellect, and volition belong to the soul, and sensibility to the body.

What is 'Nikephorian' in the account of man's creation is the emphasis on man's corporeality. Because man was created from created matter, earth, it follows that his body "necessarily is visible, tangible, and therefore, circumscribable." It is absurd to consider man as uncircumscribable. Since his nature is circumscribable, he can also be iconographically represented.[4]

## The Reality of God's Natural Law

An inseparable element in the divine-human relation is the reality of God's natural law. An innate part of man's existence, God's law directs our being to the Holy One. It manifests itself in the spirit of the written law, which also is worthy of respect. Natural law is the binding of the internal communion between God and man.[5]

Nikephoros is aware that natural law carries its consequences. To obey the law will enable man to inherit a blessedness comparable to that of the angels, thereby preserving the true purpose of man's creation as a free being. To disobey the law is to break the direct union with the creator, and will result "in the worst and [most] miserable fate."[6]

## The Fear of God

Man's relation to his creator is defined also by the fear of God.[7] Like natural law, this notion is innately part of human nature. It is not a fear of dread, but a fear in the knowledge of that inseparably close and personal relationship between man and God. Whenever speaking of the fear of God, the patriarch associates this with the honor and veneration appropriately directed to the holiness of God: "To us and all men, the fear of the Lord is implanted, and the holy are taught to be respected and honored."[8]

## The Image-likeness to God

The most important expresssion of the divine-human relation is man's image-likeness to God, mentioned first in Genesis 1.26-27.[9] Not unfamiliar in patristic circles,[10] this notion gains special significance for the iconophiles of the eighth and ninth centuries. Nikephoros' discussion, in fact, is an example of the iconophiles' use of the image-likeness concept which supports the image-archetype similitude in their theology of icons.

By citing Wisdom 2.23: "For God created man to be immortal, and made him to be an image of his own eternity," the patriarch affirms the character of this divine-human relation.[11] It is because of the will of the Triune God that man is created in God's image. The choice of scriptural passages to support the claim is not accidental: Genesis 1.26: "And God said, Let us make man according to our image and likeness"; 1.27: "And God made man, according to the image of God he made him"; 5.3: "And Adam...begot a son after his own form, and after his own image, and he called his name Seth"; and 1 Corinthians 15.49: "And as we have borne the image of the earthly, we shall also bear the image of the heavenly."[12]

The passages support the claim that man's ontological worth lies in his likeness to God. Image is the essence of man, and likeness is the potential to become a participant of grace in the perfection of that divine-human relation. Both image and likeness inseparably point to that perfection. This is what the iconoclasts want to deny. For them, man, "who is born in the image of God," cannot possibly be an image of the incorporeal God. By not recognizing the divine-human relation in terms of image-likeness to God, the iconoclasts debase the ontology of man. Once human corporeality is denied, it is just as easy to object to the humanness of the divine Logos. The patriarch concludes that man is an image-likeness to his only archetype, God (Christ).[13]

Nikephoros' use of similitude or likeness to explain man's unique place in creation is a *modus argumentum* which also fits in the aesthetic-philosophical discussion of the icon. As a relational term defining the divine-human relation, similitude is also the link in understanding the relation of an icon to its archetype. In both cases similarity means approximation, if not assimilation, with perfection. Moreover, in both the patriarch's aesthetics and anthropology, similitude implies something more than mere association with its archetype.[14] In aesthetics, the icon is like its archetype because it assimilates the latter's form. In anthropology man is like God by being a follower of Christ, thereby partaking of God's divine nature.[15]

## PRIMORDIAL STATE, ADAM'S SIN, FALL OF MAN

Once again, the patriarch is consistent with traditional patristic explications.[16] Man occupied a unique position in the primordial state. Accompanying his creation were certain gifts which defined his relative perfection. "Imprinted in our nature" by God, these included volition, the intellect, and "rule over all [creation]."[17]

The responsibility for Adam's sin lies with man himself. Supported by scriptural evidence, the patriarch does not place the responsibility for man's fall either upon God nor upon his creation of man. The participation of the devil, "through the deceit of the serpent," however, connects the fallen angel with man's original sin.[18] For Nikephoros, the cause of sin is the devil, but its recipient is man who willfully transgresses against God.

By defining fallen man as "guilty (*katakritos*)" and Adam's sin as "a transgression (*parabasis*)," the patriarch, in fact, understands that the fallen state is the rebellion of man against God and the reduction of the divine-human relation. The consequences of original sin include deceit, natural corruptibility, death, and a "myriad of passions."[19] Nikephoros is very much aware that evil exists as a negative condition of life even in post-Christian times.[20] He emphasizes that "corruptibility and death were not created together [with the nature of] the first-man."[21]

Sin, death, and corruptibility are now part of the human condition. This does not alter the fact that the body can be circumscribed. It follows that the three dimensional attributes, "physical, organic, and the sustaining power of life," define the body and are not obliterated because of sin.[22] This typically 'Nikephorian' argument reaffirms the circumscribability of man. It also has a wider significance for the patriarch's understanding of man. It presupposes that the image is not completely annihilated. As orthodox fathers before him, he asserts that "wickedness which entered in man had blackened and had made [human nature] useless."[23] He never supposes that the essence of man has been destroyed.

Anthropology does not terminate at the fall. This event becomes the prelude of man's image being restored to its pristine splendor through the Logos' redemptive act.[24] For Nikephoros, it is inconceivable for one to separate anthropology from soteriology. After describing the fallen state of man, the patriarch presents the role of Christ in his redemptive act of salvation. From the moment of man's fall, God's benevolence becomes more evident through the Logos, who took upon himself the body where corruptibility entered.[25]

## NOTES

1. See Nissiotis, "Doctrine," p. 44: "A Christian biblical or systematic theologian should begin his anthropology with a confession of weakness, realizing that it is beyond his power to theorize on the fulness of the divine mystery which is contained in human existence.... We are obliged to consider not simply man himself, but man in the light of the divine-human relationship. This is, however, a relationship which is masked by sin, and its origin is beyond understanding. For this reason we cannot pretend that this doctrine is a final explanation of the whole truth about man, his creation in the image of God and his fall."

2. *Antir.* 3.440.

3. For the history of this division, see Trembelas, *Dogmatike*, 1,469-81.

4. *Antir.* 3.440.

5. Ibid. 392.

6. Ibid. 441.

7. For a discussion of *mysterium tremendum*, see Rudolf Otto, *The Idea of the Holy: An Inquiry into the non-rational factor in the idea of the divine and its relation to the rational*, trans. John W. Harvey, 2d ed. (London, 1950; repr., 1970), esp. "Appendix 1: Chrysostom on the Inconceivable in God," pp. 179-86.

8. *Antir.* 3.481.

9. For a definitive study, see Nicholaos P. Bratsiotis, *'Ανθρωπολογία τῆς Παλαιᾶς Διαθήκης: Ὁ Ἄνθρωπος ὡς Θεῖον Δημιούργημα* (Athens, 1967).

10. See Ladner, "Image," pp. 10-13.

11. *Logos* 752.

12. *Antir.* 3.481-84. The passages are quoted correctly, with the exception of Gen 5.3, which Nikephoros paraphrases: "Adam begot Seth, after his own image and form."

13. Ibid. 484.

14. "In patristic thought the concept of *mimesis*, imitation, which had been accorded at best a relative dignity by Plato, can stand on the higher level of assimilation to and followership of God, because of St. Paul's designation of himself, and of the Christian in general, as μιμητὴς Χριστοῦ"; Ladner, "Image," p. 13.

15. Eph 5.1: "Be ye therefore followers of God (*mimetai tou Theou*), as dear children"; 1 Pet 1.4: "That by these ye might be partakers of the divine nature (*theias koinonoi physeos*)."

16. For a summary of the orthodox position as contrasted to roman catholic and protestant formulations, see Trembelas, *Dogmatike*, 1,449, n. 101; and Andreas Theodorou, "Ἡ περὶ ἀρχεγόνου καταστάσεως τοῦ ἀνθρώπου διδασκαλία τῆς Ῥωμαιοκαθολικῆς Ἐκκλησίας (μελέτη δογματικοσυμβολική)," *Ἐπιστημονικὴ Ἐπετηρὶς τῆς Θεολογικῆς Σχολῆς Πανεπιστήμιον Ἀθηνῶν* 16 (1968) 719-78, esp. 769-78.

17. *Antir. Eus.* 470; *Antir.* 3.484.

18. Rom 5.12; Wisd 1.13-14; esp. 2.23-24: "For God created man to be immortal, and made him to be an image of his own eternity. Nevertheless, through envy of the devil came death into the world"; cited in ibid. 441-44.

19. Ibid. 441.

20. *Logos* 565,604.

21. *Antir.* 3.441.

22. Ibid.

23. *Antir. Eus.* 470; cf. *Logos* 534.

24. *Antir. Eus.* 470. That the image of God in man is still there, is metaphorically depicted by Gregory of Nyssa. He likens the image to a tarnished iron needing cleaning in order to return to its former beauty; ibid. 470-71.

25. *Antir.* 3.441.

# 7

# *Christ*

Nikephoros' understanding of Christ may be discussed under three headings: the theology of economy, the hypostatic union of Christ, and the circumscription and pictorial representation of Christ. His formulations reaffirm the balanced view of Chalkedonian christology, and at the same time justify Christ's iconographic representation.

## THE THEOLOGY OF ECONOMY

The central theme of the patriarch's christological credo is the theology of economy.[1] According to orthodox teaching, divine economy is the eternal plan of God to save and restore fallen man from sin, corruption, and death by the incarnation of the Logos and by his continuous redemptive work through the Holy Spirit. Even though his discussion of economy is brief, it is characterized by its comprehensiveness. Economy presupposes a trinitarian basis, and also, accommodates two facts: the finished work of Christ (christology-soteriology), and the divinely continuous work through the Spirit (ecclesiology).[2]

There are four themes in the patriarch's explication. Economy is "a mystery" initiated only by God's ineffable mercy and grace. It is the mystery of "all that is preached and believed by us in the holy scriptures." Because it "remains ineffable and is said to be unknowable," man's understanding of it is limited.[3]

Economy is the work and cooperation of the Triune God: "With the consent of the Father and the cooperation of the holy and life-giving Spirit."[4]

The mystery becomes an objective reality for all humankind at the moment of conception: "And was incarnate of the holy Spirit, and of the holy, glorious and truly Theotokos and ever-virgin Mary...became man in all respects except sin."[5] From this moment the two natures are united in the one hypostasis.

Christ's redemptive work is sealed with his death, resurrection, and ascension "granting to us incorruptibility (*aphtharsia*)." Christ is "the roadmaker" who has placed "human nature on the road of incorruptibility." It is only through economy that "we confess to be saved."[6]

## THE HYPOSTATIC UNION OF CHRIST

The basic christological problem, for Nikephoros, is the hypostatic union of the person of Christ. The focal point of this union is the mystery of the incarnation. As did other fathers before him, Nikephoros regards the moment of incarnation as containing God's holiness and ineffable love.[7] John 1.14: "And the Word became flesh and dwelt among us" is the scriptural text on which the hypostatic union is established. The patriarch's commentary on this passage is an early sample of his formulations concerning the person of Christ.[8] Couched in terminology familiar to readers of Gregory the Theologian and John Damascene,[9] Nikephoros insists on three points.

Economy begins with the eternal nature of the Triune God. The second person, the Son and Logos, is begotten of the Father before all ages. He is "by nature God," namely, equal to the Father.[10]

At the incarnation the Logos took upon himself human nature. He became like us "not simply assuming flesh, but a rational and intellectual soul." This was done in accord with the will of the Father and in cooperation with the Spirit.[11]

> After the incarnation the one Son was the same—consubstantial with God the Father with respect to divine essence, yet consubstantial with us according to human nature—keeping and preserving...in the unity of the hypostasis the natural qualitative differences of those natures which are united without change and without confusion.[12]

Nikephoros uses two familiar patristic terms 'emptying out' (*kenosis*) and 'taking on' (*proslemma*) to express "this new and strange mixture." The phraseology of *Logos* 585 can be compared to that in the *Tome* of Leo:

> [The Logos] took on him 'the form of a servant' without the defilement of sins, augmenting what was human, not diminishing what was divine; because that 'emptying of himself,' whereby the Invisible made himself visible, and the Creator and Lord of all things willed to be one among mortals, was a stooping down of compassion, not a failure of power.[13]

Christ is considered one person (hypostasis). When talking about his passion, it is not said that the human nature suffered, but Christ suffered, because "the Emmanuel is one, both God and man together."[14]

The emphasis upon the hypostatic union of the two natures in Christ proves how Nikephoros' christology parallels, or better, is a continuation of the traditional formulations of the ecumenical synods.[15] His Chalkedonian position is clearly defined when contrasted to those who misunderstand the manner of union between the two natures, and those who misapprehend the unity itself of the hypostasis. The former are the Nestorians who 'divide' and 'separate' the two natures. The latter are the monophysites, like Eutyches, who 'confuse' and 'alter' the two natures considering the Logos as "one identical nature."[16]

The patriarch adds nothing new to the formulation of the Fifth and Sixth Ecumenical Synods concerning the dogma of the two wills and energies of Christ.[17] His position concerning two natures, two natural energies and two free wills does not suggest that the one hypostasis is a compound of two natures (cf. Apollinarios), but rather, that Christ is, in fact, one person 'in two natures' (divine and human). Nor does the patriarch's description of the human will, as being antithetical or subject to the divine will, imply a struggle between the two. Both wills operate in unity.[18] It follows that the human nature of Christ does not lose its natural attributes because of its union in the hypostasis, but instead, "the whole is transfigured toward the better through the power of the Logos."[19]

Nikephoros' christology emphasizes the 'complete' reality of each nature. Concerning the divine nature of Christ, he sees Christ "as the icon of God the Father." Likewise, the Father is reflected in the Son: "both are images."[20] It is unnecessary to repeat what has been discussed earlier concerning the 'equal' relation between Father and Son in the hypostatic union of the Trinity. The important point is that Nikephoros insists upon the reality of Christ as fully God.

At the same time, he acknowledges the human nature of Christ. Supported by scriptural evidence, the patriarch demonstrates that Christ is fully man. He is described as eating and drinking with the apostles even after his resurrection. "He also labored and was hungry and thirsty according to the physiological law, and that 'God sent forth his Son, born of a woman' [Galatians 4.4]; and God appeared in the flesh, and assumed the [human] garment, and rose making new the [human] nature which from old had been under sin."[21]

By discussing the two natures separately, the patriarch does not 'Nestorianize'. If this were so, he would consider the two natures as parallel, separate subjects (*prosopa*), united only functionally. When he considers the two natures separately, it is for the methodological purpose of establishing their place in the theology of icons.

Considered separately, the two natures are incompatible. On this point both iconophiles and iconoclasts agree. The divine is passive and noncorporeal. It is incorruptible, and therefore, also uncircumscribable. In contrast, Christ's human nature, subject to the manifold influences associated with emotion, is the same kind as ours, mortal, and therefore, is circumscribed and can be represented.[22]

To confirm that the two natures are distinct is only half the story. The patriarch's christological formulations are most precisely Chalkedonian. The two natures can be defined only within the unity of the one hypostasis. Florovsky in *The Byzantine Fathers* uses the phrase "assymetrical dyophysitism" to characterize Chalkedon. "There is but 'one hypostasis', as the subject of all attributions, although the distinction of Divine and human natures is carefully safeguarded."[23] The locution "assymetrical dyophysitism" may characterize Nikephoros' formulations also. The issue, as articulated later by post-Chalkedonian theologians of the sixth and seventh centuries, continued to be how Christ's human nature was united in the one hypostasis. The solution, as summarized by Florovsky, who drew from Leontios of Byzantium, is that "'humanity' is included in the Divine hypostasis and exists, as it were, 'within this one hypostasis'. There is no symmetry: 'two' natures, but 'one' hypostasis. The human nature is, as it were, sustained by the Divine hypostasis: *enhypostatos*."[24]

The notion of "within this hypostasis (*enhypostaton*)" provides the strongest ammunition for Nikephoros' own claim that Christ is circumscribable and can be iconographically represented. To justify the image of Christ based upon his similitude with our nature is not the most powerful demonstration for overthrowing completely the iconoclastic position. The real issue to be proved is that the divine-human hypostasis as hypostasis can be pictorially represented, and not just its human nature. For this to be true, the Chalkedonian definition of the hypostatic union of the incarnate God must be supposed.[25] Without the traditional formulation of the synods, and especially Chalkedon, Nikephoros cannot justify Christ's image.

The patriarch's objection against the iconoclasts is focused upon their misunderstanding of Chalkedon. He accuses the iconoclasts of not accepting the reality of Christ's hypostatic union. For them, the divine is still incompatible with Christ's human nature. In other words, they do not accept the consequences of the incarnation.[26]

## THE CIRCUMSCRIPTION AND PICTORIAL REPRESENTATION OF CHRIST

Nikephoros' justification of Christ's pictorial representation supposes the inseparable connection between a theology of icons and his christological formulations. The iconoclasts (*eikonomachoi*) are really "enemies of Christ (*Christomachoi*)" in disguise.[27] The icons of Christ are the living reminders of the dogmatic reality of the incarnation: "And the Word was made flesh, and dwelt among us" (John 1.4). They are the visible testimony of the continuing historical presence of Christ as the God-man.[28] However relatively, the icons participate in, imitate, and are like the hypostasis, Christ, not only as man, but as God.

Arguing for the reality of the Incarnate Word in two refutations (*An-*

*tirresis* 1 and 2), the patriarch devotes an important part of his exposition to the justification of Christ's pictorial representation. Working within the assumptions of his christology, he presents an involved and sophisticated argument which presupposes the philosophical distinctions found in his aesthetics. Responding to objections made by his interlocutor, Constantine V, the patriarch labors to elucidate the difference between dogma and heresy.[29] To the modern reader much of the refutation might seem to be a futile exercise in logical semantics. But we must be fair to Nikephoros. As Florovsky reminds us, "faith or confession requires philosophy.... These Fathers had conviction and we must come to terms with the convictions and not merely with the terms. The style of the 'Patristic' age cannot be abandoned."[30] If Nikephoros' demonstrations appear to be redundant and logically awkward—as in many instances they are—this does not mean that he misses the point.[31] His thoroughness, seen in his method of presenting Constantine's objections verbatum, and then refuting them sentence by sentence, is evidence of his acumen.

More than any other writing, *Antirresis* 1.231-328 is the fruit of Nikephoros' labors concerning the justification of Christ's pictorial representation. His teaching on the inseparableness of Christ and the theology of icons mark the text as an important contribution in the patriarch's christology. A reconstruction of the argument is in order.

Constantine V presents the problem of the relation between christology and the theology of icons by asking the iconophiles: "How is it possible to picture (*graphesthai*), that is to represent pictorially (*eikonizesthai*), our Lord Jesus Christ, the being who is one person from (*ek*) two natures, immaterial as well as material, united without confusion?"[32] It becomes immediately apparent that the positions of the iconoclasts and iconophiles are diametrically opposed. Constantine's remark is based upon a christological misconception which refuses to acknowledge the unity of the one hypostasis. Nikephoros accuses him of not seeing the relation (*syngenes*) between the two natures in terms of the hypostatic union in the one person. The single premise which Constantine holds is that the two natures are separate because of their incompatible nature. One is "immaterial (*aylon*)" and the other is "material (*enylon*)."[33]

Both patriarch and emperor are aware of the antithesis between the two natures. The latter's mistake is to examine only their separateness. By considering Christ, not in his hypostatic union, but merely from each nature, the iconoclast holds to the absolute irreconcilability of the natures. According to Nikephoros, this results in the confusion of the two, and worse, in their identification as the same. If Constantine's position is accepted, the divine nature is not divine and the human nature is "certainly not human."[34]

The patriarch acknowledges the natural properties common to each nature, but also their "unconfused" unity in the hypostasis. His formulation accomodates the principle of the sharing of natural properties (*antidosis idiomaton*) whereby a sharing of names is possible between both natures just because of their unity in the hypostasis.[35] To separate the natures, as Constantine does, leads to the absurdity that the name of a part *eo ipso* is the common name of the whole. The patriarch explains that the parts of a house, such as stones or wood, by themselves do not name the house. The sharing of names does not work under the model which has been proposed by his interlocutor. The case is otherwise for Nikephoros. Neither soul nor body by themselves name man "but both together as a whole comprise man." As Christ "is both God and man, it follows that he is both capable of being depicted and incapable of being depicted."[36]

In summary, Constantine's position by beginning with the separateness of the natures, offers two rigid choices: to consider Christ either "wholly uncircumscribable or wholly circumscribable." The patriarch's contention, which is based upon the unity of the hypostasis, offers the more sophisticated solution. Christ's icon, a work of art, is identical with its archetype as to his divine-human hypostasis; but not identical as to his divine, uncircumscribable nature. The basis for debate has now been established. The remaining contentions and refutations are the working out of the consequences of these initial positions.

Constantine's second christological thesis, presupposing the irreconcilability of both natures, reads:

> Since [Christ] has another immaterial nature which is conjoined (*synenomenen*) with the flesh, and with these two natures [he] is one, and his person (*to prosopon*), that is, his hypostasis, is inseparable from the two natures, we cannot suppose that it is possible for [Christ] to be circumscribed [i.e. we hold that he cannot be circumscribed]. Since what is characterized is one person, he who circumscribes that person has clearly circumscribed the divine nature also, which is uncircumscribable.[37]

Nikephoros considers Constantine's objection as an opportunity to clarify the notion of circumscription as it applies to the hypostasis. Remarking that the emperor does not make the distinction between painting and circumscription, he derives two consequences from Constantine's position. While admitting that Christ is one hypostasis, the iconoclast denies the natural properties of each respective nature. He does not accept Christ's human nature, which is naturally more recognizable to us, as circumscribable.[38]

By reconstructing Constantine's reasoning, the patriarch reveals the premises which lead the emperor to these conclusions. He is led to the first consequence because he conceives the one hypostasis as being simple and incomposite, and therefore, incapable of ever being circumscribed. Nikephoros' alternative is to consider "the one hypostasis and the unity of the two natures in one hypostasis." As a hypostatic unity, Christ is circumscribable. In contrast to Constantine, who considers that Christ is uncircumscribable because the hypostasis is simple, the patriarch considers uncircumscription only in relation to the divine nature. He does not, however, remain here. The christological justification for representing Christ iconographically is the recognition that the whole hypostasis is circumscribed because of the hypostatic union of both natures. Because of this union, it makes sense also to say that "the divine and ineffable nature" is "co-circumscribed."[39]

Constantine's second consequence supposes a premise which depreciates the unalterability of the Logos, and destroys the unchangeableness of the human nature by deifying it.[40] The iconoclastic tenet: "The flesh which is united to the Logos was made divine,"[41] betrays its monophysitic colors when contrasted to the orthodox position: "The Word became flesh" (John 1.4). In other words, human nature is incorrectly exalted to a higher ontological status than it actually has.

The patriarch reiterates that circumscription is the defining factor which limits a body spatially and temporally. "To say, therefore, that the body is not circumscribed, is the same as to say that it is not in place. And what is not in place, is not a body. Then, what follows from these things, but that the body is not a body?"[42] By accepting all the other natural qualities of human nature, "such as figuration, three-dimensionality, the tangible, physiological composition," and refusing to accept circumscription, the iconoclasts "would take away the essence of the body too." Nikephoros supports his thesis of the inseparableness between body and circumscription:

> If a man would not retain his [property of] being rational, he would not be a man. Similarly, if his mortality, his erect walk, his moving, his being animate, or any of the other properties which when combined would constitute the nature and definition of man, were lacking, he would not be a man. And if somebody takes away the ability to neigh from the horse, or that of barking from the dog, there will be neither horse nor dog. Therefore, the humanity of Christ if deprived of one of its properties is a defective nature, and Christ is not a perfect man. Rather, he is not Christ at all, but is lost altogether if he cannot be circumscribed and pictorially represented.[43]

According to the patriarch, the iconoclastic position moves in two directions. It deprives Christ's complete human nature (*atreptos*) by denying its circumscribable character; and it changes the divine nature *(analloiotos)* by transferring a property of it to another nature. As to the first direction, Nikephoros labels their position as Arianism. He taunts those who hold such views to explain this supposition: "If Adam sinned only half as much, his adoption and salvation would be half; but if he is totally united to God, the whole [man] also is saved."[44]

The patriarch exposes the absurdity of the second direction as well. Since Constantine imposed uncircumscription upon Christ's human nature, by logical necessity, he must also apply the other properties of the divine nature to the human nature. The addition or omission of a property from either nature results in the mistaken identification of the human nature with Christ's divine nature: "Since the flesh is according to you, consubstantial with the Word, and the Word consubstantial with the Father, then, based upon your reasoning, let it be that the flesh is consubstantial with the Father, and similarly with the Spirit."[45]

Constantine's third contention reveals how the iconoclasts see the consequences of Christ's pictorial representation.

> The subject [we are dealing with, the hypostasis] is inseparable after that union, as we confess in dogma. If, then, someone makes an image of only the flesh, it follows that [the artisans] give to the flesh its own person. This becomes a foursome[46] in the whole godhead, that is, three persons in the godhead and one person of the human nature, and this is wrong.[47]

Constantine's original premise is that Christ cannot be represented pictorially. His second contention supports this premise by considering it impossible to circumscribe Christ because of his divine nature. It is misleading to suppose that he has changed his position in conceding that it is possible to represent Christ in his human nature. An icon can neither depict the human nor the divine nature of Christ, because he, for Constantine, is the one simple and incomposite divine hypostasis.[48] The emperor's ploy, rather, is to accuse the iconophiles of Nestorianism.[49] In other words, having an image of Christ means that one divides the natures of Christ by hypostasizing the human nature resulting in adding another separate person to the Godhead.

The patriarch once again affirms that the divine nature is visible, and therefore, circumscribable, because the hypostasis has visibly appeared. Nikephoros cannot determine just what kind of Christ Constantine accepts, since by the latter's own admission Christ has two natures. He asks a crucial question which is directed to the iconoclast and in a sense reflects the Chalkedonian problem of 'who' is Jesus, the Christ and Lord: "You, then, who have supposed in your contentions two natures, which of them do you confess concerning the form of Christ, and the person of him who has been seen and appeared?"[50]

Nestorianism, directed originally against the iconophiles, is turned now toward Constantine. According to Nikephoros, the heresy denies

Christ's true union. Because the divine nature is uncircumscribable, it cannot accept union with another person. By dividing the one hypostasis, separating the human nature from it, Constantine makes "Christ a creature only, without the divine nature as part of his essence." The emperor "dogmatizes considering Christ a mere man." For the patriarch, however, there is no tension between what is circumscribed and uncircumscribed. Whether Christ is performing miracles (common to his divinity), or suffering (common to his humanity), the properties of both natures are attributed always to the person of Christ.[51]

Constantine's fourth contention reads: "That only upon the flesh can one circumscribe the same person of an ordinary [mere] man (*psilou anthropou*)."[52] The iconoclast's remark is deceptive. While holding that Christ cannot be circumscribed, he seems to offer an alternative, that Christ may be circumscribed only as an ordinary man. Once again, the emperor misuses the term 'circumscription' to signify 'pictorial representation'. His position, in fact, has moved beyond his third contention, which accused the iconophiles of creating another person in Christ's image. This time the emperor accuses the iconophiles of depicting only an ordinary person when making an image. Underlying his objection is the refusal to accept the Chalkedonian tenet that humanity is "within the one hypostasis."[53]

The patriarch correctly argues that 'ordinary man' is no person at all, namely, an empty abstraction; it is not Christ. Constantine's Christ stands "naked, alone, separated from the Logos." The consequence of "considering Christ a mere man" is that his human nature is changed, and therefore, the hypostasis itself is not consubstantial with the other persons of the Trinity. Constantine, not the iconophiles, adds to the Trinity a completely different hypostasis which is neither fully divine nor fully human.[54]

Constantine's fifth contention completes his accusation that the iconophiles are Nestorians: "That is, [the artist] who characterizes [depicts] the person, makes Christ a mere creature, without the divine nature belonging to him [Christ]."[55]

Nikephoros' response to this charge is well formulated. By identifying Christ as creature, it follows that there can be no condition for union of the two natures. Since there is no human nature, there can be no relation to its visible archetype. By considering the represented image as consubstantial with the thing represented, Constantine has identified the Logos with "a mere creature." Thus, Christ and his image are "identical."[56] This is exactly the mistake which the emperor charges the iconophiles with making each time they represent Christ in his image. But while Constantine understands Christ to be an ordinary man who is thus already uncircumscribable, he accuses the iconophiles of relegating him to the status of creature.

That Christ is only a creature is an erroneous contention when one considers both natures: his human, because we are more cognizant of this visible part in the hypostasis; his divine, because he appeared with his divine nature also. Nikephoros maintains that since Christ appeared, he can be characterized. This includes his divine nature:

> Not only is Christ's visible, human form introduced by means of the memory and the likeness to the archetype, but also the Logos. Even if he is not circumscribed together nor pictorially represented, since according to his own nature, he is a being invisible and completely intangible, he is, nevertheless, one and undivided from the hypostasis. For this reason, his [Logos] memory is also brought out together.[57]

A mere creature is something which is not circumscribed. Nikephoros compares it to a lifeless statue not identified with the essence of man. To divide the soul from the body in a man and still name him 'man' is absurd. The same happens when the iconoclast either identifies Christ as 'ordinary man' or as creature (*ktisma*). The patriarch bases his reasoning on two premises: since Christ received flesh, it follows that he is circumscribed; and one cannot take away any attributes, including circumscription, which make up the human nature.[58] The iconoclasts commit themselves to a notion of non-being: "For what else is death than the separation of the soul from the body?"[59]

Nikephoros accuses Constantine of separating what is really not separated in the hypostasis, namely, its activity or operation (*energeia*) from its sensibility (*aisthesis*). The separation is made by attributing activity to the divine nature and sensibility to the human. Constantine's mistake is to divide these qualities absolutely in Christ: "He separates [the hypostasis] into God's own and man's own." This absolute division can only lead to the heretical teaching that the Logos could have suffered even before the incarnation. Nikephoros concludes that Constantine is not justified because activity and sensibility are joined naturally and inseparably in Christ. This remains a mystery which even human reason is unable to comprehend or express fully.[60]

Constantine's sixth contention reads: "But if [the hypostasis] is not divided, it is surely co-circumscribed."[61] The emperor appears to concede to circumscription, but circumscription is of the "uncircumscribable Logos" (a *reductio ad absurdum* claim). The patriarch argues that it is impossible to depict Christ (*eikonizein*) without at the same time acknowledging that his humanity is circumscribable. This claim is based upon accepting the inseparableness of both natures in "the united divine Logos." This is precisely what Constantine denies. He attempts to clarify his Christ ('ordinary man') as a hypostasis consisting of soul but not body. By separating the soul from the body, the hypostasis is considered a non-corporeal, and therefore, uncircumscribable existent. The consequence of Constantine's claim, as interpreted by Nikephoros, is that Christ has become an inanimate entity, and thus, incapable of movement. The iconoclast has stripped the hypostasis of its nature to be circumscribed, and has degraded Christ to a non-moving (passive) entity incapable of resurrecting and freeing the dead, because he himself is dead.[62]

Constantine claims that an icon of Christ is "the same" and "consubstantial" with its archetype because of the distinction between activity and sensibility.[63] As seen in his fifth contention, these two qualities are separate in the hypostasis. Now the division is extended to include the archetype's image. Nikephoros, in contrast, reaffirms that as activity and sensibility are inseparably united in the one hypostasis, they are closely joined in the image. He reasons that as Christ moves and acts, this action is transmitted or transferred to the believers. Likewise, Christ's icon, because it is an image which "assimilates this divine and sacred character" of the hypostasis, transfers this action and sensibility to its beholders. Nikephoros describes this process as a "magnetism" of the archetype which presents itself to the artist, who in turn through his craft makes the icon 'animate' as its animate prototype.[64]

The patriarch dispels the fear that a representation of Christ divides the hypostasis by holding that the true image of Christ is to depict him as he appeared, with both his natures. To represent the Logos iconographically does not mean that he will suffer again because he suffered once; nor does it deprive the hypostasis of anything no matter how many representations are made. "[Christ] whom we have seen with our eyes through faith, and whom our hands have touched, is the one we depict and represent, without dividing or separating...the flesh which has been once united to the divine [nature]."[65]

Constantine states his seventh contention: "It is impossible for something to be an icon which does not show the essential, characteristic feature of the person of its prototype."[66] The emperor comes closest to the iconophile position by admitting that an icon must point (*delousan*) to its archetype. The patriarch could not have agreed more. According to him, Constantine's contention is based upon two premises. If Christ has "a form and character," the icon is capable of representing him. If the icon does not characterize, it means that it represents something which is "without form, uncharacterizable, and impersonal."[67]

As to the first premise, Nikephoros believes that Christ has "a form and character" found in his human nature, and as such he is substantial and can be represented. The patriarch accepts the second premise also, because it expresses the same view as the former, now stated from the perspective of the icon rather than its archetype. In contrast, Constantine cannot really accept the first premise because he has denied Christ's humanity; the second premise is incidental for him.

Nikephoros centers his refutation on the fact that Constantine does not truly characterize the archetype. Proper representation refers to its proper archetype. By analogy, the proper impression used in a wax seal belongs only to that one person. The patriarch draws the following implication from the iconoclast's contention. Since the emperor has defined that "Christ is non-personal, without form and character, and therefore, non-hypostatic," the icon is nothing more than an idol. In other words, the image of Christ is an "insubstantial fiction (*anaplasma*)," and not "a similitude" of its archetype.[68] If Constantine's contention is taken seriously, we are left with an image which represents nothing since what it depicts is without hypostasis.

Constantine's eighth contention, a clarification of his first thesis, reads: "It is not possible, therefore, to represent pictorially a person having one nature since he is a being who is of two natures in one person. It follows that the one [nature] becomes non-personal."[69] He denies the icon of Christ on the basis that its archetype is a nonperson. The patriarch condemns the iconoclast's misuse of logical methodology. Leaving aside all biblical and patristic evidence, the emperor uses his imperial position to convince his audience of these dogmatic illiteracies.

Constantine's ninth contention reiterates the iconoclastic definition of Christ: "The icon is an icon of a person, and in this [icon] the divine nature is impersonal, as it happens to be uncircumscribable."[70] The patriarch argues on the following points. By considering Christ as "only a mere God" Constantine has defined the Logos as consisting of the divine nature only. It follows that the hypostasis is non-personal, and therefore, incapable of being represented.

By isolating the uncircumscribable in this manner, Constantine has stripped the divine nature of all its other qualities (such as, the simple, passive, incorruptible, incomprehensible, unintelligible) and has made him anything but God. The emperor has refused to accept the antithesis between the natural qualities pertaining to each nature, and at the same time, their unconfused union "seen in the one and the same person of Christ" because he identifies "the opposites [i.e. two natures] as one and the same."[71]

Nikephoros compares Constantine with Areios, Apollinarios and Eutyches, who divide and confuse the two natures, and in effect, deny the complete humanity of Christ. Their heretical teachings have this in common with Constantine's contentions: Christ is one person understood as one nature which consists of "God in the divine glory."[72] The patriarch correctly insists that the emperor's definition of Christ as one nature = essence (*physis* = *ousia*) composed from two is heretical. What had been seen in Constantine's first contention is only now rebuked: "It should be noted as before that he dogmatizes here that Christ is of (*ek*) two natures.... Nowhere before does it appear that he says he is in (*en*) two natures."[73]

According to the patriarch, the formulation "Christ is of two natures" identifies Constantine as a follower of extreme Agraptodoketism.[74] Undoubtedly, he is an advocate of one essence. The formulation 'of two natures' to refer to the one essence in Christ was rejected as heretical by the Fifth Ecumenical Synod.

Constantine's tenth contention reads:

> Since Christ is one person from twofold (*ek diplotetos*),[75] if the divine is co-circumscribed in this image, or if Christ is understood as only a mere man [and upon his flesh only is defined the person][76] and is pictured as such, [either way] the image is an image of the person, and the divine is uncircumscribable.[77]

The iconoclast maintains that if Christ has a double hypostasis, he cannot be represented; just as if he is a mere man, his likeness cannot be represented. The former premise presents what the iconoclasts understand to be the iconophile position, while the latter premise is a disguise of the emperor's own thesis, as interpreted by Nikephoros. For Constantine, both are on equal ground because they presuppose the iconoclastic tenet of the irreconcilability between image and its archetype.

Nikephoros first challenges Constantine's second premise. He reminds his readers that even though Constantine admitted earlier that the Logos did not lose its passivity by being united with its humanity, the latter, in fact, denies the uniqueness of the incarnation. It makes no difference to the iconoclast whether the body is united in the Logos or united in such a way as to be "substantially and inseparably joined in it."[78] This is the model by which the circumscription of Christ is understood. For Constantine, however, the flesh remains uncircumscribable because the Logos is uncircumscribable. There is no other justification.

Nikephoros justifies Christ's circumscription by his all-knowingness, a characteristic of his divine nature. Christ knew of Nathaniel's conversion and Lazarus' death. His power and foreknowledge was acknowledged before his ministry by John the Baptist: "There standeth one among you, whom ye know not" (John 1.26); also, during his ministry by his apostles: "Lord, even the devils are subject unto us through thy name" (Luke 10.17); and even after his resurrection "to the end of the ages."[79]

An important part of the patriarch's argument consists in relating Christ's foreknowledge to the other persons of the Trinity. He disputes Constantine's minimization of Christ's passivity: "The divine essence neither happened to be at one time inactive nor was [his] activity without substance; because it is said that 'my father worketh hitherto, and I work'" (John 5.17). Even before the incarnation, the Logos knew about his incarnation as God-man because he was "consubstantial with the Father."[80]

Economy, which consists of Christ's foreknowledge in cooperation with the other persons of the Trinity, is a notion which categorically refutes Constantine's 'ordinary man'. To separate the Logos from his humanity, as the iconoclast proposes, is a false premise for justifying Christ's circumscription. The patriarch concludes with a corollary argument. Since creation is circumscribable, it follows that Christ's body is circumscribable, and therefore, Christ is also.[81]

The importance of Nikephoros' refutation of 'ordinary man' cannot be overestimated. By defining Christ as "being like us essentially, but as to activity and worth only, these pertain to God the Father," he has rendered the emperor's position, that Christ is an abstract essence and activity, ineffective. Arguing from Christ's divinity, namely, consubstantiality with the Father, Nikephoros never places Christ on a secondary or dependent level: "He saw what was ahead [knew the future], and as God who is present to all, is not considered as a mere activity, according to some."[82] Eternally in cooperation within the Triune Godhead, Christ is always acting. His power and providence are the attributes which associate him with the Trinity's activity directed to the salvation of man (Psalm 138.7) and creation (Jeremiah 23.4). Christ, then, is circumscribable because he wants it to be so – a manifestation of his infinite power and foreknowledge.

Nikephoros returns to refute Constantine's first premise which considers Christ a "twofold" hypostasis. The patriarch contends that the emperor does not preserve the double nature of Christ either by saying that Christ equals two natures or by giving the name 'Christ' to refer to the existence of two natures. Neither alternative suffices for an orthodox formulation. Constantine must grant circumscription to the human nature which he has omitted de facto from the hypostasis. If not, he falls either into Nestorianism or monophysitism.

If Christ is simple, it follows that the hypostasis is non-composite, and therefore, 'ordinary man'. This is Nestorianism, a denial of the two natures altogether. If Christ is to be defined as a twofold hypostasis, this would mean that he is a composite of two natures. This is a guise for monophysitism. Constantine's inconsistency is immediately apparent. He blurs both premises which, when compared with each other, are irreconcilably antithetical:

> If the deity (*to theion* = Christ) is uncircumscribable because it is simple and non-composite, what is that which is of a twofold and composite [nature]? One would have to say, even if he did not want to admit it, that it is circumscribable; besides, that is the meaning of a composite – it is understood by all of us as being circumscribable.[83]

Constantine's position, then, is a conglomeration of both Nestorian and monophysitic errors.

From the emperor's definition two consequences follow for the iconographic representation of Christ. If an artist was to represent Christ (one hypostasis which is of a twofold nature), he would then have to consider Christ as only an ordinary man (Nestorianism). If one considered Christ and icon as the same, he could not even attempt to depict the prototype. The iconoclast's position, then, dismisses that Christ can be represented at all.

Constantine's eleventh contention is really a statement of the iconophile position: "The maker of that icon says that [this] is the icon of Christ. And the name 'Christ' is known because it denotes not only man, but also God."[84] The statement is meaningless for Constantine who denies that an icon is an image of Christ because it does not refer to either nature. Consequently, the name 'Christ' which refers to his icon is non-referential.

The patriarch adds that the name refers to the person, Christ. It is incorrect, however, to signify by that name a hypostasis which confuses the two natures. The absurdity of this is evident when the iconoclast refers the name "to the one [person] which is either wholly circumscribable or wholly uncircumscribable." The patriarch argues that Constantine's formulation "of contraries joined to one," which may be interpreted as the hypostatic unity of one essence, is in contrast to his concession in the tenth contention, namely, that there are two natures. Nikephoros asks "what is the reason for not giving to each of these [natures] their own and what belongs to them [attributes]?"[85]

The difference betweeen the positions of both interlocutors is apparent. Constantine has accepted that the hypostasis is twofold but not that Christ is circumscribable because he is "in two natures." He is unwilling to take the further step of recognizing the natural properties (*ta oikeia kai prosekonta*) of each nature in the one hypostasis. In other words, he has not disavowed his premise that the hypostasis is a unity of one nature (*physis = ousia*). The iconophile painter, according to Nikephoros, "on the one hand, recognizes what is signified by the name, and on the other hand, knows what is denoted by the person."[86]

Constantine's twelfth contention reads: "Concerning the name of God and man, which signifies the divine nature and human, and which we have denoted upon this icon, how are we possibly to characterize only the human nature, and not the divine and incomprehensible nature?"[87] By identifying once again the one nature with one name, and holding to the impossibility that an icon represents two natures, Constantine has returned full circle to his first contention.

The patriarch's discussion of the sharing of natural properties becomes the coup de grace of his refutation against all of Constantine's objections.[88] First, he reiterates that the name 'Christ' refers to the whole hypostasis. He illustrates his premise with such examples as the cross, which is not the cross "of the human nature only...but is called the cross of Christ"; the tomb of Christ; and the ascension, where the body of

Christ remained true and "had its character completely." The name denotes not only both natures, but "without a doubt the duality (*ten dyada*) of the natures presented to us in the one hypostasis."[89]

Second, there is no contradiction, as Constantine would have us believe, when Christ is referred to as the Son of man as well as the Son of God. This is understood consistently along the reasoning of the sharing of properties, of which the emperor is "completely ignorant." Because he defines Christ as 'ordinary man', which neither denotes the hypostasis as the Son of man nor as the Son of God, the patriarch condemns the iconoclast for being not only "an adversary against the name (*onomatomachounti*)," but moreover, "an adversary against Christ (*christomachounti*)."[90]

Third, the patriarch introduces three locutions which indicate three ways of understanding the relation between the natures as presented in the scriptural and patristic tradition. The affinity of properties (*oikeiosis idiomaton* ) means that each nature has its own natural properties which do not pertain to any other than itself. For example, "neither is the divine [nature] said to be created or passive; nor, on the other hand, is human nature called uncreated, incorruptible, or passive." This is one perspective which emphasizes the preservation of the non-confusion (*asyncheton*) of each nature. Reciprocity of properties (*antidosis idiomaton*) is when the divine renders the human, and vice versa, its respective natural properties because both are united in the one hypostasis.[91]

Both affinity and reciprocity are accomplished through permeation (*perichoresis*). Also understood as an appropriation (*idiopoiesis*) of the respective natural properties, sharing is based upon "the unity of the hypostasis." In other words, each nature shares and receives the other's properties. This does not mean that the natural properties are combined or conjoined (cf. Nestorianism), but rather, that there is "a co-suffering [sharing] with each other" within the hypostasis. This, of course, does not imply a loss or change in the character of the hypostasis. Sharing is the orthodox answer to monophysitism. The latter mistakes the transfer of properties of one nature to the other with respect not to the person of Christ, but to each nature considered in itself. "As the fathers have dogmatized," it makes sense to Nikephoros also to talk about the Logos suffering "since he is one [hypostasis]...inasmuch as it is said that the Logos by economy made his own the sufferings of the same flesh."[92]

The christological discussion of the sharing of natural properties and its consequences for the hypostasis, especially for the human nature receiving "the riches of the divine energies...without...the loss of any of its natural attributes,"[93] becomes a justification for the pictorial representation of Christ.

> As the sufferings of the body are appropriated by economy, and as, indeed, the body of the divine Logos is said to have been ap-

> propriated, in this manner also the icon and similitude (*aphomoioma*) of his all-holy body is referred as familiar to him. Thus, [the icon] having made its own and taken on the common name of [both] natures, is called homonymously [as] the archetype.[94]

Without confusing the respective character of each, the patriarch has preserved the unity of the relation between the image and its archetype. This relation becomes a familiarization and an elevation of the material side of an icon directed toward a close harmony with its archetype which it represents. As in the nature of the archetype-Christ, by analogy there is an affinity between the icon of Christ and its prototype. Icon and archetype form a bond of one activity which directs itself to continuing the historical presence of Christ.

The conclusion which may be drawn from Nikephoros' argumentation is that a theology of icons is not possible without an orthodox christology. It is how one sees the archetype-Christ that determines how one considers pictorial representation. The patriarch's characterization of Constantine and his followers as being not only iconoclasts, but also "adversaries against Christ," must be taken seriously, for it is a condemnation which centers on the issue of Christ's nature. A Chalkedonian definition of hypostasis is the only assurance of correctly determining the relation between image and archetype.

## NOTES

1. *Logos* 584-89.

2. See Gregory of Nyssa's formulation of this twofold understanding of economy in *Εἰς τό, ὅταν ὑποταγῇ αὐτῷ τὰ πάντα, τότε καὶ αὐτὸς ὁ Υἱὸς ὑποταγήσεται τῷ ὑποτάξαντι αὐτῷ τὰ πάντα*, PG 44.1312; cf. Eph 3.16-19.

3. *Logos* 584, cf. Jn 3.15-18; ibid. 589.

4. Ibid. 584.

5. Ibid.

6. Ibid. 584,589.

7. Ibid. 584; cf. Maximos the Confessor, *Περὶ θεολογίας καὶ τῆς ἐνσάρκου οἰκονομίας τοῦ Υἱοῦ τοῦ Θεοῦ* 1.66, PG 90.1108, trans. Philippou, "Mystery," p. 83: "The mystery of the incarnation of the Word contains in itself the meaning of all the symbols and all the enigmas of Scripture, as well as the hidden meaning of all creation both sensible and intelligible. But he who has grasped the mystery of the cross and the tomb knows also the essential principles of all things. Finally, he who pursues even further, and finds himself initiated into the mystery of the resurrection, apprehends the end for which God created all things from the beginning."

8. *Logos* 585-89.

9. Cf. the canons of the Christmas matin service by Cosmas the Melodos, bishop of Maium (Gaza) (ca. 750) and by his contemporary, John Damascene in *Menaion of De-*

*cember*, pp. 309-15. The latter's canon, written in iambic verse and containing an acrostic in heroic hexameter, draws from the Christmas sermon of Gregory the Theologian; see G. Papadopoulos, *Symbolai*, pp. 231-35.

10. *Logos* 585.

11. Ibid. 584. The fathers did not use the phrase "man deified (*anthropon apotheothenta*)," but "God incarnate (*Theon enanthropesanta*)," to emphasize that God himself was the direct cause of the incarnation.

12. Ibid. 585.

13. Trans. Hardy, *Christology*, pp. 363-64; cf. Phil 2.7.

14. *Logos* 585-88.

15. The Chalkedonian definition of faith (*horos pisteos*) in part reads: "We confess...one and the same Christ, Son, Lord, unique; acknowledged in two natures without confusion, without change, without division, without separation—the difference of the natures being by no means taken away because of the union, but rather the distinctive character of each nature being preserved, and [each] combining in one Person and hypostasis—not divided or separated into two Persons, but one and the same Son and only-begotten God, Word, Lord Jesus Christ"; trans. Hardy, *Christology*, p. 373; for Greek text see Karmiris, *Mnemeia*, 1,175. It must be noted that the first two phrases "without confusion (*asynchytos*)" and "without change (*atreptos*)"—adverbs in the original— assert the permanence, and the last two, "without division (*adiairetos*)" and "without separation (*achoristos*)" the inseparability of the two natures of Christ. The former is the orthodox answer against monophysitism; the latter speaks against Nestorianism.

16. *Logos* 588.

17. Ibid. 588-89. A part of the definition of the Sixth Ecumenical Synod reads: "Believing our lord Jesus Christ to be one of the holy Trinity and after the incarnation our true God, we say that his two natures which shone forth in his own subsistence, in which [he performed] both the miracles and [endured] the sufferings through the whole of his incarnate life, and that not in appearance only, but in every deed, and by reason of the difference of nature which must be recognized in the one hypostasis, for although joined together yet each nature wills and does the things proper to it; for this reason then, we confess two natural wills and two operations, concurring appropriately in him for the salvation of the human race"; see Greek text in Karmiris, *Mnemeia*, 1,224.

18. *Logos* 588-89. The passage can be closely compared to John Damascene's explication in *Ekd. pisteos* 1068-69; trans. Karmiris, *Synopsis*, p. 50: "The flesh of the Lord is not said to have been deified and made equal to God in respect of any change or alteration, or transformation, or confusion of nature: whereof the one being deity, the other was deified, and, so to speak, boldly made equal to God...but rather the economical union, I mean, the union is subsistence by virtue of which it was united inseparably with God the Word, and the permeation of the natures through each other, just as we say that burning permeated the steel. For, just as we confess that God became man without change or alteration, so we consider that the flesh became God without change. For because the Word became flesh, He did not overstep the limits of His own Divinity, nor abandon the divine glories that belong to Him; nor, on the other hand, was the flesh, when deified, changed in its own nature or in its natural properties. For even after the union, both the natures abode unconfused, and their properties unimpaired. But the flesh of the Lord received the riches of the divine energies through the purest union with the Word, that is to say, the union in subsistence, without entailing the loss of any of its natural attributes. For it is not in virtue of any energies of its own, but through the Word united to it, that it manifests divine energy: for the flaming steel burns, not because it has been endowed in a physical way with the burning energy, but because it has obtained this energy by its union with fire."

19. *Antir.* 1.272. Note Nikephoros' use of *metestoicheiotai*, and not *metamorphoutai*,

for "transfigured."

20. *Antir.* 3.405,485.

21. Ibid. 461-64; cf. 1 Jn 1.1; Acts 10.41.

22. *Logos* 585.

23. Cited in "Discussion: Concerning the Paper of Father John Meyendorff [entitled 'Chalcedonians and Monophysites After Chalcedon']" in *Papers and Minutes*, p. 34. In contrast, Florovsky characterizes Nestorianism as "a symmetrical dyophysitism."

24. *Papers and Minutes*, p. 34.

25. Cf. *Prol.* 247 with *Antir.* 3.464.

26. *Logos* 781,585; also, *Antir.* 3.460-61.

27. *Antir.* 1.253,328.

28. *Logos* 784. In many orthodox churches there is a tier of icons directly above the principal icons of the *iconostasion* which depict the stages of Christ's temporal life from the annunciation to the ascension; see Leonid Ouspensky, "The Iconostasis" in Ouspensky-Lossky, *Icons*, pp. 59-64.

29. These objections are extant fragments taken by Nikephoros from thirteen published tracts of Constantine. They are in the form of questions inviting an answer which may help to refute an opponent and are called *erotapokriseis* or *peuseis*; see Alexander, *Nikephoros*, pp. 48-53; Gero, *Constantine V*, p. 37, n. 1; and Hennephof, *Textus*, pp. 52-57. Concerning the contribution of the emperor's writings toward the definition drafted at the iconoclastic Synod of Hieria, see Alexander, p. 53; Ostrogorsky, *Studien*, pp. 15-22; and Gero, pp. 37-45.

30. "Discussion: Concerning the Paper of Archbishop Tiran Nersoyan [entitled 'The Lesson of History on the Controversy Concerning the Nature of Christ']" in *Papers and Minutes*, p. 132.

31. Alexander in *Nikephoros*, p. 211, agreeing with Ostrogorsky, *Studien*, p. 45, believes that both iconoclasts and iconophiles "talked at cross-purposes." Even though this may be true, the following comments: "in spite of all the array of learning he [Nikephoros] did not even attempt to refute it [the dilemma which Constantine presented]," and "Nikephoros' comments miss the point," are generalizations which are open for debate.

32. *Antir.* 1.232.

33. Ibid. 232-33.

34. Ibid. 233.

35. Ibid. 236. Meyendorff in *Christ*, p. 188, incorrectly accuses Nikephoros of a "Nestorianizing confusion," and "his tendency to minimize the value of the *communicatio idiomatum*, which, for him, merely manipulates 'words' (*psila onomata*)"; see also, Schönborn, *L'Icône*, pp. 214-17.

36. *Antir.* 1.236.

37. Ibid.

38. Ibid. 237.

39. Ibid. 240; see also, 256.

40. With respect to Chalkedon, Florovsky in *Papers and Minutes*, p. 34, discusses the importance of this distinction: "The special difficulty was really to interpret 'hypostasis' in regard to the union of the two natures. Chalcedon emphasizes the *atreptos*. This implies that in the One hypostasis of the Incarnate Logos humanity was present in its absolute completeness—*teleios anthropos*, although it was the proper humanity of the Logos. The term *physis* is used in the Chalcedonian definition precisely for the purpose to emphasize this 'completeness'. In fact, *atreptos* and *teleios anthropos* belong indivisibly together. Again, the 'complete' human 'nature' is free of sin, sin being a reduction of human nature to subhuman condition."

41. *Antir.* 1.240. The Latin translator has rendered the verb *tetheotai* (root verb *theoo*) as "contemplamur." This is a misreading based upon another verb *tetheatai* (root verb *theaomai* or *theomai*).

42. Ibid. 241.

43. Ibid. 244.

44.Ibid. 245.

45. Ibid. 248.

46. MS Coislinianus 93, cited by Ostrogorsky, *Studien*, p. 9, n. 2, correctly has the word *tetras* instead of *teras* which appears in the Migne ed., PG 100.249.

47. *Antir.* 1.248-49.

48. See above, p. 72 for Constantine's second christological objection. For the identification of *prosopon* with the meaning of *hypostasis* in Constantine's writings, see Ostrogorsky, *Studien*, p. 19.

49. Constantine's 'quartenity' argument is not uncommon in the anti-Nestorian arsenal; see Gero, *Constantine V*, p. 42, n. 25.

50. *Antir.* 1.249,232,236,248.

51. Ibid. 252,249.

52. Ibid. 252.

53. *Enhypostatos* "indicates a different status of Christ's humanity in comparison with the humanity of 'ordinary' men—*psiloi anthropoi.* It is humanity of the Logos. Yet, in its character it is 'consubstantial' with the humanity of men. But Christ is not a man, although *kata ten anthropoteta* [according to his human nature]. He is *homoousios hemin* [consubstantial with us]. The 'status' of His humanity, however, is different from ours: *choris hamartias* [without sin]"; Florovsky, *Papers and Minutes*, p. 34, interpolations mine.

54. *Antir.* 1.252,249.

55. Ibid. 253.

56. Ibid. 256,257.

57. Ibid. 256.

58. Ibid. 260,273. A corollary argument follows which justifies Christ's circumscription based on the humanity of the Theotokos in 265-73; see below, p. 100.

59. Ibid. 276.

60. Ibid. 284.

61. Ibid. 285.

62. Ibid.

63. Ibid. 285-88.

64. Ibid. 288.

65. Ibid. 292.

66. Ibid. 293.

67. Ibid.

68. Ibid.

69. Ibid. 296.

70. Ibid. 297.

71. Ibid. 297,300.

72. Ibid. 300. When the Chalkedonians speak of two natures (*physeis*) after the union, they mean two essences (*ousiai*), whereas Eutyches believed in one essence after the union, nature being synonymous with essence; see Romanides, "Cyril," pp. 96-100.

73. *Antir.* 1.300.

74. Ibid. 268. The Agraptodoketai held that Christ's body could not be represented

because of its incorruptibleness after Christ's ascension.

75. Add *hen prosopon*; see MS Coislinianus 93 in Ostrogorsky, *Studien*, p. 9, n. 4.

76. Add *kai epi tes sarkos autou mones prosopon didein*; see ibid. n. 5.

77. *Antir.* 1.301.

78. Ibid.

79. Ibid. 304-05.

80. Ibid.

81. Ibid. 305.

82. Ibid. 304.

83. Ibid. 305,308. The use of the term *to theion* is indicative of Constantine's refusal to distinguish between essence, which must refer to nature, and person or hypostasis, which refers to an individual; cf. John Damascence, *Ekd. pisteos* 997. Also, note the iconoclast's use of circumscription instead of painting (*graphein, eikonizein*).

84. Ibid. 309.

85. Ibid.

86. Ibid.

87. Ibid. 313.

88. Ibid. 313-28.

89. Ibid. 317.

90. Ibid. 316,313.

91. Ibid. 320.

92. Ibid.

93. John Damascene, *Ekd. pisteos* 1068-69.

94. *Antir.* 1.324.

# 8

# *Mission and Salvation*

Anthropology cannot be separated from soteriology. It is also true that orthodox soteriology is bound inseparably to christology. Christ's redemptive work of mission and salvation is the basis of man's relation to the Triune God, as formulated in the Nicene-Constantinopolitan Creed:

> [2] And in one lord, Jesus Christ,...[3] who for us men and for our salvation came down from heaven[s] and was incarnated from the holy Spirit and virgin Mary and became man. [4] And was crucified on behalf of us under Pontius Pilate and suffered and was buried. [5] And resurrected on the third day according to the scriptures. [6] And ascended to heaven[s].[1]

Four main events which characterize Christ's redemptive work are mentioned in these articles: his incarnation which inaugurates our redemption; his exemplary life as divine teacher and moral legislator which "adds to the wandering mind of man";[2] his death by which, as high priest, he frees us from sin and reconciles us with God; and his resurrection by which, as omnipotent king, he raises us from death to life by establishing and governing his Church, and thereby seals our redemption. These events provide the foci of Nikephoros' discussion concerning Christ's redemptive work.

With the exception of the mystery of incarnation which has been discussed under the hypostatic union of Christ, the patriarch's soteriology can be presented under two headings: the mission of Christ as exemplified by his threefold role in the world: prophetic, priestly, and royal; and man's participation in his salvation.

## THE MISSION OF CHRIST

The presence of Christ in the world is an important theme in the patriarch's discussion of Christ's mission. Man's salvation is possible only because Christ acts visibly. Concerning our salvation specifically, his mission is direct and inclusive. Nikephoros understands Christ's mission on a grand scale of universal conversion, and, at the same time, a catharsis of the world from a sinful past condition.

In characteristically epic style, the patriarch begins his description of this twofold task by asserting that man's redemption is a mystery of God's eternal will. He is the only one who inaugurates and "has worked out all the mysteries of our salvation." This is done by giving the Mosaic law, sending angels and prophets, and finally, apostles to teach the nations, "re-establishing them upon that easy and most direct redemptive path." The triumph of redemption comes with Christ, whose glory and strength is directed to breaking that bondage of falsity (idols, devil, and unbelief), inasmuch as "he destroys the temporal and mundane ways of those who have surrendered to the idols."[3]

Addressing those who formerly had been followers of iconoclasm, Nikephoros compares their return to the Church by describing the process of universal conversion as experienced by the first century gentiles. In the latter's previous state, the dominant factor was their unfaithfulness perpetuated by the devil. This led to a belief in idols and everything else associated with them (*ta cheiropoieta*). The nations' conversion begins with "relearning what is proper,...understanding the truth of those things pertaining to redemption." Cognizant of their condition, they enter upon a new state, that of grace. The gentiles' conversion is made possible by an acknowledgment of Christ. As the savior had exposed all the falsity of their previous condition, they too, now work "to censure the unholy,...and to expose those things which tend to make the mysteries [of salvation] arbitrary."[4]

Related to Christ's presence in the world is his work as the savior. Nikephoros emphasizes that an important contribution was a cleansing (catharsis) of the world from idols and demonic influence.[5] The savior overthrew the devil, "the father of lies," whose intent was the "destruction of the world and its decency." The savior also destroyed the devil's followers whose deceitful influence held humankind under their spell. "It was his voice that renewed the nature of man, cleaned the air, threw open the heavenly gates for us, opened the entrance to the holy of holies for us, established men as companions of angels, loosed the barrier [of death], and reconciled us, who were adversaries because of [our] sin, with God the Father." Catharsis, as accomplished by Christ, is another manifestation of "God's knowledge and name."[6]

## His Prophetic Office

Nikephoros acknowledges Christ's dual role in his prophetic office, as the divine teacher and shepherd. Christ, the divine teacher, is the truth. One aspect of his ministry was to make man conscious of the need for redemption. The patriarch praises Christ's teaching methods: "The one who is mild and humble in heart, who is without commotion and always proper, and indeed, willing to show leniency and to be accessible, was teaching in the synagogues the word of salvation,...not laying down laws,...but preaching the heavenly kingdom." Inseparably related to his teaching was the healing "of every sickness and malady in the people." The consequence of this teaching ministry was the giving "of divine philanthropy to all who came forward in faith."[7]

Christ, the shepherd, is the comforting leader who protects his flock from the snares of evil. Supported by scriptural references, especially John 10.14-15: "I am the good shepherd, and know my sheep, and am known of mine...and I lay down my life for the sheep," the patriarch emphasizes the care, protection, and concern which is enjoyed by Christ's followers. They, in turn, see their shepherd as their only truth and eternal comfort.[8]

## His Priestly Office

Christ's sacrifice on the cross marks the focal point of his high-priestly (*archieratikon*) office. The patriarch emphasizes the reality of this redemptive sacrifice offered by Christ himself: "Giving his own life-giving and saving blood as a ransom for all of us, and enduring the suffering and cross for us, he ascendend on high and converted our captivity by taking it captive." The sacrifice on the cross is inseparably bound to the belief that God, "the creator of all," has made a covenant of peace with man (Ezekiel 37.26) "which has clearly been shown to us by the savior."[9] God's love, then, has "established the gift of peace" in the world. Peace becomes a reality through the crucified Christ. He "is our peace, the mediator between God and man; through him we have been reconciled to the Father, we who have been enemies because of sin." Referring to Ephesians 2.14-17 and Colossians 1.19, Nikephoros sees Christ's priestly ministry not only as a reconciliation of God and man, but a commencement of a new era for humanity. Gifts, as "grace" and other "eternal and lesser goods," are consequences of Christ's sacrifice which establish man as a spiritually new existent (Hebrews 13.20).[10]

Nikephoros' explication of Christ's priestly office is consistent with orthodox tradition. The sacrifice on the cross, a mystery which requires faith and diligent study on man's part, is not to be separated from the entire ministry of the redeemer. The patriarch cannot be accused of discussing the death of the savior out of context from the other facets of his mission on earth;[11] of regarding the sacrifice of the cross separately from the regeneration of the believer's heart and from the good works which are to follow. Neither can he be accused of limiting soteriology only to Christ's resurrection and disregarding the importance of his priestly office.[12] Even though the savior "gave himself to be sacrificed once for the salvation of sinners," his sacrifice continues "perpetually" to sanctify the believers.[13]

The patriarch emphasizes the theme of Christ eternally sanctifying the Church through his priestly office. His account is reminiscent of the liturgical description found in the liturgies of John Chrysostom and Basil. Christ is "our high priest (*archiereus*)" and is exalted as "high priest remaining forever." Nowhere is his priestly office so dramatically felt as a mystery of the savior's ever-presence than in the liturgical setting: "He, indeed, is both priest and sacrifice, he is the one who sacrifices and is slain for us; who is sacrificed and offers the chosen people to God the Father."[14]

## His Royal Office

Supported by biblical references, Nikephoros' narrative reveals his feeling of deep and complete awe for Christ's kingship: "Nations have been subjugated, not simply, but all nations; because [Christ] is king and lord of all." He alone "is seen as the author, rather than the teacher, toward the fulfillment of those things [the law and prophecies]."[15]

Christ's royal office is understood by the patriarch in other ways as well. First, Christ is the warrior-king. He is described as the new king—the only true king—who has the strength to "crush and sack the booty of the enemy." The incarnate Logos comes to destroy the devil and to crush all his possessions, the works of evil.[16]

Second, Christ the warrior-king, is inseparably connected to the characterization as Christ our liberator. He is the one who grants our freedom from "the persuasion of the reigning enemy." The liberator's power is all-inclusive. He "not only saved those living under the tyranny of the evil one," but descending into hades, he "preached freedom...to our ancestors who had lived before, during the times of ignorance, in atheism and impiety."[17]

Third, Christ is the just ruler of his kingdom. His soteriological mission and its consequences, namely, the founding of his Church, are the presuppositions of "establishing us as the chosen people." He "rules and reigns over us to the ages." On the one hand, his justice involves discipline. Sitting on the throne of David, he is depicted as "a holy messenger (*angelos*) who disciplines the foolish." On the other hand, his justice is the direct antithesis of the earthly kings who are perpetuators "of every lie and impiety." Indeed, Christ's rule is the only true and just one. Supported by Ephesians 1.17-23, the patriarch contends that under Christ's rule the subjects are not subordinated tyranically to their ruler, but rather, "those who have hope in him are rendered inheritors of the kingdom."[18]

Fourth, Christ is the king "of love and faith" and has led the nations to a recognition of the true faith. In fact, "this [was done] without demonic deceit."[19]

Fifth, Christ is the king-servant "who assumes the form of the servant" for our redemption. The incarnate God is the ruler of all, and "he is justly named king." He is and is still called "ruler and lord," even though he has assumed human nature. "He who is descended from the seed of David according to human genus is and shall be our ruler for all ages. He is the eternal king, whose sharpened and shining arrows will hit his enemies." As God-man, Christ "rules as the one from the seed of David according to the flesh [human nature], and according to divine nature, the same only-begotten Son of God the Father." Christ as ruler-servant, then, is seen dually by Nikephoros. His "rule and command are eternal, and glory indestructible." At the same time, they are made known to us through his person: "Becoming as us a man, he stemmed death and at the end obtained sovereignty."[20]

Nikephoros clearly maintains that the work of Christ is principally of a redemptive nature. Salvation comes to man through Christ's threefold mission to the world as prophet, high priest, and king. To claim that one office is of more or less importance than the other is to disregard the fact that salvation is based upon the unity of the person of Christ. Through his hypostasis salvation is objectively offered to all people. Legalistic formulations common in Western medieval expositions, which attempt to define the link between objective salvation and the inauguration of each man's subjective salvation as perfected in and through the Spirit, are foreign to Nikephoros' thought. He, instead, acknowledges the mystical concept of salvation as a twofold act of redemption: a redemption from sin, death, moral and natural evil, and a restoration of man's unity with God through Christ.[21]

## MAN'S PARTICIPATION IN HIS SALVATION

Man's active participation in his salvation is based upon his restoration; namely, his regeneration through his participation in the glory of God.[22] As discussed earlier in anthropology, man's salvation is directed toward his potential capabilities of achieving likeness to God. Created in God's image, man's nature, according to orthodox teaching, has not been annihilated because of Adam's sin. In agreement with patristic soteriology, Nikephoros emphatically remarks that man's nature, described as "the ancient beauty," has not changed, but rather, "has been washed away by the foreign shame derived from sin." The patriarch compares man's state to gold which is temporarily stained, but later returns to its former brightness thanks to its cleansing by fire.[23] This purging agent is, of course, Christ who returns man to his former position "in the way he was created by the creator." As a result of Christ's incarnation human nature did not change, but became renewed, in the sense of being restored "and elevated to immortality and incorruptibility."[24] The paradox and novelty of man's restoration is that the image of God, darkened and disfigured in the 'old Adam', was restored through Christ, the 'new Adam.'[25]

The divine factor as a supposition for man's active participation, namely, that God became man to save man, is a theme which Nikephoros consistently maintains. The savior "has granted us complete cleansing and purification of our souls, and has freed us from [our] sins." We have been elevated in the communion of his glory because of his incarnation. Consequently, "we have appeared as legitimate worshipers of the Trinity."[26] The patriarch once again affirms that man's salvation lies with Christ. The argument has a Nikephorian twist. Man's salvation becomes possible only when the Logos assumes human nature: "Because the [human] nature had need of re-formation (*tes anaplaseos*), it was necessary that Christ become in nature similar in all respects."[27] This is the key phrase for soteriology. Re-formation is possible because man is always under the embrace of God's providence: "If he did not want to save, how does he create from nothing?" Providence, as well as salvation, comes from the beneficence and goodness of God.[28]

The activity of God, as seen in the christological framework of justification and redemption, remains a mystery to man. It is within the unity of faith that man approaches an understanding (*epignosis*) of the Son of God. The iconoclasts fall short precisely because of their lack of faith. "For this reason, those who do not believe do not know the power of Christ's mystery.... They do not understand that without faith it is impossible to please God."[29] In addition to having faith, man must actively participate in his salvation.

Nikephoros characterizes the human dimension of soteriology as a unity composed of both faith which accepts the reality of Christ and works which are the manifestations of a new life in him. The importance which the patriarch places upon man's active participation through faith and works is evident in his choice of twenty-six patristic passages which insist on the necessity of faith.[30]

The result of man's salvation is that he becomes a new man. The end of justification is his glorification, being similar to God (*kath' homoiosin*).[31] Citing passages from Cyril of Alexandria's commentary on Paul's epistle to the Romans,[32] the patriarch considers man's likeness to God to be a consequence of soteriology, which is based upon a restoration of his relation to God through Christ. The relation is seen as an adoption by the Father through the Son: "As images are [related] to the archetype, so we also, the adopted sons, [are related] to the one who is declared [Christ], who is truly the nature and strength of the Father."[33] Distinct from the Christ-Father relation which is essential and natural, man's relation to God is by adoption. Through Christ our relation is "by adoption and grace" in contrast to the Son's relation to God the Father which is "essential and true." The term 'sonship' (*hyiotes*) does not apply to man's relation which is defined as 'adoption' (*hyiothesia*). As Cyril remarks: "We too are defined as sons. Rather, not in quality, but by grace, are we worthy of the call, earning that thing by the one will of God the Father."[34]

Considering redeemed man in this way, Nikephoros arrives at two important soteriological conclusions. First, through Christ's justification, man is brought back to the glory of the archetype (*kat'eikona Theou*): "As we have borne the image of the earthly, we shall also bear the image of the heavenly" (1 Corinthians 15.49). Second, because of his similitude with God (*kath'homoiosin*), man's own nature has been glorified as a result of Christ's kingly rank.[35]

The consequences of these formulations of mission and salvation for the theology of icons are not difficult to see. The soteriological perspective of man's likeness to God as a true image of the prototype can be applied by analogy to the problem of image-archetype. Moreover, the distinctions made in Nikephoros' soteriology between man, Christ, and God the Father support the thesis that the iconophiles distinguished between the various images in an ontological hierarchy of images. Ladner explains: "One is introduced into a world of images which extends from Christ through the divine ideas, through man as image of God, through the symbols and types of Holy Scripture down to the memorials or monuments of literature and art."[36]

## NOTES

1. Karmiris, *Mnemeia*, 1,77. The numbers in brackets indicate the particular article of faith.

2. *Antir.* 1.328.

3. *Logos* 661.

4. Ibid.

5. See below p. 141.

6. *Logos* 745,641.

7. Ibid. 716-17.

8. Ibid. 708-09. It must be remembered that Nikephoros directs his remarks to the iconoclasts who are attempting to minimize the importance of Christ and his mission in the world in order to suit their aims and theories.

9. Ibid. 680,733.

10. Ibid. 733-36.

11. See ibid. 584-85,680,733-36. Eusebios of Caesarea in *Εὐαγγελικῆς ἀποδείξεως* 4.12, PG 22.284, discusses the manifold dimensions of Christ's sacrifice which includes teaching, erasing our sins, freeing the world from demonic influence, as well as establishing the sanctification and hope through his living voice and deeds for the whole creation.

12. See *Logos* 733. J. L. Neve, *A History of Christian Thought*, 2 vols. (Philadelphia,

1943-46), 1,166, represents a view—still prevalent in some circles—which assumes that orthodox soteriology is limited only to Christ's resurrection, and therefore, it "failed to appropriate the Pauline idea of justification."

13. Ibid. 716.

14. Ibid. 716,724. The liturgical high priest is also an iconographic motif found in an icon by Biktoros (date unknown) in the Museum of Zakynthos with the title "The King of Kings and Great High Priest."

15. Ibid. 681,684.

16. Ibid. 664.

17. Ibid. 689.

18. Ibid. 680,681,684,685.

19. Ibid. 684.

20. Ibid. 729,732.

21. Ibid. 729.

22. *Antir.* 1.321.

23. *Antir. Eus.* 430; cf. the iron metaphor of Gregory of Nyssa above p. 66, n. 26.

24. Ibid. 430,431.

25. Ibid. 430. Christ is "the one who is made new...so that man by grace becomes God."

26. *Logos* 729,724.

27. *Antir.* 1.273.

28. *Logos* 796,797.

29. Ibid. 804,801.

30. Ibid. 812. Man assumes his fullest participatory role as a member of the sanctified body of Christ, the Church; see below, p. 160.

31. *Epikr.* 315. Terms which describe this beatific state are *makariotes*, *doxa*, *theosis*.

32. *Antir.* 3.421-25; see PG 74.7.773-76.

33. Ibid. 421.

34. Ibid. 420,424,421.

35. Ibid. 424.

36. "Image," p. 8. Ladner correctly contrasts the image hierarchy of John Damascene to platonism and neoplatonism: "John no longer calls the 'non-human things of nature' images. While for Plato 'these latter' had been the images *par excellence*, and for Philo, Plotinus, and Proclus, both intelligible and material natures were images, it was in the nature of Christian thought that material natural creatures should stand both above and below the dignity of images: above as creatures of God; below, if compared, for instance, with an image of Christ"; ibid. p. 9.

# 9

# *Church*

Nikephoros' ecclesiological formulations are unique in the history of patristic thought because they were used to combat the iconoclastic challenge against the Church. The inseparable connection between ecclesiology and christology is seen precisely in this challenge. By rejecting the incarnation, the iconoclasts implicitly deny the fulfillment of the Old Testament prophesies in Christ and his Church, and consequently, reject the apostolic and patristic tradition of the Church.[1]

The patriarch makes no attempt to introduce a definition of the Church's nature. Instead, he utilizes many scriptural and patristic metaphors which express its nature as well as its mission in the world.[2] A striking description is given at the beginning of *Apologetikos*:

> The holy Church of God stands securely and firmly upon the foundation of the apostles and prophets, having as the cornerstone Christ, our true God, and being decorated and beautified by all the holy and divine dogmas. Within her there is, by no means, any defense or debate concerning our correct, pure faith and worship.[3]

The passage is important because it presents an inclusive description of the Church's nature which is consonant with the creedal formula found in the ninth article: "[I believe] in one, holy, catholic, and apostolic Church."[4] Nikephoros' account is a descriptive unpacking, so to speak, of this formula. With these creedal distinctions, one, holy, catholic, and apostolic, the patriarch's notion of the Church can be elucidated.

## THE CHURCH IS ONE

Nikephoros regards the Church as one in origin, and also, inherently one. One in origin means that the Church was part of the eternal will of the Triune God. Its origin is heavenly and supernatural, not earthly and natural. By describing it as "the holy Church of God," the patriarch underscores that its essential oneness is based upon the oneness of the Triune God.[5] God and the Church are, in fact, inseparable; it is against both that the iconoclasts wage a futile battle.[6]

In addition to being one in origin, the Church is inherently one within itself. This internal unity, while strengthened by the Holy Spirit and by the love of those within the Church, is manifested externally as unity in faith, worship, and polity. The phrase "within her there is, by no means, any defense or debate concerning our correct, pure faith and worship" proves how seriously Nikephoros regards ecclesial unity.

The 'heavenly Jerusalem' is an important image which illustrates the mystery of the Church's oneness. The relation between the heavenly Jerusalem and the Church on earth is understood as a revelation of the former and a participation of the latter in the heavenly: "The heavenly things are revealed to those on earth,...and the kingdom of the heavens is made within us." Consequently, we already share in the heavenly Jerusalem which we shall fully inherit in the next life.[7]

Utilizing terminology similar to that of Gregory the Theologian, Nikephoros maintains that God is "the craftsman and creator of it [the heavenly Jerusalem], to which the Church of the first-born, who are enlisted in the heavens, celebrates with the divine powers [the angels]."[8] The faithful, then, belong "to the heavenly Jerusalem and the metropolis of the first-born, which is the Church of Christ." The heavenly Jerusalem is revealed to the faithful in all its magnificence and glory by Christ, its "great king."[9] In a stirring metaphor, the patriarch compares the Church to a city which is surrounded by a strong wall and whose cornerstone is Christ. Each section of the wall is linked with his beneficence and goodness. The prophets' sermons, the apostles' teachings, and the holy fathers' dogmas are the fortified towers which secure the kingdom. Surrounding the city from above, the incorporeal powers guard and protect it from all heretical intrusion.[10]

The oneness of the heavenly, invisible Church and the visible Church on earth is possible only through Christ's incarnation. He "has established one Church and celebration of angels and men in heaven and on earth." The character of such a unity, as "a celebration of angels and men," finds its ecclesial expression in the orthodox liturgical setting. In the performance of their liturgical duties, the priests "are imprinted in the likeness of the high super-mundane [powers] and orders [of angels]." Even the decoration and plan of the church edifice are "imitations and figures" which represent the heavenly court.[11]

Ecclesial unity through participation is best illustrated in another of Nikephoros' metaphors which depicts the Church as the mountain of God. The heavenly Jerusalem is the house set upon the summit of the highest mountain which is called the Church. "To this mountain and house the nations from afar come." It is here that "the faithful begin their climb," advancing above the earthly ideals to a contemplation of the holy, all the while being enlightened by the lives and teachings of the holy apostles and saints. Even though the lord's paths make for difficult climbing, they are true and secure because the climbing itself is from the lowest unbelief to the highest contemplation of the divine. Nikephoros reiterates that the faithful belong to the heavenly Jerusalem which is "the temporally endless, great city of the saints."[12]

Three conclusions may be drawn from these passages concerning the patriarch's notion that the Church is one. First, there are not two, but rather, one and the same, "Church of God"; originating outside of time, it reveals itself temporally in history. Second, the Church explicitly becomes known to us through Christ and our active participation. Third, the Church on earth is the icon or figure of the heavenly one. The glory of the latter is made known to us through the Church on earth.[13] Our sanctification is possible, then, in the holy temples which "are scattered throughout the world," and are compared "to mountains covered with lush foliage...which purge [us] of sin, sanctify souls and bodies, and fill all those people with divine grace who approach with devotion and desire."[14]

## THE CHURCH IS HOLY

Nikephoros' description "the holy Church of God" predicates what is relevant to the meaning of the Church. It is holy because of Christ. Its holiness is derived from its sanctification by him: "Christ also loved the Church, and gave himself for it; that He might sanctify and cleanse it with the washing of water by the word, that He might present to himself a glorious church, not having spot, or wrinkle, or any such thing; but that it should be holy and without blemish" (Ephesians 5.25-27).[15] There is an inseparable connection between holiness and Christ. The affirmation that he is "our lord and God" testifies to the holiness of the Church within Christ. It is holy in its mission because it recalls all people to holiness. Its mission as directed by Christ, finally, is sanctified by the Spirit through the sacraments.[16]

## THE CHURCH IS CATHOLIC

The patriarch's notion of catholicity is uniquely nonconfining. He regards the Church not merely in a quantitative sense, within local and temporal boundaries, but also in a qualitative sense, namely, "metaphorically, theologically, and metaphysically."[17] His position will be elucidated under these two aspects.

### Catholicity in a Quantitative Sense

Nikephoros intimates what may be understood as the Church's 'ecumenical openness'. In contrast to pagan mysteries in which only the initiate members were allowed to participate, and to Judaic tradition where worship was confined to one place, such as the temple of Jerusalem, Christ's Church is for all people. "Not being within the spatial limitation of the synagogue, which is composed of the Israelites, the Church, rather, is designated as catholic [because] of its numerical strength."[18] Nikephoros, nevertheless, distinguishes its membership from other groups. Christians are Christ's people: "We are his special people, a royal priesthood and eternal inheritance; to say it summarily, [we are] his elect and most intimate possession."[19]

The members of the Church which the partriarch focuses on are the Theotokos, the martyrs, and monks. These individuals exemplify catholicity in its uninterrupted historical continuity by their witness to the ecclesiastical norms (*ekklesiastikoi thesmoi*) both in their lives and in their manner of death.

## THE THEOTOKOS

Like other orthodox fathers, Nikephoros regards the Virgin Mary in her special role in Christ's incarnation. He characterizes her as "the all-pure mother of God descended from the genus of the root of Jesse and the seed of David." His agreement with the Third Ecumenical Synod (431) is seen in his identification of the Virgin Mary as the Theotokos. The use of the terms "all-pure" and "mother of God" makes this allegiance to Ephesos perfectly clear. Because of Christ's unique nature as the God-man, she "is known to us mainly and truly as the Theotokos." At the same time, because of the Logos' incarnation, her virginity was "sheltered" even after conception. This remains an "indescribable" mystery to all.[20]

These locutions reveal a creedal basis which defines the Theotokos and her relation to Christ's incarnation: "[He] was incarnate of the holy Spirit and of the all-holy, glorious and truly Theotokos ever-virgin Mary."[21] The special place which she occupies in the orthodox choir of saints, not to be interpreted in the later roman catholic sense of her immaculate conception, is due to her role as the bearer of Christ.[22] Our giving "due respect to the venerable icons of our all-holy, pure lady and true protectress ever-virgin Theotokos," is based upon her role of bringing God in the flesh "without seed, inexpressibly and extraordinarily" as our lord and savior Jesus Christ.[23] A justification for the iconographic representation of the Virgin Mary, then, is our acknowledgment of her role as the mother of God.

When Nikephoros discusses the Theotokos, most often it is within a christological framework which verifies her inseparable relation to the hypostasis of Christ. Even though the subject of the Theotokos is subsumed under the panoply of christological objections directed against the iconoclastic emperor, an understanding of the patriarch's position concerning her can be gained.[24]

Nikephoros presents a corollary argument against Constantine's fifth contention which supposes that Christ is "a mere creature." He interprets the iconoclastic position to mean that Christ is uncircumscribable.[25] The patriarch's argument for the proof of Christ's circumscription, and therefore, his humanity, is based upon the humanity of the Theotokos. In other words, his argument attempts to settle the question of Christ's human nature by comparing it with hers. How it is possible for "the Logos, who took on our nature...and according to the flesh came from her, to be uncircumscribable" is answered on the basis of his natural relation to the birth-giver (*ten tekousan*).

> Since God the Father is uncircumscribable, it is affirmed that Christ, inasmuch as he is God and consubstantial with him, is also uncircumscribable. But because the mother [Virgin Mary] is circumscribable, and therefore, also human according to our nature, it will be affirmed then that Christ too, inasmuch as [he] is man and the same nature as her, is circumscribable.[26]

Nikephoros' rebuttal against these iconoclastic objections reveals how he understood the Theotokos. First, if Christ's nature is uncircumscribable, as the iconoclasts claim, it follows that his birth from the Virgin Mary is without sensation, and therefore, uncircumscribable. "If it is impossible that the body is uncircumscribable, it is more impossible [to maintain] that to be born according to human nature is uncircumscribable."[27] The iconoclastic tenet leads to the impiety of denying that the Virgin Mary gave birth to Christ.

Second, by maintaining that Christ is uncircumscribable, the iconoclasts have reached the illogical position of transferring other qualities as well which belong to him, such as incorruptibility, immortality and impassivity, to the Virgin Mary. Consequently, they demote the Logos to a secondary position ("mere creature"), and at the same time, elevate the Theotokos to a higher place. The patriarch rhetorically demands: "What, then, ought to differentiate the God of men?" Since we are circumscribable, it follows that Christ also must be circumscribed in order to save us. If he were otherwise, "it would be superfluous that he lived among us."[28]

Third, if uncircumscription is attributed to the Virgin Mary, the relation between her and Christ is inverted completely. The inversion follows from the thesis that her nature is also uncircumscribable. Not even 1 Corinthians 15.53, which deals with corruptibility and incorruptibility, implies a substitution or obliteration of her nature rendering it uncircumscribable. He scoffs at the suggestion that the iconoclasts can justify the non-representation of the Theotokos on the grounds that her nature, like Christ's, is uncircumscribable. Nikephoros concludes his objection by reiterating "but certainly the Virgin is circumscribable, and therefore, the body of Christ is circumscribable, as coming from a circumscribable body [Theotokos]."[29]

The patriarch inserts a curious *appendum* to the argument for the Theotokos' humanity which identifies his interlocutors with docetism. He refers to "an old phantasy" wherein "the teachers dogmatized that the Logos from above [the heavens], becoming incarnate, passed through the Virgin as a channel (*dia solenos*) in order that neither one ought to participate in the other." The iconophile fears that the iconoclasts can easily resort to this heretical opinion in order to justify their thesis of the non-affinity of Christ's nature with humanity. On these grounds they are linked to docetism.[30]

The patriarch considers this theory untenable because it denies the humanity of Christ, more specifically, his similitude to us based upon the reality of the Theotokos. Docetism implicitly questions the humanity of the Virgin Mary also. Christ's humanity must be connected to ours because he is "the son of the all-holy Virgin." This is precisely what docetism denies. At the same time, our humanity is made known to Christ through "our sublime, all-holy lady mother of God, who is the first over those things pertaining to the saints and of all those things performed in creation."[31]

## THE MARTYRS

Considered an important group in the Church, the martyrs especially interested the patriarch because their icons were targets of attack by the iconoclasts.[32] His purpose is specific: to argue for the martyrs' iconographic representation. As in the case of Christ, the justification of their images lies in acknowledging the reality and sanctity of the archetype.

Without referring to any particular martyr, the patriarch has in mind "those innumerable" persons who gave witness to Christ through their death during the Church's first three centuries.[33] He defines them as those "workers of God, who carried the cross throughout their life, who followed Christ and were crucified also, and became imitators and followers of his life-giving passion and death." They are characterized as saints, and their perfection lies in their imitation of him through persecution and witness. The prefix *syn* with the verbs *synestaurothesan*, *syndiokontai*, and *sympaschousin* emphasizes the fact that their lives are conformed to Christ's.[34] As he suffered, so too, they suffered as imitators of him.

The suffering continues, moreover, in the desecration of their icons by the iconoclasts. This impiety has the effect of transferring the insults to the archetypes, the martyrs themselves. "What happened before to the archetypes, this and now, in fact, is shown [to happen] with the holy likenesses." The result of the present desecration of their icons is "a duplication of the [martyrs'] contests upon a duplication of persecutions and insults." Their reward, however, is to be doubly crowned by Christ.[35]

Nikephoros strongly believes that there exists an intimate affinity between the martyr and Christ. This is not confined merely to a present commitment of suffering and martyrdom, but, at the same time, transcends the temporal life of the martyr. For their suffering, "they co-rule with him to the age." The phrase "they live always with God and are in peace" is not to be taken only figuratively. It expresses an existential fact of the martyr's inseparable relation with his prototype, Christ—a fact which encompasses his present persecutions on earth and includes his crowning and co-rule in the eschatological future.[36] The patriarch beautifully describes the connection between present and future circumstances:

> It follows that the bodies of the saints which have suffered...will become conformed to him, transformed from corruptibility to imperishableness and conformed to the one sitting on the right of the father's glory and above all principality and power, and worshiped by every power, when he will come from the heavens as the expected one. Then too, the saints will be conformed to Christ, co-illuminated with him, transferred from the present humility to the high and celestial, and possessing the heavenly government.[37]

This bliss or beatitude is recognized by all the faithful. Such an acknowledgment finds its expression in the liturgical experience, particularly "in the hymns chanted by us everyday." At the end of the *ephymnion melos*, which was recited (*recitativo*) by the clergy, the congregation responded in chant with the last verse called *to akroteleution*. One such verse has been preserved by the patriarch: "Bless the lord, spirits and souls of the just."[38]

In almost mystical language, Nikephoros describes the intimacy between the martyr and Christ as "mixing together (*anekrathesan*)" which is a result of their love for him. "Their souls have been wounded by love for Christ." This "inseparable" joining has been actualized by becoming "martyrs of sufferings." Their suffering for Christ has enabled them "to become communicants (*koinonoi*) of his life-giving death, resisting sin to the point of blood [i.e. death]. And now having been exempted from these [earthly concerns], they have appeared as participants (*metochoi*) of the recently stirred up persecution and insult against Christ." By being "communicants" and "participants" in Christ's life, the martyrs have become in a real way imitators of his death and have given their lives "for the common salvation of us all." Nikephoros believes that once again they must suffer with Christ because of the iconoclastic attack against their images: "Again they suffer together in order that they may be glorified together anew."[39]

The patriarch's description of the martyr's life follows the traditional metaphors and characterizations. A martyr is a soldier. Nikephoros embellishes the pauline theme of the martyr who is armed with faith and hope. "Looking toward future things as if those were already present things...despising all temporal things as temporary and corrupt...raising the cross...receiving, indeed, the strength from above,...they have shown themselves to be invincible soldiers of the great king and most courageous athletes."[40]

A martyr is an athlete. To be a good soldier implies being a courageous athlete too. Their martyrdom is a training of body and spirit. "They are strengthened in the temptations and tribulations," and moreover, "they are perfected in [their] witness to Christ." The patriarch beautifully describes this process: "Tempered in the furnace of tortures, and as the tested gold discovered and shining, these victorious martyrs shine more than the sun [and] blaze beyond the stars." As Christ was the sacrificed lamb, so too, they have become "the rational and perfect victims, and [their] sacrifice is most favorable and pleasing to God."[41] As a result of their contest, "they have been awarded most rightly the unfading crowns from the prize-giver God." Even "the angels are astonished at their boldness, and the super-mundane powers exult in their feats."[42]

The martyr's only goal is the eternal crown of salvation. "They endure all [torments], looking to one [end], regarding the prize of the high calling." The prize of eternal salvation is won by their "invincible faith, inexpressible love, certain hope,...willingness and haste to the higher and heavenly things." These have enabled them "to win over nature and hover above creation."[43]

A martyr's life is a fight "against every machination of the enemy," namely, the forces of evil. Through all forms of persecution they "have shamed the wounded devil together with his apostatic powers." Their fight against him has been won: "Indeed, as mortals they have shaken the invisible powers and have won over the evil [powers]."[44]

A martyr, finally, is an image of God's glory. The glory of God's name has been preserved and "kept before nations and kings" through their witness, manifested in their fight, endurance, and preference for death against "the threats of the tyrants." Moreover, the martyrs "were seen [as] the unshakable towers of our faith, pillars of the Church and consolidation, base of piety and unshakable foundation, great glory and ornament for us the faithful. As bright and intellectual torches, they light the ends [of the world], the rays of their feats and faith radiating brilliantly."[45]

The soteriological unity between God and man is seen from this characterization of the martyr. "The power of God" and the martyr's "good disposition" to be saved are in mutual cooperation. The patriarch emphatically insists that both factors are involved.

On the one hand, "the power of God" is manifested in "the exceptional holy gifts [of the Spirit]" which strengthen and encourage the martyr on his road to perfection. The witnesses of Christ endure "the instruments of punishment" with dispassion as if they were experiencing delight, and, at the same time, "conquer the insolence of the evil one," only because "of the divine synergistic grace and power" which sustains them.[46]

On the other hand, the martyr's "disposition" is exemplified in his "greatness of soul." This magnanimity is a sense of thanksgiving which is felt by him. His martrydom is a reflection of God's glory: "On behalf of the saints that are in his hand, he [the lord] has magnified all his pleasure in them" (Psalm 15.3-4). They are the exemplars of the soteriological mystical union between God and redeemed man. His glory is reflected through their deeds, and "they become imitators of the divine" through him.[47]

The desecration of the martyrs' icons is a consequence of the iconoclastic irreverence toward Christ's image. Nikephoros suggests that there is a causal connection between these two circumstances. The reverence one attributes to Christ by honoring his icon will have a bearing upon one's attitude concerning the martyrs and their images. As in the case of Christ and his image, the justification for representing a martyr iconographically is based upon an 'orthodox' understanding of the archetype.

Nikephoros' characterization of the martyrs as witnesses of the faith and imitators of Christ has reaffirmed their uncontested place in God's kingdom. Because of their status as saints, they have received the power of the Holy Spirit "to cure every malady and every sickness." Does the patriarch's characterization also justify that there should be images of martyrs? He believes that the premise "the honor rendered to the image passes to the prototype" likewise applies to them.[48] The image-similitude seen in the saint's life as he relates to Christ, his archetype, can serve as the framework for understanding the connection between the martyr and his material image. Their images become the visible reminders of their invisible subjects. Supported by passages from Paul, John Chrysostom, Cyril, and Basil, the patriarch reasserts "that the saints are seen through their similitudes, since they too are holy."[49]

Nikephoros' discussion of the saints' veneration implies that "the honor rendered" is directed not only to the material image, but includes all that is related to the martyr himself: "We honor their feats, we venerate [their] holy relics, [and] we kiss ardently their holy icons." Moreover, the honor that is given to them is also proof of our honor for Christ. This idea of inclusiveness becomes clearer when seen in conjunction with the saint's memory and our seeking his intercessions. By destroying their icons, relics, and books which have described their feats, the iconoclasts haved supposed that they "have completely erased the memory of them." Consequently, asking for a saint's intercession would be impossible to do under these circumstances.[50] For Nikephoros, however, honoring the images of the saints already implies "acknowledging [their] memory and entreating [their] intercessions." Only "those who appeal and entreat are able to be assisted and helped by them [the saints] in unity with God's power and grace, because they live in God and act in him."[51]

In an effort to minimize the importance of the martyrs, and therefore, to deny their iconographic representation, the iconoclasts have cited an unusual argument of Epiphanides. The heretic contends that it is impossible to represent in an icon the future glory of the martyrs. The patriarch believes that a link exists between Epiphanides and Eusebios on this point. As Eusebios taught that Christ cannot be represented iconographically because the hypostasis has changed completely into a divine essence, so too, Epiphanides contends that the saints cannot be pictured because they have been transformed to a future bliss.[52]

In response, Nikephoros argues that the saints' glory really begins in this life through their witness to Christ. He admonishes Epiphanides for being like the foolish farmer who thinks that it is easy to harvest without the tools for sowing, and even without seeds. Drawing from this analogy, Nikephoros contends that the feats of the saints were done in the present; these, in turn, will be the cause of their future bliss. The saint "is pictorially represented, not as he might be, but as he who was or is now."[53] The justification of a saint's icon rests with Nikephoros' insistence that an icon presents "the present" and "the historically seen" events, rather than future things which as yet have not occurred.[54] Its true motif is just these historical events (*ta historoumena*), which in themselves manifest the real glory of the martyr.

## THE MONKS

In many respects these individuals are similar to the martyrs. They too have left the transitoriness and pleasures of this world and "have exercised in the ascetic palaestra." Rather than being in the arena of martyrdom, the monks have chosen to dedicate their lives to "living purely."

They have fled to the desert "far from the noises of everyday life,...conducting themselves as [if] they were spiritual beings still in the flesh and striving after the angelic state." Their sanctity is manifested in the curing of incurable diseases. They too have broken and chained the power of the demons. Without further detail, the patriarch characterizes the monks as "lights in the world."[55]

As persecution was directed against the martyrs of the early Church, likewise the same tactics were meted against the monastic communities. The patriarch has in mind his contemporaries who have identified openly with iconophilism. His description of persecution methods as employed by Constantine V discloses the resilient spirit and true character of monasticism. Against this iconoclastic opposition, the monastic ideal is tested.

Nikephoros characterizes this ideal with a list of virtues which each monk ought to possess. They are "temperance, humility, meekness, calmness, forbearance, sleeping on the ground, poverty, solitude, and the separation from the world and mundane things."[56] Any persecution against monasticism will attempt to compromise the ascetic principle of "the separation from the world and worldly things." By attempting to secularize monasticism, and at the same time rejecting these virtues, the iconoclastic attack was no different. Constantine's tactics, besides being physically brutal—monks were tied in sackcloths and thrown into the sea—were directed to breaking the spirit by substituting secular vice for monastic virtue. Such humiliating acts as shaving the monk's head and cutting his beard, or marching him into the theaters and forcing him to wear other than the monastic habit, were directed toward this end. The patriarch's characterization of these persecuted members of the Church as "the venerable men (*hoi hosioi andres*)" is a worthy accolade.[57]

The pain experienced by the monks was certainly no different from that of the earlier martyrs. The eighth and ninth century situation, however, was uniquely different. Although the attack was directed against the icons of the martyrs, it included the supporters of their images, the monks. Since the monks were the painters of these images—there is no reason to deny this—it makes sense to suppose that a persecution against the makers of images would mean a diminished supply of images, and eventually, an eradication of the memory of an image's archetype. By publicly denouncing the monks as "the unmentionables," Constantine and his iconoclastic cohorts thought that they had completely erased the memory of icon veneration. If the monk who was the painter as well as the venerator of the image was ostracized, it followed that the image and its archetype, the saint or Christ, were also "the unmentionables." As a monastic in exile, Nikephoros could readily identify with the monastic ideal of "tested faith and works which were bright and visible."[58] His favorable characterization of monasticism, finally, suggests that he, too, as other orthodox Byzantines before and after him, regarded the monks "as being an essential, and indeed the highest, expression of Christianity."[59]

### Catholicity in a Qualitative Sense

Nikephoros regards catholicity as that which transcends all local and temporal limitations. The martyrs, monks, and other members of the Church have formed an uninterrupted continuity of faith in Christ and unity of fellowship with each other which links all believers irrespective of their specific historical experience. Catholicity means that personal and individual feats, persecutions, and eternal victories are common and made public to the totality of the Church. The patriarch arrives at two conclusions in his unique treatment of catholicity: the saint's image is a reminder of the historical presence of its archetype; and the believer's honor and veneration of the image perpetuates the memory of the saint. These confirm that catholicity was understood by him also in qualitative terms, namely, metaphorically, theologically, and metaphysically.

Catholicity in a qualitative sense means that the Church is understood beyond mere numerical strength. The Church is the intimate bond of fellowship between the 'chosen people' and Christ. Belief and teaching among its members are the expressions of this visible fellowship. These are guided by the work of the Holy Spirit. For Nikephoros, belief or faith means "a concord (*ten symphonian*)" with orthodoxy in contrast to heresy.[60] His statement, "within her there is by no means any defense or debate concerning our correct, pure faith and worship,"[61] defines catholicity precisely in terms of a theological agreement between faith and dogma.

From the vantage of his contemporary situation, the patriarch argues that catholicity means oneness in orthodoxy:

> If they [iconoclasts] remain in this heresy, and perhaps are able to lead astray some others who are poorer and more ignorant, and even if they can cause a sedition and gather a throng of followers, they are outside the sacred domains of the Church. But even if only a very few remain in orthodoxy and piety, these few are the Church. And the authority and protection of the ecclesiastical norms repose in them, even if they must suffer for their piety.[62]

Catholicity understood quantitatively, then, is reflected in its qualitative aspect. The latter, in turn, is the impetus for the former.[63]

## THE CHURCH IS APOSTOLIC

Recognized as divinely instituted, the Church, as Nikephoros insists, is also a visible institution which "stands securely and firmly upon the foundation of the apostles and prophets."[64] Its apostolicity is confirmed by its historical beginning, teaching, and uninterrupted apostolic succession. Nikephoros understands church polity, namely, the composition of the Church, primarily in terms of apostolic succession. We will focus on his views concerning the governing hierarchy of the visible Church and postpone discussion on apostolic origin and teaching until chapter eleven.

The patriarch's account of the priesthood is set against the background of his time wherein many members of the hierarchy became iconoclasts. The sanctity and indelibleness of the priesthood unmistakably may be discerned in his discussion. The orthodox clergyman, according to Nikephoros, should have the fear of God; preserve the holy tradition, "all the canonical and divine legislation which has been well established by the teachers through the Spirit"; and honor the sanctity of his ordination vows.[65]

The actions of those priests who have become iconoclasts are proof that they have forsaken these characteristics. That some in his flock "have denied the office of the priesthood which has been confirmed to them" on the day of their ordination, is an apprehension which is deeply felt and expressed by the patriarch. Reflecting upon the third characterization, he believes that a priest's unworthiness lies in compromising his vows of ordination: "Forgetting the vows which they [iconoclasts] confessed before the holy altar...they were ordained unworthily." Upholding the indelibleness of the priesthood, Nikephoros reaffirms that any deviation is a further denial and insult to the faith of the Church's members. Even though the iconoclast clergy are still called priests, "they have broken themselves off as rotten and disfigured members of the great and indivisible body of the Church."[66]

Citing Old Testament prophetic passages (especially Zechariah 10.3;11.17), the patriarch defines the mission of the priest by the relationship which exists between a shepherd and his flock. An important part of the priest's task is to deepen his understanding concerning the sacred: "Her priests also have set at nought my law, and profaned my holy things: they have not distinguished between the holy and profane, nor have they distinguished between the unclean and the clean, [...] and I was profaned in the midst of them" (Ezekiel 22.26-27).[67]

To distinguish between what is sacred and profane as outlined by the Old Testament prophet, presupposes a stability in the priest's personal character. Unfortunately, this is completely absent in those bishops who, because of iconoclastic pressures, have yielded and are cooperating with the opposition's cause. They have forgotten "to be servants of God"; instead, they "are concerned to please men." A true hierarch is one who does not deviate from "the straight road [of truth]," and, moreover, stands firmly "within the ancestral faith."[68]

In contrast, the iconoclast bishops are characteristically irresponsible. They condemn themselves by being "inconsistent (*akatastatoi*)" in their ministry. Nikephoros posits them as saying: "We are double-minded, inconsistent in all our ways, and we are like the raging waves of the sea which are tossed and blown [here and there]." The patriarch insists that an unstable character manifests itself in "the evil of unbelief which has neither stability nor foundation, but is forever at variance,...presenting and changing itself in this or that manner."[69] To be a heretic, especially a supporter of the fight against icon veneration, for Nikephoros, is the worst thing that a clergyman could do. An iconoclast's refusal to honor the images ultimately means denying his faith in Christ and the dogmatic tenets of his Church.

The image-archetype relation existing when priests in their liturgical functions represent the likeness of the heavenly orders is a reaffirmation of the kind of character an apostle's successor should emulate. The use of the verb *apotypoo* (*o*) is not an accidental choice. The priests more than represent the angelic character. The angelic likeness is formed on them, as one would stamp an impression upon wax. When Nikephoros contrasts the orthodox from the iconoclast priest, this meaning of *apotypo* is implied. What the psalmist affirms: "Thy priests shall clothe themselves with righteousness" (Psalm 131.9) is impressed upon the character of the priesthood (*to hieratikon schema*). Their resemblance to angelic conduct, as mirrored in the virtues of their priestly office, entitles them to be recognized as "honorable" by the pious members of the Church.[70]

The apostolicity of the Church cannot be understood without the sacred and indelible character of the priesthood. Nikephoros emphasizes that it lies with the clergy, as successors of the apostles, to be above all honorable in preserving the apostolic teaching and tradition as handed down by Christ. Without this apostolic succession, which insures the continuation of the apostolic kerygma and sacramental life, it is difficult to envision the Church as apostolic.

## NOTES

1. See O'Connell, *Ecclesiology*, pp. 79-80. This study is the first major work since Alexander's *Nikephoros* (1958). The author focuses on church polity in the pre-Photian era between East and West through Nikephoros' ecclesiology. Gero's important criticisms in BZ, 68 (1975) 409-11, are directed against the latter's interpretation of Nikephoros' passages which relate to an understanding of the relation between the Eastern pentarchy and Roman

primacy. He correctly criticizes "O'C.'s contention that in employing the 'patriarchal' concept, N. 'admits the doctrinal primacy of Rome' (p.194)."

2. See a listing in ibid. pp. 80-83.

3. 833-36.

4. Karmiris, *Mnemeia*, 1,77.

5. *Apol.* 833; also, *Chaps. 12-PK*, 454.

6. *Prol.* 233.

7. *Logos* 789; *Prol.* 236-37.

8. *Logos* 680; cf. *Εἰς τὴν ἀδελφὴν ἑαυτοῦ Γοργονίαν ἐπιτάφιος* 8.6, PG 35.796.

9. *Prol.* 236.

10. Ibid.

11. *Logos* 585; *Antir.* 3.484.

12. *Logos* 660.

13. Ibid. 657,661,680.

14. Ibid. 661.

15. Cf. ibid. 693 for other scriptural references.

16. Ibid. 697,692-93.

17. See Karmiris, *Synopsis*, p. 92.

18. *Logos* 692-93. Admiration for the Church's expansion is also expressed in 645.

19. Ibid. 744.

20. Ibid. 677.

21. Ibid. 584.

22. Ibid. 585; cf. *Antir.* 1.265.

23. *Logos* 589; cf. *Antir.* 2.341.

24. *Antir.* 1.265-73.

25. See above, pp. 75-76.

26. *Antir.* 1.265. The terminology is very specific concerning Christ's two natures. Terms which define his relation to the Father are *symphyian* and *homoousios*; those which relate Christ to man (via the Theotokos) are *syngeneian* and *homophyes.*

27. Ibid. 268.

28. Ibid.

29. Ibid. 269; 3.468.

30. Ibid. 1.269. Nikephoros does not identify these teachers of the old phantasy. His closest contemporaries of heresy were the Paulicians who made their appearance in the middle of the seventh century in Armenia. They "were docetists and on this point [Christ's incarnation] were identified with the Gnostics and Marcionites, but sometimes they impersonated that they agreed with the Nestorians"; Stephanides, *Historia*, p. 256, n. 4. The Nestorians, who were also against icon veneration, took a 'heretically' more moderate position concerning the manner of Christ's incarnation. They "accepted, that the divine Logos was not born of the Virgin Mary, but simply passed through her, the Logos taking up residence in the man Jesus who was conceived simultaneously. They did not consider the incarnation of Christ a phantom; they were not docetists, but they denied the name Theotokos and the honor proper to her"; ibid. It can be implied, then, that in *Antir.* 1.269 the patriarch seems to identify the iconoclastic thesis with the extreme docetism of the Paulicians, rather than with the Nestorian non-docetic position. For the historical connec-

tion to the Valentinian gnostics, who "taught that the body of Jesus was a heavenly psychical formation, and sprang from the womb of Mary only in appearance," see Adolph von Harnack, *History of Dogma*, trans. from 3d German ed. Neil Buchanan, 7 vols. bound as 4 vols. (New York, 1961), 1,259-60; 260, n. 1.

31. *Antir.* 1.273,269; 2.341.

32. A reconstruction of Nikephoros' views on martyrs is based on these passages: *Logos* 644; *Antir.* 2.341-44; 3.468-77; and *Antir. Epiph.* 305-17.

33. *Logos* 644.

34. *Antir.* 2.344; *Antir. Epiph.* 312.

35. *Antir.* 2.344.

36. Ibid.; cf. 3.473-76.

37. *Antir. Epiph.* 311-12.

38. *Antir.* 3.476.

39. Ibid. 469.

40. Ibid. 469-72.

41. Ibid. 472.

42. Ibid. 473. The athletic motif whereby God, the prize-giver (*ho athlothetes*), awards the crown to the victorious martyr (*ho athlophoros*) also is seen in *Logos* 644.

43. Ibid. 472-73.

44. Ibid. 472.

45. Ibid. 473.

46. Ibid. 473,472; *Logos* 644.

47. *Antir.* 3.473.

48. Ibid. 476.

49. *Antir. Epiph.* 310-13. For the patristic references, see Pitra, SS 4.310, n. 1,5; 312, n. 3. Paul's reference is Phil 3.20-21.

50. *Antir.* 3.476,477.

51. *Logos* 589.

52. *Antir. Epiph.* 309,316.

53. Ibid. 317. Based on Nikephoros' citation of Cyril earlier at 311, the following conclusion may be drawn. The patriarch believes that future bliss is an eschatological condition, categorically different from the martyr's historically present circumstance in which relative glory is experienced. This will be completed in the next life.

54. Ibid.

55. *Logos* 644. "Though not theologians as such, through their contemplative life they developed what might be described as a 'monastic' theology. It was the monastic world which produced the countless hymns, troparia and canons which enriched the liturgy. It was the great monastic directors who left instruction and meditation on the spiritual life"; J. M. Hussey, "Byzantine Monasticism," CMH 4, pt.2,183. For social outreach outside the confines of the monastery, see pp. 181-84.

56. *Antir.* 3.516.

57. *Antir. Eus.* 377-78.

58. *Antir.* 3.517.

59. Hussey, "Byzantine Monasticism," p. 184.

60. *Logos* 744.

61. *Apol.* 833-36; see above, p. 97.

62. Ibid. 844; see also, *Logos* 621.

63. If *Logos* 684 is to be understood as referring to the hope of the messiah belonging both to the pagan nations and the Jews, it follows that catholicity may be interpreted in the broadest sense to apply in some measure even to those pagans, such as Socrates, "who taught and lived as Christians"; see Theodorou, *Theologia*, p. 104. Nikephoros nowhere mentions the doctrine of the 'seminal word' (*spermatikos logos*) which is Justin's explanation as to how the pre-Christian pagans acquired a partial knowledge of the divine truths of Christianity. The patriarch accepts that the Church has revealed itself in three historical phases: as the heavenly Church of the angels, as the earthly Church from the creation of man to the time of Christ, and as the Church of Christ; *Logos* 657-65; cf. Karmiris, *Ekklesia*, p. 6. Like other fathers before him (Irenaeus, PG 7.1069-70; Basil, PG 29.288; John Chrysostom, PG 62.75, cited in Karmiris, pp. 10-12), Nikephoros understands the second phase as including those gentiles who lived faithfully and justly. It follows that Christ, "even if partially, acted in the pre-Christian period of humanity too; his work is for all men, indeed universal"; Theodorou, p. 106.

64. *Apol.* 833.

65. *Logos* 545,548.

66. Ibid. 548.

67. Ibid. 577. The phrase "and have hid their eyes from my sabbaths" is omitted by Nikephoros.

68. Ibid. 593,596.

69. *Antir.* 3.484.

70. Ibid.; also *Logos* 600.

# 10

# *Sacraments*

## ORIGIN, NATURE, AND SCOPE OF A SACRAMENT

Nikephoros' discussion, even though not extensive, presupposes a framework which defines the origin, nature, and relational scope of a sacrament. Consistent with other orthodox formulations, he defines the sacraments as "the innermost and hidden mysteries according to Christ's economy." As a means of transmitting grace, they are "the highest and sacred mysteries (*aporreta*) of theology." Avoiding any scholastic definitions concerning the sacramental nature, Nikephoros characterizes their nature as lying within the mystery of the incarnate Logos, and for this reason they are "the treasures of knowledge and the innermost of wisdom." The initiator of the sacraments is Jesus Christ. The mysteries were revealed first to his disciples and through them to succeeding generations.[1]

There is an intimate and inseparable relation between Christ, the sacraments, and the Church. The efficacious character of the sacraments is manifested in their action, namely, to sanctify man. Their sanctification (*hagiasmos*) is "toward a benefit" or "healing." Nikephoros affirms the prominence of the mysteries as the direct instruments of sanctification in the Church. Through them the faithful actually participate in the life of Christ. This does not imply a 'symbolic', but a 'real' dependence upon him.[2]

Sanctification plays an integral part in the believer's "unity and communion." By being "a partaker of the secret mysteries," the believer is in communion with Christ "who sanctifies as the head and author of salvation, the giver and lord of all sanctification." The members are "those who are made anew by being sanctified in the partaking of his grace."[3] This participation, transmitted through the sacramental life, is the visible expression of what Nikephoros describes as the Church's brotherhood or "brotherhood in the unity of Christ."[4] No comparison can be drawn between the sacraments, based on their origin, nature and function, and the pagan rites, as the iconoclasts would suggest.[5]

Even though the patriarch does not refer to each sacrament separately, he does not deny that there are seven sacraments. It must be remembered that his discussion of the sacraments is also directed toward apologetic ends. Besides ordination, which has already been explicated,[6] he discusses two other sacraments, baptism and the eucharist.

## BAPTISM

Nikephoros' references to baptism must be seen as one further objection against the iconoclastic claim that icon veneration is idol worship. That he emphasizes certain characteristics, and not others, concerning baptism is to be understood within this apologetic background.

Baptism is a sacrament "of regeneration by washing and of renewal by the holy Spirit."[7] Nikephoros' explication of its nature is a repetition of familiar orthodox formulations. His metaphorical description, which compares the undiminished abundance of the Spirit's gifts with the oveflowing waters covering the seas, is a true literary gem.[8] Of note is the patriarch's insistence upon the tri-immersion and "the invocation of the supreme Trinity." The mark of baptism is to be baptized in the name of the Trinity. Within the baptismal water is "the fire of the Spirit." The laver of regeneration enables "us to wash away the salt of the previous condition of unbelief.... Thus, by shedding the old Adam, we are clothed with the new and recreated [man] in Christ."[9]

Baptism has a sacred and indelible character as well. The patriarch cannot imagine that the iconoclasts' impiety would lead them to deny the validity of baptism. They find it necessary to be rebaptized "in the name of Constantine" on the ground of rehabilitating the sanctity of the sacrament. The indelible character is visibly present "once [the believers] have been illuminated and tasted the heavenly gift, and have become participants of the holy Spirit." It is unthinkable to consider re-baptism or re-ordination because the nature of the sacrament "ought to be well-accepted or trustworthy."[10]

Baptism is also a sacrament of historical continuity. Its historicity is seen in Christ's command to his apostles to teach and baptize all nations in the Triune God (Matthew 28.19); his message through their ministry; and finally, the conversion of both Jews and gentiles. Nikephoros adds that the covenant of God to Abraham is made complete and universal with Christ's message and the baptism of his followers.[11]

The historical continuity of baptism finds its expression in the unity of faith among all the baptized members of the Church. "The catholic Church of Christ is formed and gathered from those who agree to one faith of confession." The sacrament cannot be compared to any pagan initiations because its uniqueness lies in the confession of faith directed to God. The initiants are "in the knowledge of the Trinity." Like the bond between Abraham and God, baptism is that inseparable unity between Christ and his illumined followers "who are filled with the glory and knowledge of him." This can never be achieved by any pagan rite.[12]

Finally, inseparably related to unity through faith is the perpetuation of baptism's sanctity in the believer's life. Even though the iconoclasts have also been baptized, thus acknowledging all the characteristics of this sacrament, according to Nikephoros, they have desecrated that sanctity by their actions. They have succumbed to "the operation of the unclean spirit [the devil]," and consequently, "either have never yet put on (*endysamenoi*) Christ or have taken [him] off." The sacrament is thus perpetuated from the moment that the believer desires "to be teachable by God" in the knowledge of divine things.[13]

## THE EUCHARIST

Of all the sacraments the eucharist is the one most discussed by Nikephoros. In his earlier writings, the sacrament is contrasted to pagan sacrificial rites. Being the body and blood of Christ, the eucharist cannot even be compared with the pagan sacrifices: "And what concord hath Christ with Belial? or what part hath he that believeth with an infidel? and what agreement hath the temple of God with idols?" (2 Corinthians 6.15-16).[14] Quoting Hebrews 9.13-14 and 1 John 1.7, he reiterates the qualitative difference by emphasizing the eternal sanctity of the sacrament which enables the believer to progress further as a sanctified member of Christ's mystical body, the Church.[15]

The patriarch also examines the eucharist from the participant's perspective. Whoever is inactive in his faith, distorts the truth of the sacrament, loses sight of the 'lord's supper' (*kyriakon soma*) as the incarnate Christ, and considers the sacrament by nature impure and corrupt.[16] Worthiness is based upon the faith of the participant. One who subjects the mystery to rational scrutiny is worse off than the unbeliever. Such a person is filled with "foolishness and defiance, made known from the sin of unbelief. Since they do not approach the holy [sacraments] with faith, they have sinned, regarding the holy as [something] common,...not distinguishing between the holy and the profane." Impurity, then, is not within the nature of the sacrament, but, rather, rests with the partaker.[17]

Nikephoros' purpose for discussing the eucharist at greater length in his later writings is apologetic; namely, to refute the iconoclastic claim which characterized the eucharist as the only true image of Christ. This claim, formulated by Constantine V in his second inquiry and later used by the Synod of Hieria in 754, was the logical outcome of the doctrine proposed in the first inquiry: that the true image has the same essence as its archetype. Accordingly, the image of a saint, or even of Christ, as discussed earlier, does not meet the conditions of the iconoclastic claim. Only the eucharist is the true image. To see this as a further polemic against icon veneration is to appreciate the intensity of the patriarch's own refutation. An examination of his responses to Constantine's theses completes the picture of Nikephoros' eucharistic theology.[18]

Constantine begins his examination concerning the nature of the eucharist by tracing its origin and perpetuation in this fragment: "According to his [Christ's] divinity, foreseeing his death, resurrection, and ascension to the heavens, and in order that we who have believed in him may have endlessly, day and night, the remembrance (*to mnemosynon*) of his incarnation."[19] What appears to be consistent with iconophile teaching proves to be logically incompatible even on iconoclastic grounds. The patriarch's criticism strongly condemns the emperor's position on the eucharist as being like the latter's other erroneous theories. Constantine approaches the problem equipped with his earlier formulations concerning archetype-image distinctions, and also, with his thesis that the incarnate Christ, as "God without flesh," is uncircumscribable. These views are diametrically opposed to those of the iconophile patriarch.

Nikephoros begins his refutation by defining what Constantine means by the term 'remembrance' or 'memorial.' The emperor's use of remembrance to refer to the eucharist is not offensive to the orthodox position. That his usage presupposes a heretical view of the incarnate Logos will be the basis for Nikephoros' later argumentation. For now, his criticism is directed against Constantine's refusal to extend the term to include the icons, which *sui generis* are the remembrances of their archetypes. To want "the remembrance of his incarnation" already justifies having images "which mark (*diasemainousin*)" all events of Christ's temporal life.[20]

Constantine continues his contention: "[Christ] commanded his holy disciples and apostles...to pass on the type for his body;[21] so that through priestly invocation, even if it [type] becomes by participation and adoption [Christ's body], we may receive it as principally and truly his body."[22] Nikephoros understands Constantine to mean "that which is brought about (*to teloumenon*) by participation and adoption, through priestly invocation becomes principally and truly the body of Christ." If Constantine "somewhat confesses that this [body] is the same as the body [of Christ], which, indeed, was taken on from the holy Virgin," then his position commits him to accept that Christ is circumscribable. The proof lies in the fact that the eucharist is visibly present, handled, and even consumed. The patriarch convincingly argues that "if this [lord's supper] is circumscribable and becomes the same as that body [of Christ] which the incarnate Logos took on from the beginning, and since it refers to [Christ], then, that too [the body of Christ] is circumscribable."[23]

The opportunity to expose the emperor's inconsistency when he defines the eucharist, on the one hand, as "type for his body," which suggests an arbitrary and symbolic nature of the sacrament, and, on the other hand, as "principally and truly his body," which confirms the consubtantiality of the sacrament with Christ, is not argued at this time by Nikephoros. The inconsistency is more evident in Constantine's noncommitment to the reality of the eucharist; the phrase "even if it becomes by participation and adoption" is stated in the subjunctive.[24] The patriarch, instead, has turned aside his interlocutor's uncertainty in order to argue against the assumption that "what is brought about" "becomes (*ginetai*) principally and truly the body of Christ." Moreover, he has stated his opponent's position in the indicative. The implications of Constantine's vacillation concerning the nature of the eucharist, whether it is "type" or "principally and truly his body," are not presently refuted by Nikephoros.[25]

For now, the patriarch has established two facts. Since Constantine recognizes "the remembrance of Christ's incarnation," it follows that he must accept the remembrance of icons. Since he accepts that the sacrament becomes the body of Christ, it follows that he must acknowledge its circumscription as well. Taken together, both facts are another justification for the iconographic representation of Christ considered from the perspective of the reality of the eucharist.

Constantine clearly maintains that the eucharist is the image of Christ's body: "If we may want to consider it as an image of his body as sent down by him, we have it [the sacrament] in the shape of his body."[26] In speaking against the emperor's thesis, Nikephoros presents the clearest account of his own position. By viewing the eucharist exclusively in symbolic terms, Constantine supposes two premises: the distinction between image and prototype, and a christology which views Christ as uncircumscribable because his divine nature is so.

Concerning the first premise, Nikephoros objects to the iconoclast's radical move in considering the sacrament not "principally and truly the body of Christ," but instead, "an image of his body." Constantine's eucharistic doctrine, then, supposes a distinction between image and prototype, which in fact was not held. "As indeed, the wise [Constantine], being deceived, said above,[27] [that] image and prototype do not differ in anything from one another."[28]

On the contrary, the distinction between image and archetype, for Nikephoros, does not apply to the eucharist: "We say, then, that these [elements = bread and wine] are neither an image nor a type of his body, even if they are celebrated symbolically, but they are that deified (*tetheomenon*) body of Christ." There is no biblical basis, moreover, for calling the eucharist an image. Citing John 6.53: "Except ye eat the flesh of the

Son of man, and drink his blood, ye have no life in you," the patriarch unequivocally affirms the reality of this sacrament. "And this [Christ] gave to his apostles; saying 'Take, eat [this is] my body,' not [saying] the image of my body" (Matthew 26.26).[29]

According to Nikephoros, then, the following two claims are accepted. First, the nature of the eucharist is understood only in reference to its prototype; it is "principally and truly the body of Christ." Second, the ontological distinctions found in the image-archetype relation do not apply when defining the reality (essential nature) of the eucharist: "As indeed the bread, the wine, and the water[30] which are eaten and drunk are changed into the body and blood [of Christ] naturally (*physikos*), and do not become another body distinct from the former."[31]

Concerning Constantine's second premise, Nikephoros argues for Christ's hypostatic union based on the unity of the eucharist. The patriarch understands this unity within the mystery of consecration: "These [elements] we do not understand [as being] two, but we believe that they become one and the same [body of Christ]."[32] He makes the important distinction that, whereas before the consecration the elements may be referred to as "antitypes" of the body and blood of Christ,[33] after "the invocation of the priest and descent of the holy Spirit, these change supernaturally into the body and blood of Christ."[34] The eucharist is the whole Christ.

The patriarch's characterization of the sacrament as "antitypes" before the consecration is consistent with the restrictive use found in the patristic tradition,[35] and especially the Byzantine liturgical experience.[36] The interest lies in the fact that, while Nikephoros utilizes 'antitypes' for the restrictive purpose of relating the elements to the eucharist before the consecration, the term and its connotative meaning of "historical prefiguration"[37] is absent both from Constantine's inquiry and from the iconoclastic definition of 754. For the latter, the eucharist is defined as 'type', 'image', but not 'antitypes'. For the iconoclasts' purposes, 'antitypes' in its restrictive usage does not characterize the essence of the sacrament. It is unlikely, then, that they would want to use antitypes synonymously with either type or image.[38]

From Constantine's christological thesis Nikephoros draws the logical inference for the eucharist: "Since he said that if you circumscribe, you divide Christ, or you also circumscribe the Logos. It follows to say to him, that 'if you sacrifice, you divide Christ for you sacrifice the body, not the divine nature.'"[39] Nikephoros accuses Constantine of supporting Eusebios' contention, "that all the flesh [of Christ] has changed completely" because of its relation to his divine nature.[40] This can lead to the "manichaean phantasy," which claims that we receive only the divine nature of Christ in the eucharist. The same kind of absurdity follows from Constantine's christological thesis: "Now, according to your word, either you sacrifice the Logos [the divine nature] through the one hypostasis, or by sacrificing you divide the human [nature]." In contrast, the patriarch affirms that the unity of the eucharist is the reality of the hypostatic union of Christ. He is "our great high priest, sacrifice, lamb and victim, inasmuch as he is and is called man."[41]

Constantine continues: "What then? That which we receive is both an image of his body and the bread, [the bread] figuring (*morphazon*) his flesh, as becoming the type of his body."[42] Nikephoros calls attention to Constantine's vacillating position. There are three inconsistencies. By using the conjunction 'and' (*kai*), it is unclear whether the emperor implies two distinct and separate images, one being "the body of Christ" and the other the material element (the bread). His use of the term 'image' (*eikon*) for the eucharist is inconsistent with his earlier position, where objecting to iconophile icon veneration, on the one hand, "he was not afraid to call it [the icon] an idol"; on the other hand, "he brings the image to the similitude of the prototype."[43] He still is inconsistent by not resolving whether the eucharist is "this body principally and truly," or "the image of the body," all the while attempting to verify his heretical views with "scriptural history and tradition."[44]

The patriarch, moreover, contends that Constantine's premises lead to considering the eucharist as an empty sacrament. If the body of Christ is uncircumscribable because of "its unity with the Logos," as the emperor contends, it follows that his image also is uncircumscribable. "According to your opinions, there is no body of Christ nor image of his body. Then, if you should say that [the eucharist] is circumscribed because it is enclosed by lips and teeth, it is not Christ's body, nor is it united to the Logos." The emperor's contention that the eucharist is an image of Christ's body leads to a distortion of what it is to be an image. "On the other hand, if you say [that the eucharist] is an image of the body [of Christ], not only is it rejected as an image, but also as that which divides the physical body from the unity with the Logos." The patriarch sardonically adds that if we take Constantine seriously even "this bread is uncircumscribable...and does not have a [physical] nature."[45]

Nikephoros' purpose in this rebuttal has been to prove conclusively that whatever position his interlocutor accepts, each is invalid and leads to an absurd conclusion, because it presupposes a distorted image-archetype theory which is untenable even on the grounds of the iconoclast's own heretical christology.

Constantine's last contention is most curious because it defines the sacrament as the true "made-without-hands (*acheiropoietos*)" image: "Not all bread is his body, as indeed not all wine is his blood, unless by sacerdotal consecration the offered [i.e. elements] are transferred from that which is made by hand to that which is made-without-hands."[46] Nikephoros could not agree more with Constantine's claim that only those elements that are offered constitute the eucharist. This, however, is not an issue to be debated seriously. The important point, according to the patriarch, is the reality of the lord's supper.

Constantine's conclusion that the eucharist is the true image, namely, the 'made-without-hands' icon, denies this reality. By distinguishing the eucharist as the true image of Christ from the other images of the Theotokos and the saints made by the artisans, the emperor unjustifiably confines the sacramental nature within an image-archetype framework. The characterization 'made-without-hands' has not enabled him to abandon the thesis that the eucharist is the one and only true material image of Christ. By considering the sacrament as 'made-without-hands', and therefore, a "non-anthropomorphic symbol,"[47] Constantine has widened the drift between a symbolic view and an essential view of the sacrament. The predication 'made-without-hands' is not a step in the orthodox direction for accepting that the essentiality of the sacrament is consubstantial with Christ himself.

The refutation against considering the eucharist as an "image of the body of Christ," and specifically as a "non-anthropomorphic symbol," is provided in Nikephoros' argument for circumscription. The reality of the eucharistic sacrifice is confirmed by its circumscription. This is based upon the fact that Christ is circumscribable because his human nature is so. The patriarch's objection, finally, is forcefully articulated in a rhetorical summation: "How and whence is this sacrifice, the great, immaculate and venerable, the cleansing victim and salvation for all the world to be known?... If for no other reason than it is also circumscribable."[48]

## NOTES

1. *Logos* 665.

2. Ibid. 737-40.

3. Ibid. 737,608. Even though Nikephoros has baptism in mind when describing the sacrament and its relation to the believer, his explication in 737-40 can also apply to the other sacraments.

4. Ibid. 737,739. "Forasmuch then as the children are partakers of flesh and blood, he also himself likewise took part of the same" (Heb 2.11;14).

5. Ibid. 613.

6. See above, p. 109.

7. *Logos* 629.

8. "Ὡς ὕδωρ πολὺ κατακαλύψαι θαλάσσας, τὸ ὑπερπλῆρες καὶ ἄφθονον τῆς ὑπερβλυζούσης χάριτος, ἐν τῇ ἀνελαττώτῳ χύσει τῆς ἐπιχορηγουμένης τοῦ ἁγίου Πνεύματος δωρεᾶς, ἧς ἐν τῷ σωτηρίῳ βαπτίσματι οἱ πεπιστευκότες ἠξίωντο"; ibid. 628.

9. Ibid. 628,609,628-29.

10. Ibid. 609.

11. Ibid. 608,629.

12. Ibid.

13. Ibid. 629,739-40. Nikephoros contrasts "ignorance (*agnosia*)" of the Triune God as experienced by the pagans from "knowledge" of "divine science (*theognosia*)" acquired through baptism.

14. Ibid. 608. Nikephoros' argument verifies Gero's observation in "Doctrine," p. 20, n. 69: "The motif of the true eucharist image of Christ, the counterthrust to the heathen cult images, may well have been a more prominent feature of the insistent parallelism drawn between demon-inspired heathen cult and worship, and true Christian spiritual sacrifice and prayer, than is immediately apparent from extant early Christian apologetic."

15. Ibid. 729; cf. John Damascene, *Πρὸς τοὺς διαβάλλοντας τὰς ἁγίας εἰκόνας* 3.26, PG 94.1348: "Men participate and become communicants in the divine nature; as many as receive the holy body of Christ and drink his blood."

16. Ibid. 805. For the connection between the lord's day (*kyriake hemera*) and the lord's supper or body (*kyriakon soma*), see Alexander Schmemann, *Introduction to Liturgical Theology*, trans. Asheleigh E. Moorhowe, 2d ed. (New York, 1975), pp. 62-64.

17. Ibid. 808. The notion of unworthiness is expressed also in the communion prayers of the liturgy of John Chrysostom: "Tremble, O man, seeing the divine blood. For it is to the unworthy a burning coal. The body of God both deifies and nourishes me. It wondrously deifies [my] spirit and nurtures [my] mind"; N. Papadopoulos, *Leitourgia*, p. 55.

18. *Antir.* 2.332-40. Gero's contribution in "Doctrine" lies in his efforts to trace the iconoclastic doctrine of the eucharist back to "certain, somewhat obscure, yet genuine, components of exegetical tradition"—in this respect his extensive footnote references are indispensable—notwithstanding "the statements of the medieval monophysitic and Nestorian theologians"; p. 21, n. 75. It must be noted that he does not commit himself fully to the latter thesis: "In short, it does not seem that either Nestorian or monophysite formulations (which themselves of course are derivatives of earlier patristic thought) can account for the iconoclastic synthesis; provisionally, one could say that, though a homoousios eucharistic doctrine is more congenial to monophysite than to Nestorian Christology, the 'image' language and the notion of 'thetic' body appear to be more akin to the Nestorian doctrines of personal, not 'natural', union"; p. 22, n. 75.

19. *Antir.* 2.332.

20. Ibid. 332,333.

21. The preposition *eis* in *typon eis soma autou* is not translated as genitive, but with the accusative only. The exception, which does not apply here, is *eis* with the genitive by ellipsis; cf. Herbert Weir Smyth, *Greek Grammar*, rev. Gordon M. Messing (Cambridge, Mass., 1956), p. 376. Gero in "Doctrine," p. 5, inaccurately has translated the phrase to "type of His body."

22. *Antir.* 2.333.

23. Ibid.

24. Ibid. "The thought underlying Constantine's and the *horos*' statement is that the eu-

charist is an 'arbirtary', not a 'natural', begotten image—hence it is an εἰκὼν θέσει, not φύσει"; Gero, "Doctrine," p. 11, n. 42.

25. See ibid. 336.

26. Ibid. The phrases "type for his body," "image of his body (*eikona tou somatos autou*)," and "shaping of his body (*morphosin tou somatos autou*)" refer to a symbolic view of the eucharist. For a comparison with the iconoclastic definition of 754, see Gero, "Doctrine," p. 12.

27. Ibid. 1.225.

28. Ibid. 2.336. For differences in the application of the consubstantial notion to images between Constantine and the iconoclastic definition, see Gero's explications, pp. 10, n. 40; 11, n.41-42; esp. n. 40: "I think, the *horos* perhaps passed in silence over the homo-ousios definition of 'image' as being irrelevant to the question at hand, but put even greater emphasis on the eucharist as the one and only true material image of the Savior."

29. Ibid. 336; "this is (*touto esti*)" omitted by Nikephoros.

30. The custom in Palestine was to take the wine which already was mixed with some water. For the justification of using wine mixed with water, which after the consecration is the blood of Christ, see Trembelas, *Dogmatike*, 3,157-58.

31. *Antir*. 2.336.

32. Ibid. Nikephoros unequivocally affirms the reality of the eucharistic consecration in *Antir. Eus*. 440: "We believe most firmly and we confess that by priestly invocation and by the descent of the all-holy Spirit, [the elements] which are constituted mystically and invisibly are the true body and blood of Christ."

33. *Antir*. 2.336. In the context of a passage from Anastasios of Sinai (seventh century) who argues against the unqualified use of antitype in *Odegos*, PG 89.297: "Gaianites [the interlocutor]: Let it not be, that the holy communion be called by us antitype of the body of Christ, or simple (*psilos*) bread. The orthodox: Christ did not say this is the antitype of the body," Gero defines antitype as the "historical pre-figuration, the ordinary matter of bread and wine"; "Doctrine," p. 14, n. 46. The following clarification, however, should be added. In the state of pre-consecration they are the ordinary matter of bread and wine 'to be offered' for the consecration. In other words, these, and no other material products, are the 'offered' antitypes or "historical pre-figurations" of Christ's blood and body; cf. *Antir. Eus*. 440: "We also offer now on the basis of being a symbol these, I mean the bread and the wine."

34. Ibid. 2.336. A cautionary scholium is in order concerning Gero's phrase: "Nicephorus of course denies the existence of any biblical basis for calling the eucharist an image, though he admits that to call it 'antitype' before the consecration is permissible"; "Doctrine," p. 8. The eucharist of pre-consecration is not the same (essentially) as that of post-consecration. The former consists of the offertory material elements, and as such, the patriarch defines this state as "the antitypes" not "antitype": "If perhaps they are referred to as antitypes, they are called that not after, but before this consecration"; ibid. 336. After the consecration, "the eucharistic elements themselves are certainly not a τύπος, but reality itself"; Gero, p. 12, n. 44, citing Cyril of Alexandria. At the same time, the material of the offered elements is preserved: "As the worth of the sacrifice of Golgotha lies in its anthropological basis in Christ, in the same manner, therefore, the position in the Mystery and worth of the elements of bread and wine as natural products neither is removed nor diminished through the things which act upon them and through them"; Siotis, "Eucharistia," p. 173. Cf. *Antir. Eus*. 440, where Nikephoros emphasizes that the bread

and wine, characterized as "food and drink," are not something "incomprehensible, indescribable, and ineffable," but rather, "the grace [Spirit] in them truly is inexpressible and not to be laid hold of."

35. "If many times by these phrases of the Fathers [i.e. image, type or antitype, similitude] the impression is given that these characterizations refer to that essence of the Mystery, in reality these refer always either only to the material form of the bread and the wine or to the state of their offering in the Mystery, never to the essence of the Mystery. In other words, the whole Mystery of the Holy Eucharist is never characterized by them. This point, [namely,] the fact of the impossible discernment of the bread and the wine after their consecration from the essence per se (*kath'hauto*) of the Mystery, creates a certain difficulty. To this difficulty is due the sometimes improper use of the above-mentioned characterizations. At any rate, these are used exclusively to denote not the Mystery, but its material elements, which are understood either as physical or in their mystical ontological change in the Mystery"; Siotis, "Eucharistia," p. 172. I agree with Gero that "now, most probably under the influence of the pronouncements of the council of 787 and the iconoclastic controversy, the restriction of the term ἀντίτυπα to the elements 'before' the consecration became normative in Byzantine and later Greek Orthodox theology"; "Doctrine," p. 14, n. 46. (For a comparison between Nikephoros and John Damascene, see *Ekd. pisteos* 1148; 1152-53.) The fact that Nikephoros discusses antitypes only in this sense proves that his position is not identical with the iconoclastic symbolic notion of the eucharist.

36. See the prayer of consecration (*anaphora*) in the liturgy of Basil: "Wherefore, O Master, all-holy, we also your sinful and unworthy servants...boldly come near your holy altar; and presenting the antitypes of the holy body and blood of your Christ, to you we pray and to you we implore...that your Holy Spirit come upon us and upon these gifts which are presented here, bless them, sanctify and manifest [them]"; N. Papadopoulos, *Leitourgia*, p. 75.

37. Gero, "Doctrine," p. 14, n. 46.

38. A stronger position than that proposed by Gero in ibid. p. 7, n. 21: "It is not at all certain that the iconoclasts themselves appealed to the liturgy, and the characterization of the eucharist as τὰ ἀντίτυπα.... I think one has to look elsewhere for the patristic sources of the iconoclastic terminology," must be taken which suggests that the iconoclasts purposely avoided the term.

39. *Antir.* 2.336; cf. the communion prayer in the liturgy of John Chrysostom: "The Lamb of God, who is broken and not divided, who is always eaten and never consumed but sanctifying those who partake, is broken and distributed"; N. Papadopoulos, *Leitourgia*, p. 54.

40. Ibid. 337. In *Antir. Eus.* 442, Nikephoros accuses the iconoclasts of following Arianism which, by considering Christ's human nature "without form," regards the eucharist as simply bread and wine. An inseparable connection exists between the iconoclasts' symbolic view of the eucharist and Eusebios ("his students considering these holy, venerable, and divine mysteries an image of the body"); and between their notion of the hypostatic nature of Christ and Arianism. Indeed, "this is typical of Nicephorus who throughout his works sees a renascent Arianism as the root cause of iconoclasm"; O'Connell, *Ecclesiology*, p. 89.

41. *Antir.* 2.336-37; cf. the petition during the cherubic hymn in the liturgy of John Chrysostom: "For you are the offerer and the offered, the acceptor and the distributed, O Christ our God"; N. Papadopoulos, *Leitourgia*, p. 46.

42. Ibid. 337.

43. Ibid. This statement does not convey what the patriarch really means to say about the

emperor's position, namely, that the image is consubstantial (identical) with its archetype.

44. Ibid.

45. Ibid.

46. Ibid. Gero in "Doctrine," p. 19, n. 61, suggests that "the application of this precise word to the eucharist is unique; there may be a very real polemical counterthrust to the widespread characterization of miraculous images as ἀχειροποίητος: the eucharist is the true ἀχειροποίητος εἰκών."

47. The locution is Gero's description of an icon 'made--without-hands'; ibid. p. 18, n. 60.

48. *Antir.* 2.340.

# 11

# *Tradition: Its Place, Role, and Twofold Expression*

Tradition, for Nikephoros, holds an important place within the life of the Church. To describe its various facets, he employs a constellation of terms that is consistent with earlier patristic descriptions.[1] He is most concerned, however, with the practice of tradition in the believer's life called *praxis*. As "the custom which has been handed over in the Church, tested by a long time and permanently lasting," practice is inseparably connected to the believers' desire for the holy things, as exemplified in their "pious, entirely unwavering will, and vigilance."[2] Tradition, then, is the life-stream of the Church: "For this reason, also now, every spirit [person] follows that which is in the sound teaching of the Church, as it came from God and above, [and] comes to honor and is taken up by it."[3] Moreover, the place of tradition is found in the catholicity of the Church, in its members. Its strength is safeguarded by the Spirit of God. It exercises the role of polemic against heresy and schism which challenge faithfulness to tradition.

By defining tradition in the widest possible sense to include "what has been handed down to us from above [and of old] both written and unwritten,"[4] Nikephoros does not suppose that it is comprised of two sources. It is one tradition; its source is apostolic and it is transmitted to us in both written and unwritten form. Both written and unwritten tradition are derived equally from the apostles, and consequently, from Christ, and their expression is guaranteed by the Holy Spirit.[5]

The patriarch emphasizes the parallel relationship between written and unwritten tradition. The latter is "the groundwork and foundation of those [customs] used in [our] life." Tested by time, these customs become habits and ultimately a natural way of life. The scriptural message was given to men not "in paper and ink" nor "on stone tablets." God, rather, "placed these [natural laws] in [men's] souls; these were engraved and imprinted in spirit, not by letters." Christ's message, "as everyone knows," was presented orally and later written down.[6] This argument is supported by Luke 1.1-3: "Forasmuch as many have taken in hand to set forth in order a declaration of those things which are most surely believed among us, even as they delivered them unto us, which from the beginning were eyewitnesses, and ministers of the word." It is precisely because of unwritten tradition that the orthodox talks about tradition being older and richer than the scriptures; the latter, as Karmiris states, "embody but a small portion of Sacred Tradition."[7]

Nikephoros notes that "not a few things which are traditional and kept have come down to us from unwritten [tradition]." These include worship services, the liturgy, much of sacred hymnology, the veneration of the holy relics and cross, the paschal celebration, the creed, vigils, fast periods, feastday celebrations, even the manner in which the sacraments are administered, and finally, "all those things which the beauty of sacred order [i.e. rubric] demands." Recognizing that each locality commemorates its own saints and has its own local holiday too, he concludes:

> These things which have come down to us, we have received from unwritten custom and tradition. We honor and venerate them all, and gladly accept and hold on to them no less than what is prescribed to us in scripture, since both receive their guarantee [*to asphales*] from the apostolic teaching.[8]

Written tradition, for Nikephoros, in the narrowest sense consists of the scriptures, both Old and New Testaments. But written tradition is not confined to these alone. Apostolic tradition is preserved and transmitted through the tradition of the fathers, namely, the patristic teaching.[9] The divine truths as revealed in the scriptures, witnessed and interpreted in the patristic teaching, and in a wider sense, asserted in doctrine through the synods is what Nikephoros, on the one hand, understands to be written tradition. Unwritten tradition, on the other hand, is the practice of the Church.

The twofold expression of tradition, its universal teaching and practice, is the life-stream of the Church. For the patriarch, an appeal to tradition is the best guarantee of truth. This claim is based upon the irrefutable fact that God's Church has the knowledge of the truth, and because of this rightly understands the 'meaning' of revelation. It is this certainty of the authenticity of tradition which is reflected in Nikephoros' statement: "Everything, therefore, which has been handed over in the Church of God, both written and unwritten, is venerated and honored, and sanctifies bodies and souls; and concerning these things there is no doubt among the faithful."[10]

This twofold expression can be explored further under subjects which have attracted the patriarch's attention, either because they constitute or challenge tradition. These are under written tradition: the scriptures, the fathers, dogma and synods, schism, heresy, and idolatry; and under unwritten tradition: miracles, architecture, the cross, and the icon.

## NOTES

1. These terms are canon (*kanon*), definition (*horos*), law (*nomos*), legislation (*thesmothesia*), rescript (*typos*), legal decrees (*thespismata nomika*), instruction (*didaskaleion*), apostolic or patristic teaching (*apostolike; patrike didaskaleia*), ecclesiastical teaching (*ekklesiastike didaskaleia*), ordinance (*thesmos*), ethos, lesson (*didagma*), customary usage (*synetheia*), tradition (*paradosis*) which is frequently qualified as apostolic, patristic, canonical, authorized (*enthesmos*), or inspired (*entheos*); see listing in O'Connell, *Ecclesiology*, p. 91.

2. *Antir.* 3.392.

3. *Epikr.* 303-04.

4. *Logos* 808; also, *Antir.* 3.460.

5. *Antir.* 3.388.

6. Ibid. 385.

7. *Synopsis*, p. 6.

8. *Antir.* 3.388.

9. "'Ecclesiastical understanding' could not add anything to the Scripture. But it was the only means to ascertain and to disclose the true meaning of Scripture. Tradition was, in fact, the authentic interpretation of Scripture. And in this sense it was coextensive with Scripture. Tradition was actually 'Scripture rightly understood'"; Florovsky, "Function," pp. 74-75.

10. *Antir.* 3.381.

# 12

# *Written Tradition*

## THE SCRIPTURES

Nikephoros' high regard for the scriptures is evident from frequent citations found throughout his writings. Knowledgeable in both the Old and New Testaments, he unequivocally accepts them as God-inspired, as the word of God. Not concerned, as was John Damascene, with enumerating the books established by scriptural canon, he accepts what has been said on the subject.[1] The patriarch's attention, instead, is directed to the content of the written testimony through which God's providence to man is made manifest. Even though his use of scripture is directed toward apologetic ends, it is possible to isolate several themes which are important to him. Of no less significance is his understanding of the relationship between the Testaments as he presents these subjects.

A favorite theme is the movement of God through history. He guides man toward a better and more perfect state.[2] This movement is the history of man's salvation through the patriarchs, the prophets, the laws of the Old Testament, and finally, the complete fulfillment in the incarnate Word as explicated in the New Testament. Both Testaments are placed in historical perspective by Nikephoros. The providence of God, as manifested through the law, is fulfilled in the grace of Christ. What happened was ultimate and new: "The Word became flesh"(John 1.14). "The grace in Christ renewed our piety toward completion and perfection. That which failed by the law was fulfilled: 'I am not come' therefore, said Christ, 'to destroy [the law], but to fulfill [it].'"[3]

A second theme is the assessment of the Old Testament law: "The law is holy, and the commandment is holy, just, and good." Both, "while under the veil of the letter and the shadows present the divine knowledge to us." Nevertheless, they take second place to the full revelation of the Word of God. Nikephoros evaluates the place of law:

> Having the shadow of future goods, the law is not that image of those things.... As to those things which it offers [i.e. sacrifices], it is not able to perfect those who turn to it. The commandment is holy, and even though it is a shadow of those future things, it is not an image of those things. Those things of which the law is a shadow, that is, grace and truth, came through Jesus Christ.[4]

The patriarch's use of the terms "shadow (*skia*)" and "image (*eikon*)" is noteworthy for two reasons. First, it emphasizes an ontological difference between a shadow and an image. While the shadow denotes something which is "somewhat less distinct and less perfect (*amydroteron pos kai metrioteron*)," the image is a true reflection of its prototype. Second, it indicates the place of Old Testament legislation: "The law does not perfect, but it is holy."[5] He explains the contrast quoted in John 1.17: "For the law was given by Moses, but grace and truth came by Jesus Christ": "The laws of grace...are not written in inanimate materials, but are imprinted upon the consciousnesses of rational beings by the finger of God and the pen of the Spirit." Our lawgiver, Jesus Christ, did not write laws; rather, these were established in the souls of men by the Holy Spirit. A lesson can be learned from the Israelites who did not take the divine laws seriously in their hearts, as did the Christians.[6]

A third theme is the connection between the Old Testament vision of the Messiah and the New Testament historical presence of the incarnate Logos. This vision is best understood in the finality of grace through Christ's priestly office. The law is holy because of the savior "who has perfected the sanctified [followers] forever in the one sacrifice (he, then, is the perfector of our faith to whom we refer)."[7] Christ himself is the meaning of the biblical vision of dispensation. In contrast to those sacrifices which were offered by the priests not only for the sake of the people, but also for their own infirmities, the high priest's sacrifice "he did once, when he offered up himself" (Hebrews 7.27). By distinguishing the sacrifices of the Old Testament from the bloodless sacrifice of the New, Nikephoros shows that the Christian sacramental life is on another and completely new level.

> So, on the one hand, the blood of the bulls and goats and the ashes of the heifer which are sprinkled upon the communicants, sanctify as far as the purification of the flesh. On the other hand, the blood of Christ purges the conscience of dead works in order that they [the communicants] might worship the living and true God.[8]

By contrasting the temple, its articles, and the liturgical practices of the Old Testament from those of the New, Nikephoros evaluates the latter as being brighter and more spiritual because of the presence of Christ. "The spiritual table" is a characterization of the sacramental life of the New Testament wherein each member of the Church mystically partakes with faith and love of "the eternal food granted to men by the Logos who descended from heaven."[9]

A fourth theme is the notion of the 'chosen people'. The patriarch notes God's providential care for the Israelites as a holy nation. The pre-Christian gentiles, "permitting the irrationality of the soul, and for this reason as deceived as the irrational animals, were ignorant of the true and natural God, who as creator gave them the breath of life and placed them under his providence." In the New Testament God through Jesus Christ "called together all the nations to the knowledge of him.... We also from the nations... have in fact become the people of God and have obtained in him the new name [Christian]."[10] The old Israel, the people of the covenant, had its chance "because when they knew God, they glorified him not as God, neither were thankful; but became vain in their imaginations, and their foolish heart was darkened" (Romans 1.21-22).[11]

A fifth theme is Nikephoros' respect for the history of the Old Testament. His references to historical events are instructive and reassuring to the persecuted iconophile members of the Church. For example, the Church of God is characterized as "the chaste Susanna."[12] At the same time his references are directed polemically against the iconoclasts. They are compared to the scribes and pharisees of old: "Again Christ is insulted and whipped; as indeed, the benevolent [Christ] was when he was visible in the flesh, so now also the forbearing [Christ] is when presented iconographically." As in ancient times, the iconoclasts are the builders of "a tower of impiety, much more detestable and irreligious" than the tower of Babel. Their tower is not composed of clay and asphalt "but constructed of propagandistic voices and repugnant theories directed against the glory of the only-begotten [Son]." Their leaders are compared most often to those biblical characters who exemplify pride, greed, and gainsaying, and consequently, are "antithetical" to God and his ministers, such as the followers of Korah (Jude 11-12), the magicians Jannes and Jambres who "withstood Moses" (2 Timothy 3.8-9), and Alexander and Hymenaeos against Paul (1 Timothy 1.20). The corruption and graft among the iconoclast leaders, finally, are identical to "the Babylonian presumptions and Chaldean brash deeds."[13]

The sixth theme is Nikephoros' admiration for the prophets. The mark of a prophet is that his actions and words are "in accord with the Spirit of God." The true prophet is distinguished from the false one because the former's words are "sayings of the Spirit." The prophets are governed by the spirit of truth and keep the commandments through the fear of God. Nikephoros extensively cites those whose characteristic temper is to "censure falsehood by the test of rightness instead of rottenness."[14] Moreover, he sees an unbroken succession beginning with the prophets of the Old Testament, extending to the apostles of the New Testament, the presbyters and teachers of the Church; all are guided by the will and revelation of the Triune God. The focal point of this continuity is Christ's redemption and revelation:

These [truths] the prophets from on high proclaimed aloud, the

> apostles evangelized, the martyrs with manly courage professed, their followers and fellow teachers of the Church amplified greatly and labored together. Through all of those who were placed by God in his Church, he guaranteed what our life needed by providing all things.[15]

In conclusion, the patriarch regards the scriptures as a coherent historical unity in which no event is disconnected from God's purpose. He is not concerned with textual criticism, nor does he seek as would an allegorist hidden meanings behind every phrase; rather, he interprets biblical events as prefigurations of things to come. Nikephoros can hold that the holy things of Israel "were not eternal, but were rather a shadow and figure of the holy things which we have, and, finally, with the coming of truth they were taken away,"[16] without denying that they were an important part of the providential meaning of salvation. At the same time, he understands the Old Testament dispensation only in the context of the christological and ecclesiological meaning manifested in the 'new' reality of the New Testament. Finally, the patriarch exhorts his contemporaries to view their situation in light of this scriptural spring.

## THE FATHERS

Nikephoros has great respect for the fathers of the Church. Terms which he employs to describe these individuals are not merely rhetorical and complimentary; rather, they denote the fathers' 'ethos'.[17] This character is reflected in their writings and in the sanctity of their life as expressed in their orthodox faith which is inspired by the grace of the Spirit.

As "sacred teachers," the fathers perform a twofold function in the Church: they proclaim the faith and dogmatic teaching, and fight against every heretical impiety.[18] By emphasizing that they follow "in the footsteps of the prophetic voices of the Spirit and the apostolic preaching," Nikephoros acknowledges an unbroken continuity between the scriptures and patristic teaching. Both scriptural writers and fathers are God-inspired.[19] The patriarch unequivocally distinguishes the fathers from those heretics whom the iconoclasts "have ordained as their own fathers and have set up as teachers, who of old had become defenders of impiety and atheism, and were driven out of reach from the catholic Church."[20] The fathers, instead, are "our theologians." They are "God-fearing as the easily-taught disciples of the scriptures, not extending beyond what is proper to more curious investigations, [but] accepting with a simple heart that which has been given by the account of faith." Their writings are characterized by "an unconfused faith in what is believed,...a straightforward opinion, and a spontaneous drive." A search for demonstrations and verbal disputations is not only useless, but very harmful, and consequently, is "the trade of heretical men," not that of orthodox fathers.[21]

By not making further distinctions, is Nikephoros blurring the difference between the roles of bishops, fathers, and members of a synod?[22] The answer must be qualified. All have this in common: they are witnesses to the Christian truth. Moreover, faithfulness to the teaching of the Church is not limited to anyone group within the ecclesial fellowship. Many fathers were also bishops (John Chrysostom, Gregory of Nyssa, Gregory the Theologian, and Nicholas of Myra), as well as synodal members (Athanasios, who was a deacon at the time). As witnesses and guardians of Christian truth, all share in the common source, the grace of the Spirit. There exists, then, a common bond between the members of the Church, whether they are martyrs, monks, or fathers, which is characterized by the witness of their faith and is most often sealed by martyrdom. Apostolic teaching is safeguarded in all generations and in the whole extent of the Church by the Spirit. At the same time, however, living tradition, originating from one source, may express itself in many different ways. From the hierarch to the most humble monk, each has a special role.

Nikephoros clearly distinguishes the role belonging uniquely to the fathers. They are the teachers, the theologians, helping and guiding the Church in its struggle against heresy. Their armament of eminent erudition and sanctity of life were forged not necessarily in the hearth of persecution, nor in the ascetic arena of deserts and caves, but rather, in the intellectual battles against the heretics. The epithet "lights in the world" given to the monks, must apply equally to the fathers in their struggle against impiety and atheism.[23] As rhetoricians and intellectuals, these men

> clung as much as possible to the right word of truth, sowed and declared the teachings of piety everywhere in the world, tore up the prickly plants of impiety by the roots, stopped and sewed up the mouths of the heretics who planned and spoke injustice against the highest. From then on, the one faith and the same confession among all Christians was hammered out and preserved.[24]

It comes as no surprise to find Nikephoros calling to remembrance the fathers for the sake of guiding the flock once again from the snares of heresy, this time from that of iconoclasm. The appeal to the fathers was made for "the reminding and benefit" of the believers "so that they might not suffer [to be] the same as those [heretics] who disobey the truth."[25] That the patriarch extensively uses their sayings (*chreseis*) to substantiate his arguments is another demonstration of his ability to work with the fathers.[26] If a compilation was made of all patristic citations in his writings, we would marvel at the number of passages used by Nikephoros. He frequently cites fathers of the third and fourth centuries, both eastern and western, though with the exception of Tertullian and Augustine.

In contrast to the iconoclasts' misuse of the fathers to suit their own theories,[27] Nikephoros' 'following the fathers' is an appeal directed not so much to their individual opinions, but more importantly, to the 'mind-set' of the Church (*to ekklesiastikon phronema*). What is at stake is the validity of this patristic consensus. For the patriarch, an appeal to the fathers is an address to the witnesses of the orthodox faith who through their erudition and sanctity of life manifest the true ethos of the Church. Their 'mind-set' is the reflection of the perennial identity and catholicity of the Church's faith.

## DOGMA AND SYNODS

The appeal to the dogmatic teaching of the Church as defined and formulated by the synods is as important to Nikephoros as the appeal to the fathers. His participation in the Seventh Ecumenical Synod as the imperial spokesman, and later his opposition as patriarch to both the illicit resident synod and the iconoclastic Synod of Hagia Sophia, placed him in a singular position of defining dogma and synods.[28] His knowledge of the history of dogma can only support the conclusion that the patriarch appears to be comfortable in the 'mind-set' of the synods. His vantage point is unique because he stands historically at the end of the Seventh Ecumenical Synod, and at the same time, is closer to the earlier synods than we are, temporally unobstructed by intervening centuries.[29]

Nikephoros' understanding of dogma is not at variance with orthodox formulation. His interest lies more in the narrow meaning of dogma; namely, that dogma is connected inseparably with the fathers who have formulated it in the official setting of a synod. The latter is regarded as 'supporting', 'sustaining', or 'making firm (*synistesi*)' the content of the common faith.[30] These "correct dogmas" are truths which express the faith and consciousness of the Church, and are, therefore, obligatory and saving for all.[31] Nikephoros expresses these ideas emphatically:

> I accept and honor the holy, ecumenical seven synods and the holy, extraordinary, and saving dogmas which were formulated and preached in these [synods] by our venerable and God-bearing fathers, whom the holy Spirit places at [a particular] time to shepherd and govern his Church.[32]

What remains to be seen is how the patriarch understands the place of the synods within tradition.

A synod is summoned when there is a crisis within the Christian community; specifically, when a question of heresy arises which can lead to schism. "For this reason, this apologetic [treatise] is written concerning those present-day empty talkers who as clergy have cut themselves off from the common body of the Church." The urgency of calling a synod is emphasized again in the concluding statement: "As has been said above, the Church summons an ecumenical synod in order to remove all contention and to be awarded the peace through the grace and goodwill of God."[33]

The synod is a forum of discussion which is guided by Christ and the Spirit. "Every dogmatic issue which has arisen in the Church of God has ceased after synodical enquiry and proclamation, and is not subject to doubt of any kind." The dogmatic discussion includes "an examination and testing...of the sayings found in the unholy [heretical] writings." A settlement is possible only "through the inspiration of the holy Spirit" which guides the fathers to steadfastness "in ecclesiastical custom and rule."[34]

An ecumenical synod is characterized by its ecumenicity. In matters of faith, the Church as a whole decides. Proof of this ecumenicity is the participation of the patriarchs (including Rome), or, in their absense, their respective representatives who are entrusted with synodical letters.[35] To suggest that a committee of patriarchs decides matters of faith is foreign to Nikephoros' understanding of the synod's role within the Church's catholicity. An example of unity in catholicity exists in the proceedings of the Seventh Ecumenical Synod:

> All who convened gathered together from almost everywhere under the sun and from every land, directed to the one aim of truth, and since they had Christ awarding them peace, agreement and unanimity shone upon them from the grace on high. For so the ecclesiastical rule from old commands: those matters in the Church of God which are doubtful and disputed are to be solved in ecumenical synods, and defined by the agreement and approbation of the illustrious hierarchs who occupy the apostolic thrones.[36]

The synod is led by the tradition of the Church. It confirms officially the teaching of this tradition. The whole body of the Church functions in agreement and unanimity through the episcopacy to restore peace and unity to the catholic Church.

The unity of the synod's purpose, first, is exemplified fully in the life of the faithful. The acceptance of its decisions is obligatory for all. Nikephoros emphatically reminds his readers that the keeping of dogmatic teaching is the responsibility of all the clergy, "the pious and faithful kings," and "all the people of Christendom";[37] "the emperors of those times, following the votes of the bishops (*ton hiereon*), both accepted and confirmed them; and none of the orthodox after the promulgation called them in question, but all Christians accepted those things proclaimed as sealed by the holy Spirit."[38]

Second, the unity of purpose is seen in the manner by which the ratification of the synod's decision takes place. Its members "according to the custom acceptable from the beginning in the Church, signed [their name], marking before it their proper crosses."[39] The signature, but more importantly, the cross before the name seals the decisions. It is not by accident that Nikephoros is prompted to preserve this protocol. He wishes to link the iconoclasts' heretical actions with their denial of "those things which they have confessed," resulting in a discredit of their own signatures. "If they deny their confession [of these dogmas], they step upon their crosses, signed by their own hands, and they submit themselves to the aforesaid anathemas, and consequently, do not stand at all within the Church."[40]

Third, the unity of the synod's purpose is manifested in the emperor's role before, during, and after the synod. In the tradition of his predecessors, Nikephoros clearly understands the extent of the emperor's participation. The Church calls (*epikaleitai*) for an ecumenical synod; thereupon the emperor's goodwill and cooperation makes it possible for the synod to be convened.[41] The patriarch, however, is very much concerned with the non-interference of the State in the actual work of the synod.

The principle of interdependence (*synallelia*) of Church and State is expressed in the imperial attitude during the discussion of the Seventh Ecumenical Synod "in which the rulers [Irene and Constantine VI] were also in agreement (*sympsephoi gegonasi*)."[42] The phrase "were also in agreement" meant that the emperor cosigned, thus attesting to the authority of the synod's decisions. For instance, during the Sixth Ecumenical Synod "the then Emperor Justinian, who had become a consenter and co-worker to them [synodal members], also declared by his own signature the illustrious and pure faith of our pious [orthodox Christians]."[43] Leo V did the opposite at the iconoclastic Synod of Hagia Sophia: "He gathered together as he decided a synod from these men (the iconoclasts), took his seat with them (*synedros*), and in fact presided (*proedros*); rather he became the precursor of the domination of the feared-for evil."[44]

The phrase "accepted and confirmed (*apedexanto kai ekratynan*)" captures the meaning of the emperor's role after the proceedings.[45] The second term denotes the stronger sense of 'holding on with the intent of making firm' the decisions of the synod. This strengthening or making firm is possible because the emperor is the defender of the orthodox faith.

Nikephoros mentions one example of imperial assertion. Empress Irene defends the faith against iconoclasts who are accused of conspiring with the Manichaeans. A few are captured and others are executed by the sword. The important phrase "to which the laws command" supports Irene's action as legitimate.[46] In other words, synodal decisions are incorporated in civil law and implemented by the power of the State. In contrast to the iconoclasts who act without regard to civil law and ecclesiastical order, indiscriminately carrying out unusual punishments and deaths, the State proceeds by law as regards its execution of heretics.[47]

## SCHISM, HERESY, AND IDOLATRY

Nikephoros repeatedly stresses fidelity, unity, peace, and harmony with tradition. It comes as no surprise that he considers schism as the ultimate evil in the Church. Schismatics are those former members who have challenged tradition and have separated themselves willingly from the one, holy, catholic, and apostolic Church. These individuals are unrepentant of their stance. What remains for them is judgment and great punishment from God.[48] His citation from John Chrysostom's commentary on Paul's epistle to the Ephesians indicates just how intensely Nikephoros abhors schism: "Nothing is able to divide the Church in such a way as the love to rule; nothing disturbs God as much as the Church being divided." The danger of schism must be known by both rulers and their subjects. Referring to schismatics of his day, Chrysostom laments that they, as members of the Church, "who are born and reared within her, and have learned her mysteries," have fallen in this manner.[49] Schism begins with ambition. As an internal dissent, it is more shameful than heresy which originates from the Church's external enemies.

Nikephoros does not make a radical distinction between schismatics and heretics. In one sense, the iconoclasts are schismatics because they have separated themselves from the Church; in another sense, they are heretics because they have espoused the teachings of other leaders of heresy.

The patriarch's attitude against the schismatics is expressed through the thoughts of another father—Pope Agathon, whose synodical letter is addressed to the Sixth Ecumenical Synod. Agathon will not accept the schismatics who persist in their ways. Others, however, will take their places "as our spiritual brothers and co-bishops...when they desire to preach sincerely concerning our apostolic faith, as ones of the same mind, as co-clergy, as concelebrants, as of the same faith."[50]

The iconophile patriarch, too, shows a condescending attitude toward those who recanted their heresy.[51] He emphasizes that the Church must accept those former heretics, such as idolaters, who have shown repentance "concerning those things which they have both studied and done without thinking." For "the one who realizes his sin and repents from the evil act by approaching the Church in penance," Nikephoros recommends that a certain time be given to him "until with a contrite heart and humble spirit, the abomination of the committed transgressions can be rubbed out by fervent and persistent confession." His yielding attitude is evident when emphasizing that while "piety and justice and every virtue" are the perfect ornaments of the soul, "those who have been freed from unbelief" must be met with "compassion and fullness, rather mercy; [this is] to say it more justly."[52]

At the same time, Nikephoros takes an unyielding stand against those unrepentant schismatics: "If they remain in that heresy, and perhaps are able to lead astray others who are less learned and crude, and even if they amass a popular gathering, they are outside the holy enclosures of the Church." The heresiarchs are incapable of contrition because "their repentance is not sincere." Like the Manicheans, the leaders of iconoclasm for awhile act like Christians, but in reality their deeds reveal that they still remain in "the same deceit and impiety." They have condemned themselves to eternal punishment. A foretaste of this awesome estrangement begins with their excommunication."They are outcasts from the apostolic, archieratical, and great thrones [patriarchal] and from all the Christians, and they have neither communion, nor share the same fate with the pious [faithful].... They become foreign to and outcasts of the Christian's hope and salvation." The iconophile patriarch unequivocally refuses to admit any communion with the Church for "the leaders of apostasy."[53]

In addition to the iconoclast leaders headed by Constantine V, there are other heresiarchs, such as Areios, Sabellios, and Eusebios, whose names and teachings are mentioned by Nikephoros.[54] He purposely identifies the teaching of his opponents with that of these earlier heresiarchs. The iconoclasts, in fact, are responsible for the resurgence of earlier heresies. Nikephoros goes so far as to admonish the latest fad—students working on and contesting over these heretical writings.[55]

The patriarch provides a caricature of the heretic and his writings. The Arian heresy, for example, is very deceptive. As a trap of impiety, it is not self-evident or easily understood by many. The heretic's writings are full of "sophistical words and twisted meanings" which easily convert and sway the illiterate to their position. He is like the unscrupulous tavern keeper who dilutes wine with water. His perversion of the truth is far from ethical. The heresiarchs and their cohorts are so blinded by the darkness of their own teaching that "they are unable to see the daybreak of truth because if they knew [the truth], they would not disgrace the lord of glory." Their teachings are the cause of the Church's worse evil, internal division.[56] The danger to the peace of the Church brought on by the heretics' work, is taken so seriously by Nikephoros, that he devotes two separate treatises, *Antirresis Eusebiou* and *Antirresis Epiphanidou*, to arguing against them.

Of all the heresies, idolatry is the one which occupied the patriarch's special attention. It induced him to write a major treatise whose full title reveals its purpose: "Apology [defense] on behalf of the blameless, pure, and sincere faith of us Christians and against those who consider that [the Christians] worship idols."[57] The problem of idolatry arises because the iconophiles are said to be idol worshipers. Having accused the orthodox of substituting the worship of created things for the worship of the creator, the iconoclasts, "the guardians of error," substantiate their accusation by mischaracterizing the historical state of the Church: "As Christians, we have worshiped idols and this [has been going on] until the time of the reign of Constantine [V]."[58] With the convening of the Synod of Hieria, which is most unflatteringly caricatured by Nikephoros,[59] the iconoclasts suppose that they have remedied this situation by formally declaring their opposition to icon veneration on the grounds that it is idol worship.

Why did Nikephoros find it necessary to refute this iconoclastic attack, especially when the argument of idol worship advanced at Hieria in 754 had been dropped at the Synod of Hagia Sophia in 815?[60] The most plausible reason is that Constantine V and his Synod of Hieria still influenced the iconoclasts during Nikephoros' time. Undoubtedly, the synod of 815 tempered its definition, something which was not done at Hieria. As Alexander observes, "into their summaries they insert skillfully a review of the principle arguments used against religious images by the earlier iconoclasts."[61] The premise from which the iconoclasts of Hieria derived their argument of idolatry, was that images were merely ordinary physical objects, and because of their 'material' substantiality, were devoid of any supernatural grace. This remained an unchanged presupposition for the iconoclasts of Nikephoros' time as well. According to the patriarch, this position as well as the argument of idol worship definitely had not been disclaimed by the iconoclasts. "I realize that the struggle against them is still raging."[62] For him, Hieria still posed a threat to the unity of the Church.

The patriarch's earliest and most lengthy response against the iconoclastic claim that icon veneration means idol worship is based upon our belief in one, almighty God; the recognition that man desires to know the truth; the traditional historical practices found in the scriptures and the Church; and the mission of Christ in the world.[63] If the argument's specific purpose is to dispel any fear that the iconophiles are idolaters, it becomes a panegyric for the one, true faith, Christianity, and, moreover, another justification for the traditional practice of icon veneration.

The steps of Nikephoros' refutation, which admittedly is not organized in the strictest logical format, are the following.[64] After formally stating the iconoclasts' accusation, the hierarch presents a confession of faith with which he proves that the only worship is that of the Triune God. "We [Christians] worship that which we know, but they [iconoclasts] do not know what we worship." The former's worship is true and not blasphemous, because its source, God, is "living and true."[65]

That Christ freed man from the power of the idols through his ministry and sacrifice, which is reenacted in the sacramental life of the Church, is a demonstration that the sacrificial holy table and Christian churches are neither temples of idolatry nor centers of idol worship.[66]

According to the New Testament, idolatry has been abolished. The patriarch challenges the iconoclasts to show how it is possible that idolatry could be practiced by the Christians. The mission of Christ, his message to his apostles (Matthew 28.19), the conversion of the Jews who "were led forth from the worship of the law to the spiritual and true [worship] of the God of all," and afterward the pagan Greeks who "were freed directly from the mania of idolatry" by the sacrament of baptism to constitute "the catholic Church of Christ," are events which prove that past idol worship has been cast away once and for all.[67]

By examining two types of idol worshipers, Nikephoros refutes the claim that if a Christian fits into either category, this is reason to justify a similarity between idolatry and Christian worship. The one type consists of the materialists, who indiscriminately perceive the rocks and wood without going beyond this sensory experience.[68] The other type is comprised of those who appear to be "somewhat more logical and philosophical...and believe that certain powers, which, in fact, are gods, inhabit the statues, and consequently, call these [statues] images of gods." According to the patriarch, the position of the first leads only to "brute stupidity." The latter falls "to the terminus of impiety and atheism" by postulating male and female gods, classes of gods, and even attributing different qualities to each. The pagans, finally, have this in common: they attempt to present their religion as unique by emphasizing their differences with respect to the sects, temples, and sacrifices of others. In contrast to Christian liturgical practices, their mysteries are "abominable and devilish," administered in secret meeting places and in such a way as to be known only by the initiants.[69]

By examining the idol in terms of the image-archetype relation, Nikephoros proves that an idol cannot be considered the same as a Christian image. The error of paganism is magnified because polytheism requires a multiplication of innumerable idols to represent the many forms and species of gods and demons. The represented image (*to bretas*) of an idol is unlike its archetype. There is an unbridgeable dissimilarity between god and idol. The idol is unlike the god in kind, and the god has no relation to its image. In Christianity, on the contrary, the truth of the archetype is "simple and indivisible because Christ is one. His image is one in species, and the character is similar [because these characteristics] eternally come from the one archetype." Christ's image is always true to form because its subject stays the same. The idol, then, is false because the archetype is false to begin with. "The idols of the nations are of silver and gold, works of human hands. These neither speak nor see; in no way do they move [the hearts of men toward the true worship of God]."[70]

To claim that the Christians are idol worshipers is to deny the message and work of the Old Testament prophets. As God-inspired, they speak against the idols. It is when the Israelites refuse to heed their prophets that they, too, raise idols made by hand.[71]

A strong argument against idolatry is found in Christ's mission. He frees the nations from the weight of those many yokes which they have imposed upon themselves by their idolatrous practices, and places upon them only the one yoke, "the clean and unblemished worship which logically belongs to God." By freeing the nations, Christ at the same time unites all under the one God and creator, lord of all. Because of him, polytheism and the true faith are clearly distinct. The victory against idolatry, as described by the prophets, especially in Zechariah 13.2, is assured because it is the word of God. Nikephoros unequivocally believes, then, that idolatry has been suppressed by Christ in all its forms and expressions.[72] By accusing the iconophiles of idol worship, the iconoclasts are, in fact, implying that Christ did not have the power to destroy idolatry.

The patriarch emphasizes the difference between Jewish and pagan worship. Judaism is the middle ground between paganism and Christianity. "Inasmuch as the worship of the Jews supercedes the superstition of the nations, ours [Christian worship] is exalted over theirs." The patriarch argues that if the Jews refused to become idol worshipers because they listened to "those prophetic voices," the case for rejecting idols becomes even stronger when seen from the perspective of Christianity, the followers of which have rejected idolatry because of Christ.[73]

Against the objection that Christians are idol worshipers, Nikephoros argues from the history of the Church. The Christian evangelical teaching whose message centers on the true worship of the Triune God is "as the ray of divine knowledge." That all nations accepted this message, and consequently, rejected the deception of idols, is an indisputable historical fact, according to Nikephoros. This fact justifies the iconophile position that

Christians are not idol worshipers. Furthermore, this historical justification finds its expression in the lives of the Church's saints, martyrs, monks, and faithful who unceasingly fought against the error of polytheism.[74]

The history of idolatry proves that idol worship is not the true spiritual worship which ought to be rendered to the one living God. There is nothing spiritual or holy about the priests and custodians of the sacrificial temples "who delight in the spilling of blood." The sacrifices that include animal and even human victims are the most impious. The pagans' gods, in contrast to the Triune God, are not remembered for their sublimity. Nikephoros harshly censures the deeds of Zeus and the escapades of other gods, such as Ares, Dionysos, Hermes, and Athena. The patriarch also speaks against the deification of Hercules who "was regarded by the atheists as a god" because of his birth and many deeds. In addition, he ridicules the belief that pagan gods have a way of appearing and changing their forms to suit "the variety and multiplicity of passions." Idolatry, moreover, is connected to magic. The gods may appear once as a bird in order to affect a suitor's amorous relations, at other times as a bull or fox for those who wish to enhance their cunningness and deceit, or even as a frog. The advocates of idolatry are "foolish, far from the truth, and delight in conjuring up dreams." They are lead by demons, who are "inventors of lies and workers of evil."[75]

The patriarch's account of the history of idolatry includes references to the pagan mysteries. Of mention is the mystery celebrated by the Phrygians in honor of Rhea, the mother of the gods. By inflicting wounds upon themselves and by rolling on the ground to increase their pain, the initiants are introduced to "abominable practices." The mysteries of Demetria and Eleusinia are held in secret during the night. The references to the oracles of Dodonaion and Delphi justify the patriarch's criticism of pagan idolatry as a vain and false undertaking. The prophetess at Delphi, characterized as giving "oblique oracles," captivates her hearers with yet deeper ignorance.[76]

Nikephoros' critique of idolatry based upon a historical survey of paganism arrives at this conclusion: since the pagan gods are impure, their worship is false, and therefore, their believers are under demonic influence; whereas since the Christian God is the lord of all, his worship is pure, and consequently, his followers are moved in spirit and truth.[77]

The history of salvation through "the prophets and evangelical word" presents two important facts: the deadening effect of idolatry upon the hearts of human beings, and the promise of a Messiah to come in the fullness of time.[78] The "return" to God from the idols is proof that even from the pagans' point of view idolatry is false. Converted "from atheism to philotheism," these neophytes were granted by God the true spiritual gifts, which never could be found in idolatry. As Christians, they did not want to forsake these gifts of grace and illumination in order to return to the darkness and deceit of idolatry.[79]

Since the Jews were not idol worshipers, it is wrong to assume that the Christians were. "Even though many times they defiled the divine worship by deceitfully worshiping the idols, nowhere did the Jews dare to dishonor them [the cherubim] by calling them idols." Even if they did not enter into the spirit of the law, their sacrifices were pleasing to God; these were acceptable because of God's economy.[80] By adopting the double premise that the Judaic sacrifices are honorable and that the Christian practices are "above all others better and surpassing them, being worthy of glory and honor," Nikephoros develops three points in this final new argument. First, if the Judaic sacrifices are pleasing to God, it follows that the Christian bloodless sacrifice is not only acceptable, but is truer since Christ himself fulfilled the law by his sacrifice. Second, if the iconoclasts acknowledge the Judaic temples of the Old Testament, they must also accept the Christian temples as surpassing the former, even Solomon's. Third, as the center of spiritual life and sanctification, God's temple cannot be compared to a pagan one, just as there can be "no communion between light and darkness."[81]

Unlike this early refutation, the argument against idolatry in *Antirresis* deals with only one aspect of the iconoclasts' attack.[82] They have called attention to the second commandment (Exodus 22.4) by stating that its prohibition applies to Christ's image as well. Nikephoros argues that this commandment refers specifically to the prohibition of idols and must be seen in relation to 22.3: "Thou shalt have no other gods before me," and 23.24: "Thou shalt not worship their gods, nor serve them," which refer to pagan gods. The patriarch insists that the purpose of the second commandment is to distinguish "the likeness of the lord and creator from an image of created and subordinate things." Even after Moses, the prophets continued to remind the Israelites that they should worship the creator, not creation.[83] The commandment is not in conflict with God's directive to build the tabernacle, the cherubim, the temple, or the tablets upon which the commandments "were written by the divine finger." Nikephoros understands this directive to mean "that you shall not make something without my command."[84] Even the altars of stone built by Jacob, Gideon, Isaiah, and Joshua were under God's command.[85] The Judaic sacrifices, too, "belong to the glory of God and are a testimony to [his] saving economy."[86]

Nikephoros concludes by reiterating that the Christian icons are categorically unlike the idols. The former are a direct and true way to the archetype. The iconoclasts' mistake is to consider the icon as no different from "images of beasts, dogs, birds, and other animals." The decorative patterns found upon vestments, or on the apses and columns of the solea, which utilize natural motifs, are only an aesthetic aid. It does not follow, as the iconoclasts accuse, that the faithful worship these. The argument from architecture also proves that the Christian, unlike the pagan, accepts and reveres only that which serves as a true spiritual aid.[87]

To substantiate their position that the use of icons constitutes an idolatrous practice, the iconoclasts have appealed to the scriptures, historical practice, and the fathers. The patriarch, as already seen, has dealt with the first two appeals successfully. In a later work, *Antirresis Eusebiou*, he refutes their appeal to the fathers, specifically to Eusebios of Caesarea.

In a letter to Constantia, the sister of Constantine the Great, the ecclesiastical historian rightly accuses the idolaters of making false idols which represent nothing because there is no archetype. But he goes on to confuse pagan with Christian worship, the latter being the only true worship directed to "the one, only living, and true God."[88]

According to Nikephoros, Eusebios' opposition to Christian images is based upon his connection to the Arian heresy "which lowers to created matter the supersubstantial being of the Logos." By espousing this conclusion, Eusebios is easily lead to the absurd supposition that even the Christians have no archetype, and therefore, cannot justify icon veneration. His claim that the sculptors of idols and their art is without purpose, that is, without relation to anything real, is a conclusion acceptable to Nikephoros. An absence of any real archetype is proof that the image is false, but also not real, since its relation is nonexistent. Eusebios' mistake, however, is to apply this argument—correct with respect to idols—to Christian icons, "not defining those [images] as being like [and thus] something toward the archetypal form."[89]

Nikephoros favorably tolerates the efforts of pagan artisans insofar as they attempt to capture in their "sculptured images" the accomplishments of their heroes. Their effort is directed to honoring their heroes with perpetual remembrance. In the tradition of Justin Martyr and the Cappadocian fathers, the patriarch does not see this expression as a contradiction to what Christians do; they remember the life and deeds of Christ through pictorial representations. This has been established irrefutably by "all evangelical history." Even the gifts offered to the Christ child by the Magi are not to be dishonored just because their bearers are pagans.[90]

This toleration does not imply that Nikephoros' view on idolatry has changed. He is resolutely committed to the denouncing of idolatry as false because its archetype is false. As his position in *Antirresis Eusebiou* shows, he can also acknowledge the efforts of the pagans in their attempt to relate image to archetype essentially. This effort is common to both pagan and Christian. In this respect their external forms of worship might be considered similar (e.g. the use of candles, censors, and vestments). The difference lies in the subject-matter or content of worship: "Things which are similar and belong with like things are not used in the same way liturgically."[91] For idolatry, the effort to relate to an essential archetype is hopelessly futile because the idol is worshiped "in itself" and not with reference to anything else. For Christianity, though, the reference to its archetype is true because its prototype (the content of worship) exists and is true.[92]

## NOTES

1. *Ekd. pisteos* 1176-80.
2. *Logos* 757.
3. Ibid. 760. Citation from Matt 5.17; "the law" added by Nikephoros.
4. Ibid. 761.
5. Ibid.
6. Ibid. 717-20.
7. Ibid. 761.
8. Ibid. 764; cf. Heb 9.13-15.
9. Ibid. 765.
10. Ibid. 617.
11. Ibid. 620. Nikephoros is indirectly attacking his iconoclastic opponents.
12. Ibid. 553.
13. Ibid. 549,552,553.
14. Ibid. 616,541.
15. Ibid. 540-41.
16. Ibid. 736.
17. These terms are great (*megas*), initiant in the mystery (*hierophantes*), God-bearing (*theophoros*), teacher (*didaskalos*), discourser with God (*theegoros*), revealer of God (*theophantor*), great teacher, holy (*theios*), divinely-inspired (*theoleptos*), initiant in the sacred (*hieromystes*); see O'Connell, *Ecclesiology*, p. 98.
18. Ibid. 813,540.
19. *Antir. Eus.* 379; *Logos* 812-13,540.
20. *Logos* 813.
21. Ibid.
22. See O'Connell, *Ecclesiology*, p. 101. Cf. *Antir.* 1.273: "Where is the teaching of our fathers, who are initiants in the mystery [priests] and theologians, who have become stewards of Christ's mysteries and inheritors to the holy Spirit?"; ibid. 3.389: "Does it not follow that we should submit to the apostolic and patristic commands...since they derive from the spiritual grace [Holy Spirit]?"; and *Logos* 537-40: "As many as were gathered together shed their light in those sacred and God-gathered synods,...and as many as purified themselves and were illustrious in their lives, lofty in word and thought presided

over sacred thrones." "Sacred thrones" could refer to Rome, Constantinople, Alexandria, Antioch, and Jerusalem.

23. *Logos* 540,644.

24. Ibid. 540.

25. Ibid. 813.

26. Of note are the *florilegia*, lists of selected scriptural and patristic quotations (e.g. ibid. 812-32).

27. Ibid. 813; also, *Chaps. 12-PK* 459: "They falsified and corrupted the books of our venerable fathers which they [iconoclasts] exhibited for the instruction and benefit of the Church. For this too, they are already subject to canon-rule."

28. See above, pp. 5-6,10-11; also, Nikephoros' earliest work, *Letter* 192-93, and his latest, *Chaps. 12-PK* 455-57, where the Seven Ecumenical Synods are summarized.

29. The patriarch does not concur with restricting theology to any particular historical period. The Church is fully authoritative in all centuries; see *Letter* 192.

30. *Apol.* 836.

31. Ibid. Nikephoros accuses "the impious Constantine of attacking...[and] breathing more vehemently against our correct dogmas."

32. *Letter* 192.

33. *Apol.* 836,848-49.

34. Ibid. 845.

35. *Logos* 597. One such letter is the synodical letter of Pope Agathon sent to the Sixth Ecumenical Synod; *Apol.* 841.

36. *Logos* 597.

37. Ibid. 597-600.

38. *Apol.* 840.

39. Ibid. Without discussing the proceedings of the Sixth Ecumenical Synod, Nikephoros only refers to the fathers' signatures and not to the crosses: "During that time, the most venerable patriarchs and others, up to two-hundred forty bishops proclaiming those canons, are signified by their signatures"; ibid. 845.

40. Ibid. 841.

41. Ibid. 848. The emperor's normal theological functions included presiding over general synods, signing the acts of the synods, legalizing the acts through imperial edicts, and as the defender of orthodoxy, protecting the empire from heresy.

42. Ibid. 840. The recognition of the principle of autonomous independence, yet reciprocal cooperation, was based upon the premise that both the Church, as the spiritual kingdom, and the State, as the worldly kingdom, are united under the common leadership of Jesus Christ. (The unity was metaphorically compared in the *Epanagoge* [879-86] to the unity of man composed of the harmonious balance of body to soul.) The key which defined the proper relations between Church and State was the mystery of incarnation, which recognizes the duality of the human and divine natures, but at the same time overcomes their ambiguity in the person of Christ. By utilizing the hypostatic union of Christ as their model, it followed that the Byzantines, comfortable with the platonic tradition of the one and many, duality and unity, allowed the separation between Church and State (the antinomy), but also emphasized their respective union (unity) in relation to their interdependence (*synallelia* = lit. 'with the other'). This principle was severely challenged by the iconoclast rulers; see Travis, "Nikephoros," pp. 40-44.

43. Ibid. 845.

44. *Elengchos*, MS Parisinus Graecus 1250, fol. 174v, trans. O'Connell, *Ecclesiology*, p. 117.

45. *Apol.* 840.

46. *Antir.* 3.501.

47. *Chaps. 12-PK* 458; *Antir.* 3.501.

48. *Chaps. 12-PK* 459; *Apol.* 844.

49. *Apol.* 844; see *Homily* 11, PG 62.1.99.

50. Ibid. 841.

51. *Chaps. 12-PK* 459.

52. *Apol.* 844; *Logos* 609,672.

53. *Apol.* 844; *Chaps. 12-PK* 459.

54. Nikephoros in *Antir. Eus.* 460, accuses Eusebios of contradicting himself by being a heretic in his theology, but an orthodox in his historical writing.

55. *Logos* 564-65.

56. Ibid. 561,565.

57. Ibid. 533.

58. Ibid. 592,577.

59. See ibid. 580.

60. Ibid. 579; see Alexander, "Council," p. 41.

61. Ibid. p. 41. A stronger assessment is given by Anastos in "Ethical Theory," p. 160: "The cardinal fact, which Alexander disregards, is that the florilegium of 815 is based upon, and derived from, that of 754." It must be noted that, unlike Alexander, the latter concludes: "The florilegium of the Council of 815 does not advance beyond the iconoclastic theology of the earlier period"; p. 159.

62. *Logos* 577.

63. Ibid. 577-789.

64. Both Alexander, *Nikephoros*, p. 169, and O'Connell, *Ecclesiology*, p. 57, summarize the argument too generally.

65. *Logos* 577,589,592.

66. Ibid. 601-04. This theme is repeated many times throughout the treatise.

67. Ibid. 608-09.

68. Ibid. 612. Found in Egyptian cults, animism, according to Nikephoros, surpasses all other pagan superstitions; *Antir.* 3.448. The Egyptians not only worshiped animals (ibid. 453), but also, according to a reference by Cantacuzenos (later than Nikephoros), incorporated all the idols of the nations into their own worship; PG 100.447, n. 51.

69. *Logos* 612.

70. Ibid. 612-13,620.

71. Ibid. 633,617-20.

72. Ibid. 633,641.The patriarch mentions that the heavenly bodies, such as the sun, moon and stars, the demons on earth, and the most illustrious men, whose fame was "in shameful passions and acts," were worshiped and honored as gods.

73. Ibid. 644.

74. Ibid. 644-45.

75. Ibid. 648-49.

76. Ibid. 652-53. Even though pagan resistance had been to a great degree stamped out

under Theodosios and Justinian, there were regions of pagan revival in Byzantium. Remnants of paganism were found as late as the seventh century on some islands in Italy, and as late as the ninth century in Mani of Peloponnesos. Not until the Christianization of Mani under Basil the Macedonian do we have records of dioceses established by the tenth century; see Gerasimos Konidaris, *Ἐκκλησιαστικὴ Ἱστορία τῆς Ἑλλάδος: Ἀπὸ τῆς ἱδρύσεως τῶν ἐκκλησιῶν αὐτῆς ὑπὸ τοῦ Ἀποστόλου Παύλου μέχρι σήμερον (49/50-1966)*; vol. 1 with Introduction 1 and 2 (Athens, 1954-60); vol. 2: *Ἀπὸ τῶν ἀρχῶν τοῦ η. αἰῶνος μέχρι τῶν καθ'ἡμᾶς χρόνων ἐν ἐπιτομῇ μετ'ἐπισκοπήσεως τῆς ἐκκλησιαστ. ἱστορίας τῆς Ἑλλάδος εἰσαγωγικῶς*, 2d ed., rev. and enl. (Athens, 1970), 1,472; 2,38-39.

77. *Logos* 656.

78. Ibid. 676-77; cf. Isa 11.10.

79. Ibid. 677,684,689.

80. Ibid. 777,788,757; esp. 776.

81. Ibid. 788-92.

82. 3.445-65. A similar argument is presented in *Antir. Eus.* 448-59.

83. *Antir.* 3.445,448-49; cf. Isa 45.12.

84. Ibid. 453,449; also stated at 452.

85. Ibid. 449-57. The same and other examples are found in *Antir. Eus.* 452-58.

86. *Antir.* 3.457.

87. Ibid. 465,464; see above, pp. 150-52.

88. *Antir. Eus.* 443-44.

89. Ibid.

90. Ibid. 444-45,498.

91. Ibid. 502. Nikephoros substantiates this thesis with sayings from Gregory the Illuminator of Armenia (ca. 240-332). The latter maintains that habit is an innate condition for the possibility of any form of worship, pagan or otherwise. It follows that this possibility for worship can find its true meaning or content when directed by Christ; e.g. from idols to icons, from wooden statues to the cross, and from bloody sacrifices to the eucharist; 499-501.

92. Ibid. 495,444.

# 13

# *Unwritten Tradition*

## MIRACLES

One might expect a ninth century Byzantine author to delight his readers with a generous dose of miracles associated with icons. This is not the case with Nikephoros. The absence of hagiographical narrative can only be interpreted in light of his literary temperament. To occupy himself with such accounts—as his contemporaries did so well—remains subordinate to the patriarch's purpose. His aim, rather, was to arm his readers with intellectually sound theological argumentation directed against the heretical misinterpretations of the iconoclasts. Besides referring to miracles from scripture, Nikephoros describes two other miracles, one of which is scripturally based: Berenike's healing and Christ's self-portrait sent to Abgar. These are worth noting because of the apologetic use made of them by the iconophiles.

The patriarch preserves a fragment from Makarios Magnes' *Responses* concerning Berenike, the matron and ruler of the city of the Edessans.[1] Berenike was afflicted with an unclean issue of blood made worse for several years by physicians. She was healed when "she touched the hem of the savior's garment." Thereafter she recorded her experience "by respectfully representing the deed in forged bronze."[2]

Crafer's observations do not help in understanding why Nikephoros refers to this particular miracle which took place earlier than the fourth century.[3] The reason is found in the patriarch's own explanation. He accuses the iconoclasts of garbling Makarios' quotations by utilizing the latter's arguments against idols for their own attack against icon veneration.[4] Makarios' position, according to Nikephoros, is not to be confused with their's. The latter degrade the power of the archetype, and consequently, are led to the absurd conclusion that Christ, like the pagan gods, is unable to perform miracles. Nikephoros draws the implication that Makarios is no friend to iconoclasm. Proof of this is Makarios' reference to this particular miracle which justifies the pictorial representation of Christ.

Nikephoros notes that Eusebios records the event in his *Ecclesiastical History*.[5] Following the historian's account, the patriarch relates that a strange species of herb grew at the foot of the monument and acted as a miraculous antidote for all kinds of ailments. This additional point is noteworthy because it supports the iconophile's belief that even the material upon which the archetype is represented is sometimes miraculously sanctified by Christ.

Nikephoros argues against Eusebios' inconsistent position. The latter appears somewhat less scandalized with the commemorative statue than pictorial images and is able to justify it by pagan habit:

> There is nothing wonderful in the fact that those heathen, who long ago had good deeds done to them by our Saviour, should have made these objects, since we saw the likenesses of His apostles also, of Paul and Peter, and indeed of Christ Himself, preserved in pictures painted in colours. And this is what we should expect, for the ancients were wont, according to their pagan habit, to honour them as saviours, without reservation, in this fashion.[6]

On the other hand, Eusebios censures the pictorial representation of Christ by considering it a degenerate form of pagan habit.[7]

By referring to these particular miracles which are associated with Christ's representation, Nikephoros is able to justify once again the inseparableness between image and archetype. The miracles are not done "according to pagan habit," but are possible because of the grace of their true archetype represented in the image.[8]

The second important miracle is also utilized by the patriarch for an apologetic end. Impressed with miracles attributed to Christ, Abgar, king of Edessa, called an artist to make an image of Christ. The incident was recorded as early as the fourth century with an added detail; namely, that Christ not only sent a letter, but a self-portrait as well. Nikephoros emphasizes that it was Abgar's desire to preserve the immediate impression which moved him to make a lasting monument.[9] The patriarch omits the further detail—most likely familiar to his readers—that this image of Christ had become the protection of the city, a phylactery defending the city from its enemies. The implication of accepting an image as such is stated by Kitzinger: "The barrier between image and subject breaks down. Christ is palpably present in His image and fulfills His promise through it."[10] If Nikephoros regards the image as a phylactery, then, his purpose for mentioning this miracle is explicit. The justification of image representation is not only directed by God, but is also supported by the believers' desire to make the object of their faith tangible.[11]

## ARCHITECTURE

The few references concerning the architecture of the Church[12] are noteworthy for two reasons: they substantiate the patriarch's theological justification of icon veneration, and they acknowledge the continuity of the practice of the Church. These references also have a historical merit because they reveal the intensity of iconoclastic persecution which included the desecration of Christian churches.

> You curse the intercession of the saints, you dig up the holy tables of the holy sanctuaries in order to put to flame their [the saints'] relics, as, indeed, your teacher Mamonas [Constantine V] did and taught,...you desecrate their venerable churches...burning their biographies (*synaxaria*) in the fire,...so that by these [acts of sacrilege] you extinguish completely their memory.[13]

Architecture is intimately connected to the theology of the Church—a fact not to be overlooked. Nikephoros' view of this art form supposes the ecclesial unity of the Church, which understands the Church on earth as an extension of the heavenly Jerusalem.[14] The edifice and its furnishings are the setting within which the redemptive events are made present, culminating in the divine liturgy. Other points follow from this understanding of architecture.

First, Nikephoros recognizes the sublime magnificence of the Christian churches. They are richly endowed with the best of creation's gifts for God's glory. They are more glorious and illustrious than even the Old Testament temples, and consequently, the iconoclasts have no basis to criticize the architectural splendor of these edifices.[15] The decorative aspects also serve the glory of God. In no way do they detract from the primary objective: God's presence in the midst of his people. "The beauty and grandeur of some of these [churches]," and their great numbers prove the uniqueness of the Christian Church, that through its sacramental life "the kingdom of heaven is within us."[16]

Elsewhere Nikephoros praises those pious emperors, beginning with Constantine the Great, who built or rebuilt many of the magnificent Christian churches.[17] Theodosios I (379-95) and Theodosios II (408-50) are mentioned as great benefactors and preservers, especially of "the images made-without-hands of the savior Christ." The patriarch lauds Justinian I (527-65), who because of his love for Christ, erected "holy temples and other edifices [monasteries]—one in particular above all,...named the Church of the Wisdom of God the Logos [Hagia Sophia]." He uses superlative terms to describe this church's immense size and exceptional beauty.[18]

Second, the patriarch unequivocably believes that the Holy Spirit is present in all parts of the church, which also includes its icons. The edifice "is, therefore, either all sacred and holy, or all accursed and impure." The iconoclasts are inconsistent because, while accepting the prayers and invocations offered in the churches named after a particular saint, they refuse to honor the saints through their pictorial representations. Nikephoros suggests that perhaps his opponents might want to espouse the absurd option of "asking for another sanctification, other consecrations and prayers, thereby accepting the invocation of another Spirit." He argues, instead, that both icon and other parts of the church have been sanctified by the same saving grace.[19] To make a distinction based upon which of the two "is first or second, and which is venerable or holy...is the crime of the unbelievers and impious." It follows, that "all things within the church of God, we recognize and confess as venerable and holy. For this reason, they are considered by us worthy of reverence, venerable as well as honorable, and nothing is without glory or dishonor."[20]

Third, the patriarch emphasizes the importance of consecration whereby the Spirit sanctifies the edifice as a holy place of worship. His stirring description of this ecclesiastical service is significant because it shows a continuity with past practices. The service, as described by the patriarch, has remained virtually unchanged to this day in the orthodox world. The clergy offer prayers to God asking for the descent of the Spirit "to bless the temple and to fill it with eternal light." The newly-consecrated edifice becomes a temple where the gifts of grace abide: "It is established as a clinic for [the healing] of the passions, a place where demons are expelled, and it is shown to be the holy of holies." The two indispensable functions of the service are the anointing with myrrh of the various parts of the church, and the depositing of the relics of a saint or martyr "in the consecrated altars (*kathieroumenois thysiasteriois*)."[21] Even though he does not refer to the holy tables specifically, it is probable that by "consecrated altars" the patriarch implies that these relics are placed in the holy tables upon which the bloodless sacrifice is to be celebrated.[22]

## THE CROSS

Nikephoros' lengthy discussion of the cross is noteworthy because it, too, is a rebuttal of an iconoclastic position.[23] As seen earlier, the iconoclasts considered the eucharist to be the only legitimate icon of the body of Christ.[24] Another non-anthropomorphic symbol acceptable to them was the figure of the cross (*ho tou staurou typos*). Whether a connection can be made between their respect for the plain cross and the Paulicians' extreme rejection of its veneration remains unclear.[25] One fact is certain: the iconoclasts were not offended by the veneration of the plain cross. The iconophiles interpreted this, however, as a rejection of Christ as 'crucified', especially since the iconoclasts refused to consider him pictorially represented.[26]

It is important to note the presupposition which was behind the iconophiles' interpretation. They moved within a dogmatic background which, while accepting the symbolic nature of the cross, insists upon its relation to what is represented, the crucified Christ. Their position is the outcome of canon 82 of the Quinisext Synod (692) with its preference (*protimomen*) for anthropomorphic representations (*anthropinon charaktera*) rather than symbolic ones.

Nikephoros' understanding of the cross also presupposes this dogmatic background. He asserts that the cross cannot be understood without its theological truth, the reality of Christ's human body. By refusing to believe in the humanity of the incarnate Word, the iconoclasts cannot accept even the cross; the uncircumscribable could not be crucified without being circumscribed. Their contradiction consists in venerating that which has been sanctified, and at the same time, despising the one who sanctified it. The patriarch reiterates that 'all things' are worthy of veneration and efficacious for salvation.[27]

Nikephoros' rebuttal ingenuously argues against the plain cross by contrasting it to the icon of Christ. His argument is divided into ten proofs, reminiscent of later Western scholastic methodology.[28]

Whereas the icon of Christ is a likeness of him because "it portrays (*hypographei* = lit. writes out) the figure of his body for us and gives notice to the species [of the archetype], and as an imitation signifies the way of action, teaching, or emotion and other things [pertaining to the archetype]," the figure of the cross is not a likeness of Christ's body. Nikephoros' first demonstration supposes the philosophical distinction that if something is like something, even in imitation, it is truer to the archetype, than something unlike. Being similar to its archetype, the icon is more familiar "and therefore, may be considered more venerable and honorable."[29]

The icon presents to us from the first glance an immediate and direct perception of its archetype; "in it we see reflected the represented [archetype]." The cross, however, is viewed 'phenomenologically': "We direct the mind first, toward the thing as perceived. Afterwards, we consider what it is, we review how it was sanctified and by whom; and thus, we share [its efficacy] through that [cross] on which Christ was crucified and which he sanctified."[30] Admittedly difficult to follow, Nikephoros' distinction is based upon the supposition that iconographic art is representational because its product, the icon, is a direct reflection of its archetype.[31] Perception, reflection, and acknowledgment are from the beginning present in the icon. The cross, though, remains a sensible object independent of its relation to a prototype. It is only when we reflect upon this perceived object as related to the crucified Christ that we are reminded of its meaning as the crucifix. This intermediary step of reflection is nonexistent for the icon; the archetype is present in its image. The second demonstration argues, then, from the nature of the cross and concludes by saying that what can be perceived directly without mediation, intellectualized abstraction or otherwise, is more honored; "the icon of Christ, therefore, is more honorable than the venerable cross."[32]

In the third proof Nikephoros demonstrates the causal relation between the cross and the hypostasis of Christ. Not denying that both are figures, he quotes Hebrews 7.7: "And without all contradiction the less is blessed of the better." He argues that "the figure of the cross which is sanctified is honorable; accordingly, the figure of the body [of Christ] which sanctifies is indeed more honorable." The proof clearly wants to establish the logical priority of Christ's body to the cross, a fact not recognized by the iconoclasts. Christ, the one who sanctifies, is logically prior, and therefore, better than the cross, namely, that which is sanctified.[33]

The fourth demonstration similarly establishes the logical priority of Christ's body. Nikephoros argues from the Aristotelian notion that substantiality is the primary sense of being. An existent's figure, which includes its natural attributes or accidental properties, is subsequential and accidental to the definition of its ontological character. It makes sense, according to Nikephoros, to speak of the body as being 'a shaped body' (*soma eschematismenon*), but not 'a corporeal shape' (*schema sesomatomenon*). Since the attributes of the body are definitionally prior, because they are ontologically prior to the attributes of the figure, it follows that "the figure of the body [of Christ] is more honorable than the type of its figure [cross]."[34]

The fifth demonstration maintains that the subject-content of the cross is more limited in scope than that of the icon. The cross presents the passion of Christ "somewhat simply and without variety"; it is conceived by the unlearned as "the symbol of the passion." The icons describe the passion more vividly and in more detail as well as other miracles which Christ performed. Consequently, these prove to be more honorable and of more significance.[35]

The sixth demonstration argues for the symbolic character of the cross. As the symbol of Christ's passion, it reminds us first, of the manner in which he was crucified; second, of his exhortation to follow him; and third, of his love for humankind. Nikephoros utilizes precise terminology to convey the subtle differences between icon and cross. The latter "traces (*diagraphon*) those things concerning Christ," whereas "his icon is the copy and likeness (*eksphragisma kai homoioma*) of the suffering [Christ]." The icon is more honorable because "it is that which manifests Christ himself to us." It is not a symbol. The cross, though, is that which "points out the manner of his passion to us."[36]

The seventh demonstration supposes what has been established concerning the ontological difference between the cross and the icon. It argues for the inapplicability of referring to the cross in the same way as the icon. The name 'Christ' may refer by equivocation to the icon of Christ.[37] When we see this icon, it is not meaningless to refer to it by the name of its archetype, 'Christ'. The case is otherwise with the figure of the cross. When we say 'Christ', this does not necessarily refer to the name 'cross'.[38]

The eighth proof defines the ontological nature of the cross by its location on the hierarchical ladder of existents. Nikephoros syllogistically argues:

> The cause precedes the caused; it is, rather, the efficient cause. That which precedes is more honorable than that of which is preceded. Since the cause of the figure of the cross is the passion of the body of Christ, and the body is the efficient cause of the figure [of the cross], it follows that the icon of Christ's body, as the efficient cause, is also more honorable than the figure of the cross.[39]

Similar to the former proof, the ninth demonstration posits that while the final product, characterized as "that which became for the sake of (*ho tinos heneken gegonen*)," is less than its maker, "through whom it became (*ekeinou tou di'ho gegonen*)," nonetheless, it is honorable.[40]

The tenth demonstration argues for the inseparable veneration of both the cross and the icon. Because the lord's crucifixion is represented in many icons as the principal theme, it is fallacious to distinguish between the honor rendered to the cross and that rendered to the icon, as the iconoclasts do. Nikephoros concludes by accusing his opponents of not really venerating the cross, since they have used it as an excuse to desecrate the icon. They desecrate the icon 'theologically' by not considering Christ's human nature 'essentially'.[41]

In summary, Nikephoros' argumentation, set within the background of his justification of icon veneration, emphasizes that all holy objects (e.g. relics, icons, crosses, bibles) deserve the worshiper's veneration; and each is what it is because of its relation to its represented archetype. The cross, for instance, is not just a bare symbol, but is related to Christ. The iconoclasts were willing to venerate the plain cross, but not the crucified Christ. To elevate the cross to the same level as the icon is inconsistent, as the demonstrations have proven. There is an 'essential' difference between icon and cross, and this is based upon the relation betwen an image-object and the thing represented. This relation can be defined ontologically, in terms of logical priority, phenomenologically, and theologically. Consequently, the closer an image or symbol is in relation to its archetype, the more honor it deserves in a hierarchical order of importance. The phrase "the cross became in virtue of the icon, not vice versa the icon in virtue of the figure of the cross" is to be understood in this sense.[42] Still, both imply a reference to their archetype, Jesus Christ, and thus, are to be honored.

Nikephoros, finally, does not separate the cross from the living unwritten tradition of the Church. The Christians by custom kept pieces of the true cross which were encased within gold and silver containers called 'phylacteries'. Hung around the neck and worn on the chest, these phylacteries derived their name from the belief that they are used as "a protection and safety of their lives,...as medicine against the passions and a dissuasion against the unclean spirits."[43] This unwritten practice becomes another important demonstration for the sanctity of the cross. By destroying these and other sacred objects which represent the theme of the crucified Christ, the iconoclasts destroy the cross itself. "It is worth calling them everywhere the enemies of Christ's cross...for they will be opportunely counted with them [the Jews and Greeks]."[44]

## THE ICON

The icon belongs properly to unwritten tradition, but its justification is based upon tradition as a whole. For this reason, the strongest argument for the veneration of icons, according to Nikephoros, is based on tradition: "It is clear to everyone that the long-standing and ancient tradition of the Church is the strongest of all, and of all proofs it is more effective and more certain."[45] The iconophile consistently maintains "that from the beginning [of antiquity] and from above [God], from both apostolic and patristic tradition, the existence as well as the veneration of the holy icons has continued to the present, and [concerning these things] the ancient Churches have given witness to and preached." In further justifying the icons he appeals to practice: "These were placed side by side with the venerable cross in the holy sanctuary for no other reason than to be venerated. Again, in the same manner [the images] were imprinted on the holy doors and sacred gates [of the *iconostasion*]."[46]

There are three reasons why the icon is an inseparable part of tradition. First, image representation was commanded by God; the Old Testament prescriptions regarding the ark and the representation of the cherubim constitute this directive. By arguing that image development is found in Old and New Testament history, the patriarch appeals to God and the antiquity of that practice which has been passed on faithfully to each generation: "As children who succeed their fathers, indeed, we [Christians] have reverently received these from above and from the beginning."[47]

Second, the present practice is a continuation of what was taught from apostolic times.

> To figure, that is, to represent Christ iconographically, has not received its beginning from us, nor is it something which began in our generation, nor is it an innovation. It is contemporary with the evangelical kerygma. For this reason, it is both venerable and honored...since these holy visions [icons] are symbols of our pure faith.... [To represent something iconographically] is a task undertaken by the apostles; it bears the seal of the fathers.[48]

O'Connell correctly remarks that "it is not the merely material antiquity of images which is being attended to here, but their location in Church tradition and the practice of the faithful."[49] By drawing a parallel between the scriptural message and the development of visual representation,[50] Nikephoros also stresses the fact that both written and unwritten tradition are equally derived from apostolic teaching, and therefore, from Christ himself. The scriptures and the icons are inseparable within the life of the Church: "The tradition which we have received from above by the apostolic and patristic kerygma of our sacred religion, we stand and glory in. We greatly give testimony [to that belief in tradition], and its holy symbols [the icons] we possess as a secure anchor."[51]

Third, Christian imagery, as practiced in the early Christian churches and dated from the event of incarnation, has a definite place in tradition. O'Connell's comment that "in the writings of Nicephorus there is no indication of the gradual stages by which the making of images of Christ was accepted in the Church," must not be taken absolutely.[52] The patriarch does distinguish between earlier and later developments with particular reference to the synods, and especially to canon 82 of the Quinisext. The canon pronounced that the images of Christ should not represent their archetype in merely symbolic figures, e.g. a lamb, but in the form which he in fact appeared "according to human character." The synodal fathers only verified officially what was known already in practice: namely, the relation between the historic event of the incarnation and its continued commemoration through representational art. Unlike earlier visual forms, venerable though they are, the icons depict the 'truth' or 'fullness' of the event.[53] The patriarch, then, was very sensitive to the historical development and continuity of image making.

## NOTES

1. *Apokritika* 1.6. Both *Acts of Pilate* 7 and Eusebios, *Ecclesiastical History* 7.18.1-3, assume that Berenike is the same woman with the issue of blood as described in Matt 9.18-26. Nikephoros follows these accounts faithfully in *Epikr.* 332-33 and *Antir. Eus.*

491-92. With different details given, the structure of the event remains unchanged in *Antir. Eus.* 494-95. Whether Berenike is to be identified with Veronika, as Crafer in *Apokritikos*, p. 31, n. 1, assumes, is debatable; cf. Pitra, SS 1.332, n. 1.

2. *Epikr.* 333. In addition to Eusebios' and Makarios' accounts, the other records of Sozomenos, Philostorgios, and Ioannes Malalas also attribute the statue at Paneas; see Crafer, *Apokritikos*, p. 31, n. 2. Greek syntax in the phrase "of the notable region and deserving esteem *(episemou choriou kai entimon)*" would verify this also. Paneas was the city in the province of Edessa; cf. Pitra, SS 1.333, n. 1. In *Antir. Eus.* 497-98, Nikephoros mentions that Emperor Julian had taken down the statue for a time. According to the chronicle of Malalas, the statue remained at Paneas until 600; Crafer, p. 31, n. 5.

3. The fragment "contains part of the answer of Macarius to an objection to the miracle of the woman with the issue of blood"; *Apokritikos*, p. xi.

4. *Epikr.* 334.

5. *Antir. Eus.* 492. The correct numbering of this chapter is 70, not 80 as recorded by Pitra; see MS Parisinus Graecus 1250.

6. Eusebios, *Ecclesiastical History* 7.18.4, quoted in *Antir. Eus.* 493; trans. Oulton, *Eusebios* 2.177.

7. *Antir. Eus.* 492-93.

8. Ibid. 496.

9. *Antir.* 3.461; see Kitzinger, "Cult," p. 103; and Ouspensky, *Theology*, pp. 59-62.

10. "Cult," p. 104.

11. *Antir.* 3.460.

12. The term 'architecture' is understood in its broadest usage to signify the church edifice, its furnishings, utensils, et al.

13. *Antir.* 3.477.

14. See above, pp. 98-99.

15. *Logos* 785-88. This is a corollary of the argument against the iconoclasts' opposition to icon veneration as idol worship; see above, p. 143.

16. Ibid. 789.

17. *Antir.* 3.520. Nikephoros recognizes a historical fact of archeological importance concerning the early churches. The Christians converted and remodeled former pagan temples into Christian churches. As recorded in *Antir. Eus.* 499, they had thrown out all pagan things and had replaced them with Christian motifs.

18. *Antir.* 3.524.

19. Ibid. 477,480.

20. Ibid. 428.

21. *Logos* 604.

22. Ibid. 601.

23. *Antir.* 3.425-36.

24. See above, pp. 116-21.

25. Without making this identification, Gero in "Notes," p. 34, comments that "there is seventh-century evidence for ascetic Armenian iconoclasts who nevertheless venerated the cross." Known as 'servants of the cross' (*Chatzintzarioi*), they "venerated the cross, rejected images, *and* supposedly had an extreme 'Nestorian' christology—there were two persons in Christ, one of whom suffered on the cross while the other watched!"; p. 31, n. 4.

26. Nikephoros' accusation in *Antir.* 3.376, couched in a rhetorical introductory clause,

must be interpreted as a declaration against the iconoclasts who have rejected "the cross and those other things in the Church of the Christians"; see also, ibid. 436.

27. Ibid. 425-28.

28. Ibid. 428-33 is reprinted as a separate treatise in an earlier edition by Mai in SR 10.157-60. A criticism against Mai and Turrianus' claim that this selection is a separate work and not a part of *Antir.* 3 is presented by Grumel, "Douze Chapitres," p. 128.

29. Ibid. 428.

30. Ibid. 428-29.

31. See above, pp. 49-54.

32. *Antir.* 3.429.

33. Ibid.

34. Ibid.

35. Ibid.

36. Ibid. 429,432.

37. See above, p. 53; also, cf. Aristotle, *Categories* 1.1a-5.

38. *Antir.* 3.432.

39. Ibid.

40. Ibid.

41. Ibid. 432-33.

42. Ibid. 433.

43. Ibid.

44. Ibid. 436; see also, 432.

45. *Chaps. 12-PK* 454.

46. *Apol.* 836.

47. *Logos* 589.

48. *Antir.* 3.380.

49. *Ecclesiology*, p. 105.

50. *Antir.* 3.380-84; see above, p. 48.

51. *Prol.* 235.

52. *Ecclesiology*, p. 102.

53. *Antir.* 1.212. For the historical development of iconographic representation beginning with early Christian symbols, see Ouspensky, *Theology*, pp. 81-134.

# 14

# *Individual*

Nikephoros considers the individual to be a dynamic part of the community of Christian believers. Like other Eastern fathers, he does not separate man from this ecclesiological context. The discussion concerning man as the summit of creation (chapter 6) and man's participation in his salvation based upon the reality of the incarnate Logos (chapter 8) are the presuppositions to the real 'anthropological' problem, namely, the individual as one with the Church. To see him as a reflection of God's glory is to address the deeper issue of each man as a unique person whose faith and practice is a manifestation of the fullness of the ecclesial community. The patriarch understands the individual by defining what constitutes an individual member of the Church. These constituents are two: the character of the individual, and worship which is an active manifestation of an individual's character.

## THE CHARACTER OF THE INDIVIDUAL

An individual's personhood presupposes that he be a Christian. His relation to the Church is defined by this fact. Using the familiar image-archetype terminology, Nikephoros compares the 'individual-Christian' to Christ. He bears the name of his prototype and becomes Christ-like "by imitation and conduct." The patriarch makes an interesting comparison between the icon, an art object, and a Christian, a natural existent, which is based on their equivocity to a common prototype, Christ: "Even though the essence and the mode of existence appear different in both [icon and Christian], still, they share the same name, and the name of Christ is predicated commonly of both."[1]

This close relationship is severed whenever a Christian acts dishonestly and disgracefully. By dishonoring the archetype in person, as well as in name, he nullifies his participation, as a communicant of Christ, in the glory of God. Nikephoros insists that if our actions are Christ-like, then we continue to bear worthily the name 'Christian'.[2] The building blocks of such a character, which he regards as indispensable, are faith, love, and knowledge.

## Faith

Nikephoros considers faith as "the beginning and foundation of our salvation." Its essential ingredients are the fear of God and "a directness of heart."[3] The first is based upon the unshakable conviction that God is real and "a rewarder of them that diligently seek him" (Hebrews 11.6).[4] The second enables an individual to accept God's message without resorting to futile questions, debates, or even demonstrations. "Faith is the simple and non-inquisitive assent of reasonings." The worst spiritual disease is unbelief.[5]

Consistent with traditional patristic views, the patriarch regards faith as the prerequisite for our knowledge of God. Faith is necessary for man's salvation. Conversely, lack of faith results in imprudence, which is characterized by disobedience, which leads ultimately to perdition. The patriarch sees an incompatibility between disobedience and piety (*eusebeia*). Using a simile, he describes doubt as "that which overshadows [i.e. obscures] the splendor of truth, like a cloud overrunning the sun."[6] Nikephoros is committed to a position of accepting faith *ipso facto*. To ask for its cause results in a futile search, a characteristic of the unfaithful.

As faith is beyond rational justifications, it is also inseparable from the Spirit. An individual's faith is closely dependent upon it, whose power operates for the individual's sanctification. What is needed is that he acquire faith. The patriarch states emphatically "that without faith it is impossible to please God."[7] Drawing from Hebrews 11, he most eloquently instructs his readers concerning the fervor of faith found among the God-fearing individuals of Old and New Testament times. Likewise, the purpose in appending the patristic *florilegium*[8] is to emphasize, as O'Connell summarizes,

> the necessity of faith, the reverence with which faith is to be received as the gift of God, the tenacity of faith in holding to the tradition of the Church.... All of this material is aimed at forming and demonstrating the simplicity of our faith (τὸ ἁπλοϊκὸν τοῦ τρόπου τῆς πίστεως) and the guileless attitude (ἀπανούργευτον) which should characterise Christians.[9]

## Love

According to Nikephoros, love is directed to God. Expressions which define the inseparable connection between faith and love are not uncommon in his writings. Both are requisites in the make-up of the Christian. Love of God most often is described as an individual's instinctive desire or longing (*pothos*) for God and the things of God, or a burning zeal (*diapyros zelos*) which is directed to the practice of the faith. This zeal is orthodoxy's security against heretical teachings.[10]

The individual's love for God finds its fruition in his love for Christ. Moved by this love, the Christian, as a faithful servant, respects all that pertains to God's glory. This desire and burning zeal of the faithful becomes another valid argument used by the patriarch for the justification of icon veneration. The faithful do not wait to receive a directive in order to express their faith in the making of images; they do this because of their piety and love for divine things.[11] Unlike the Jews who "require a sign" and the Greeks who "seek after wisdom" (1 Corinthians 1.22), the Christian faithful are moved by their own desire to express their piety. This practice is realized in the honor given to the icons.[12]

Finally, the reality of the incarnate Logos is preserved through the making of icons due to the "love for the divine and piety" of the Christian individual.[13] His faith, manifested by his love for God and guided by the Spirit, is what justifies the representation of Christ iconographically: "The making of representations is received by us who believe, accept and embrace them...because we are led by a divine longing and by the Spirit."[14]

## Knowledge

The third constitutive element, regarded by Nikephoros as most important for the personality of a Christian individual, is knowledge. It is the recognition of things taught by faith through tradition. "We being taught those things by the teachers of the Church, stand within the boundaries of piety." As with faith and love, the source of knowledge comes from God; through Christ, knowledge has new meaning.[15]

A knowledgeable Christian is one who strives with his mind to embrace the ideal of the intellect, the knowledge of Christ. Working within a familiar platonic framework, the patriarch contends that the mind must rise above the sensible and must view what is pure and perfect. It has a particular function: to assess what is true, namely, what comes "both from above and what is of divine origin," and to disregard what is satanic and worldly. The Christian's intellectual security is based upon his faith and love for Christ. The study of the scriptures and the teachings of the fathers trains his senses to distinguish the best from the worst by selecting what is useful and repelling all which is harmful.[16] What is best for the soul has been explicated by apostolic teaching, and this alone should be honored and acknowledged.

Christian intellect enables the Christian "to acquire a heavenly conduct." Its opposite is found in the heretical iconoclasts. They follow the "other teachers" who have no basis in tradition. They are characterized by uncritical reasonings which lead them to illogical contradictions. The iconoclasts' intellect has been darkened by a worldly outlook which renders them incapable of understanding the truths of the faith. For the orthodox, however, the mind is characterized by a clear apprehension of what is true. It always operates within the precepts of tradition, and its work is accomplished under the guidance of the Spirit.[17]

Christian intellect is knowledge moving toward an end. The teachers of the Church emphasize that knowledge must be utilized for the benefit of others. Nikephoros too, believes in such a teaching ministry which is directed toward the edification of his flock. For him especially, knowledge is orientated to apologetic ends, to censure heretical teachings.[18]

Knowledge, then, is never an 'autonomous' system attached to one's nature. Rather, it is a contributing 'dynamic' element in the make-up of an individual. Christian knowledge is the guardian against the possibility of falling prey to the heretics, such as the iconoclasts, who persuade the illiterate. According to Nikephoros, the greatest danger lies in exploiting the minds of those Christians who are illiterate concerning the things of God. Such an individual is one who barely listens to the evangelical teachings and dogmas. By quickly forgetting the word, he, in fact, proves that he never accepted it in his heart or mind.[19]

## WORSHIP: AN ACTIVE MANIFESTATION OF AN INDIVIDUAL'S CHARACTER

Nikephoros' account of the individual has yielded the following conclusion. A Christian is a dynamic person whose knowledge consists of the Church's teachings, and whose intellect is tempered by a deep faith and love which instinctively originate from a longing for God. Worship can be considered the consequence of a Christian's character and is the second integral component in the patriarch's character analysis.

Nikephoros correctly distinguishes between two types of worship: adoration (*proskynesis*) which properly belongs to God, and veneration (*sebas*) which pertains to the images and through them to the archetypes. The distinction between adoration and veneration, familiar to the iconophiles since the Seventh Ecumenical Synod, is accepted by his readers as common knowledge: "All who are teachable of God in spirit know the difference concerning this honor."[20] The distinction was part of the iconophiles' arsenal for the justification of icon veneration. By discussing worship as an active manifestation of a Christian character, Nikephoros further develops this distinction made by his predecessors.

In refuting Epiphanides' claim that the Christians worship the angels as gods, the patriarch makes an important clarification. There is a difference in the honor rendered appropriately to an archetype which presupposes the hierarchical position of a particular archetype. Only to God do we offer adoration, while to angels and saints "is given the honor according to worth, and through them this [honor] is referred also to him."[21]

The patriarch further distinguishes adoration from other forms of honor.[22] The adoration offered to God is the highest expression of worship and is understood in the context of spiritual worship. Other types of honor are the honor presented by the subjects to their ruler which is rendered to him because of his exalted position in the State, and consequently, due him by law; the honor given to a tyrant due him by fear; and the honor offered to the saints, which through them is rendered to God. This honor originates "willingly from the desire and faith of the believers," and in this respect is very different in kind from the former two types of honor. Finally, there is the honor bestowed upon someone closely loved which is "relative and salutory, [derived] from a friendly and sincere disposition." This honor suggests a situation where a friendly gesture or compliment is directed to one's neighbors.

If Nikephoros differentiates between these four kinds of honor, he also implies that adoration is the highest expression because it employs the combined elements of all forms of honor. In other words, desire, which is applicable in the third, and to a lesser extent, in the fourth type, is an indispensable attribute of adoration. The individual presuppposes an instinctive desire to worship God perfectly, namely, in spirit. Likewise fear, the basis for the honor rendered to a tyrant, is a component of God's adoration (*mysterium tremendum*), though God is in no sense a tyrant. The law, a feature of the first kind of honor, also applies to God's adoration, for he is the lawgiver and ruler above all creation.[23] So while adoration is distinct from other forms of honor, their respective expressions can all be found in adoration.

Nikephoros defines the adoration of God as "the spiritual sacrifice of praise, the spiritual worship (*logike latreia*) offered to God by all the nations in the Church."[24] Familiar in patristic texts, the locution "spiritual worship " means the full participation of a believer in the act of worship. By offering adoration in the full knowledge of faith (*pistis en epignosei*), the Christian utilizes his rational and sensory capabilities toward this end.[25] Worship becomes the setting for the relationship of the individual and God. The recognition of divine truth concerning God's love for humankind, then, is verified in the individual's faith, love, and desire to worship God.

## NOTES

1. *Antir.* 3.465,468.

2. Ibid. 468.

3. Ibid. 377.

4. Ibid. For Nikephoros' commentary on Heb 11, see *Logos* 801-04,816-20.

5. Ibid. 377.

6. Ibid. 377,380.

7. Ibid. 377,480; *Logos* 801.

8. *Logos* 812-32.

9. *Ecclesiology*, pp. 89-90; cf. *Logos* 829.

10. Ibid. 808; *Prol.* 253.

11. *Antir. Epiph.* 331; *Antir.* 3.460.

12. *Prol.* 255.

13. *Antir.* 3.461. One such example is Abgar; see above, p. 150.

14. Ibid. 2.372.

15. Ibid. 1.324; *Logos* 624.

16. *Logos* 657,661; *Epikr.* 303; cf. the advice given by Basil the Great to his students in *Πρὸς τοὺς νέους, ὅπως ἂν ἐξ Ἑλληνικῶν ὠφελοῖντο λόγων*. For the English translation with the accompanied Greek text, see Roy Joseph Deferrari and Martin R. P. McGuire, *Address to Young Men on Reading Greek Literature* in *Saint Basil: The Letters*, trans. Roy J. Deferrari, LCL (1934; repr. Cambridge, Mass., 1961), 4,363-435.

17. *Epikr.* 303-04; *Logos* 624.

18. *Epikr.* 304-05.

19. *Logos* 749.

20. Ibid. 589.

21. *Antir. Epiph.* 320-21. The hierarchy of the Virgin Mary, angels, saints, et al. also finds its expression in the liturgical service. Compare their order and relation to the host as they are placed upon the paten during the service of oblation in preparation for the divine liturgy; see N. Papadopoulos, *Leitourgia*, pp. 28-31.

22. *Antir.* 3.392.

23. Ibid.; cf. Rom 13.7.

24. *Logos* 692.

25. Ibid. 672; *Prol.* 256.

# 15

# *Eschatology*

Nikephoros does not separate eschatology from either christology or ecclesiology. There is a direct relation between one's ethical Christian life and the life to come; the individual's character and actions will directly affect his blessedness (*makariotes*). The patriarch urges his readers to cleanse their thoughts and actions and to lead a life that looks toward God's glory. The reality of the eschatological presence is sufficient reason to take these exhortations seriously.[1] Not only is there a sense of urgency which is reflected in this life as a preparation for the next, but there is also that real glimpse of a future glory as mirrored in the temporal lives of the Church's members (saints, fathers, and faithful).

By keeping in mind the historical circumstances surrounding the Church of the ninth century, we are able to appreciate the apologetic nature of Nikephoros' eschatological references. On the one hand, the emphasis upon the rewards of eternal life granted to those who with patience and vigilance have exercised virtue in this life, becomes an eschatological banner of hope and comfort to those iconophiles subjected to persecutions. Nikephoros' discussion of Christ's second coming and the general judgment are also reiterated for the reawakening and conversion of those orthodox members who are being swayed to the iconoclasts' cause, and thus, pose the greatest imminent danger to the unity of the Church. On the other hand, his description of the eternal damnation which awaits all those who are unrepentant of their sins, is a warning for the iconoclasts to repent of their pride and unbelief in matters of dogma and practice.[2]

Other themes follow which reconstruct Nikephoros' understanding of the last events. Unaware of the exact day of judgment, he is sensitive to the signs of the latter days. The iconoclasts most assuredly fit the descriptions of 2 Timothy 3.1-5,8-9,13.[3]

Nikephoros' vivid description of the second coming does not differ from scriptural or patristic accounts. The last day, "great and terrible," will be heralded by a trumpet and magnificent heavenly voices, after which "the judge of all, lord and God of all" will appear accompanied by a myriad of heavenly powers.[4] With the second coming the patriarch notes also the general resurrection. The work of the savior

> will be to crush and punish the disobedient and those who have passed the bounds of reason by inclining toward matter and worldly things, and those who are subject to the wishes of the secular power [Mamonas]. [Whereas] those who have served him and have loved his appearance, he will raise as worthy of the eternal and blissful kingdom [of God].[5]

The patriarch unquestionably believes in God's promises concerning eternal life, and particularly, holds that judgment will be made according to how each man has lived. God's judgment will be for all.[6] By justifying their actions with the excuse of ignorance, or with the belief that his mercy is unlimited, the iconoclasts have overlooked the fact that they too shall be judged. Their actions shall be weighed by what has been revealed in Church dogma and practice. Universal judgment, then, will take place "not separately, in secret and in a small part of the world, but publicly, in the middle of the common theater of angels and men."[7]

God's justice cannot be compared to the decisions adjudicated in secular courts of law. These tribunals are presided over by arrogant and pompous judges who manipulate the law for their own advantage, not caring for the justice of the less fortunate. Having in mind the iconoclasts, many of whom have served as secular judges, Nikephoros derides them as the new pharisees and scribes who were warned by Christ: "For ye shut up the kingdom of heaven against men: for ye neither go in yourselves, neither suffer ye them that are entering to go in" (Matthew 23.13). The patriarch's own description is even less complimentary: "They delight in new opinions and figments [of the imagination], become elated in pharisaic arrogance, appear great in their presiding positions, and are called 'teacher', becoming very haughty [as seen] by the bulging of their eyebrow." In contrast, God's verdict will be based completely on spiritual, rather than pedestrian criteria. For this reason, Nikephoros observes that God's justice will be particularly felt by the powerful of this world.[8]

Because of the reality of divine judgment, the patriarch asks that God be merciful to all those who have appeared ungrateful, or have acted profanely against the teachings and practices of the Church, and as a result, have brought upon their souls their own damnation. His remarks, addressed in the first person plural, reveal his own pastoral sensitivity. Without spitefully attacking his opponents, he presents an honest account of what already is known and believed to be true, as expressed in scriptural and Church teaching. Undeniably Byzantine in expression, his description of eschatology, in fact, reveals a forbearing character which is able to make room for God's mercy, but also to insist upon disclosing the incontrovertible state of affairs which awaits all, including the iconoclasts, if they continue in "the drunkenness of unbelief."[9]

Even though the patriarch does not present a detailed account of these eschatological events, what he does say is forceful and to the point. These events are reminders of what shall take place. For some, the eschatological reality is a source of hope and encouragement; for others, it serves as chastisement and a call to change their ways. Being the conclusion this life, eschatology is also the bridge which connects the Church on earth with the heavenly Jerusalem. For this reason, the last events are intimately ecclesiological in nature. Nikephoros is like other Eastern fathers in three further respects. First, descriptions of the future state which go beyond scriptural and Church teaching are avoided.[10] Second, that final judgment will come is accepted as an indisputable tenet of faith. Third, the fact that the final day has not arrived brings eschatology into the historical life of the Church. By positing itself as an ever-present reminder of things to come, eschatology becomes the pivotal stimulus for the Church's stance of expectation, vigilance, prayer, and perseverance.

## NOTES

1. *Logos* 537.

2. Ibid. 576,536,596.

3. Ibid. 573.

4. Ibid. 536-37. Even though Christ is not mentioned, this does not imply that the judge is other than the second person of the Trinity, the savior, as described in ibid. 668.

5. Ibid. 668.

6. Ibid. 537.

7. Ibid. 596.

8. Ibid. 557,560,577.

9. Ibid. 600.

10. Descriptions of an apocryphal nature, embellished with scenes of Christ as the inquisitor, and ideas of purgatory, retribution, treasury of the saints, are absent from Nikephoros' account. Significantly too, there is no reference to Revelation. Like his predecessors, he is cautious in interpreting this unparalleled book of eschatology.

# 16

# *Conclusion*

The theology of Patriarch Nikephoros is a defense of the faith. To assess his contribution as a polemicist, three issues must be examined: the reality of the theological problem, his unique theological contribution and achievement, and future influence and verdict.

## THE REALITY OF THE THEOLOGICAL PROBLEM

The complexity of the iconoclastic controversy must be acknowledged. Social, political, economic, cultural, and religious events interacted in such a way as to bring about an age of crisis which involved all levels of Byzantine society in a violent, bitter, and desperate struggle.[1] The importance which these elements had in shaping the character of the crisis cannot be overlooked. One, however, takes precedence: the question of whether to retain images. By becoming a doctrinal issue, this theological question was the primary factor which gave a sense of direction to what actually happened.

That an emperor placed iconoclasm officially on a legitimate pedestal suggests that the theological problem became a test case for Church-State relations. The period reveals that all too often an emperor attempted to increase his imperial prerogatives in order to assert his authority over the Church. The patriarch's unhappy exile is an affirmation that the test between what was normal imperial theological propriety and forceful assertion of increased prerogatives could not be resolved in his generation. The cooperative union between Church and State based upon the principle of respective interdependence became a test of Christian faith. It became increasingly evident that by the reign of Constantine V, as Meyendorff observes, "the issue was the defense, not of the Church as an institution, but of the Christian faith as the way to eternal salvation."[2] In this struggle the role of monasticism, and later, that of the secular clergy under the leadership of the moderate iconophile patriarchs Germanos, Tarasios, Nikephoros, and Methodios must not be underestimated.[3]

The iconophiles clearly saw the challenge of their iconoclast rulers as an attack against the person of Jesus Christ. Constantine V was a threat to the faith because there was no place in his reform for the kingdom of God, nor was there an accomodation in an imperial secular world for the incarnate Christ whose historical presence could be expressed visibly in image.[4] Nikephoros' identification of Constantine, the leader of iconoclasm, as Mamonas was not an accidental description; it was meant to be taken literally. The resolution for iconographic representation was to accept Christ's historical presence as a person. The hypostatic union was also the key to understanding the antinomy between the secular and ecclesiastical world. The reality of Christ became the theological justification for icon veneration, tested and fought for in the arena of imperial and ecclesial authority.

Expectedly, then, Nikephoros did not consider 'doing' theology an intellectual pastime. The Christian faith was at stake, and the danger of its possible demise was felt by the patriarch himself. In contrast to John Damascene, who writes in his preface to *Fount of Knowledge* : "As I have said, I shall add nothing of my own, but shall gather together into one those things which have been worked out by the most eminent of teachers and make a compendium of them, being in all things obedient to your [God's] command,"[5] Nikephoros senses an immediate need to defend the truth by responding to the charges made by both iconoclastic Synods of Hieria and Hagia Sophia. The opening paragraph of *Logos* captures the tone of this urgency. The task is to present a systematic and thorough demolition of the iconoclasts' position. Quoting Ecclesiastes 3.7: "a time to be silent, and a time to speak," the hierarch feels compelled to speak out now, lest future generations condemn him for not writing.[6] The reality of the theological problem was 'present-at-hand'.

## NIKEPHOROS' UNIQUE THEOLOGICAL CONTRIBUTION AND ACHIEVEMENT

The patriarch's condemnation of the iconoclasts presupposes that he first took their ability to argue against icon veneration seriously. There is no question that their argumentation, as Schmemann states, "was a very subtle, theologically well thought-out, rejection of the whole concept of the icon, which required the Church to exert its mind afresh, demanded creative effort and theological 'contemplation.'"[7] That they presented their case always with logical consistency may be regarded at best as a hyperbole.[8]

The iconoclasts' opposition to icon veneration may be summarized as follows. The use of images is a remnant of idolatrous pagan practices, condemned by the scriptures and Church fathers. An image, like any other physical object, cannot be a bearer of grace or a medium of sanctification. An image of Christ is not possible because it does not represent its archetype as 'both' God and man, since neither Christ's human nature can be divided or separated from the divine, nor can his divine nature be circumscribed. The only true image of Christ is the eucharist.

Admissible images of saints are not portable icons, but rather, their virtues which each Christian remembers and ought to imitate, and non-anthropomorphic symbols, as the plain cross, which are respected.[9]

Against this arsenal, the iconophiles did take a renewed look at the place of images in the Church. They justified image representation on the basis of Christian theology, drawing from scriptural and patristic evidence. Perhaps not enough credit has been rendered to them, especially to those theologians of the second iconoclastic period, for their theologically sharp and successful refutation. Meyendorff correctly acknowledges their contribution:

> In spite of its very great terminological accuracy in describing the veneration of icons, Nicaea II [Seventh Ecumenical Synod] did not elaborate on the technical points of Christology raised by the iconoclastic Council of Hiereia. The task of refuting this council and of developing the rather general Christological affirmations of Germanus and John of Damascus belongs to the two major theological figures of the second iconoclastic period...Theodore the Studite and Patriarch Nicephorus.[10]

Because he was the last known iconophile theologian, Nikephoros had an advantage over his predecessors, namely, he could draw from their writings and conclusions. The definition of the Seventh Ecumenical Synod and the works of the iconophile defenders gave the Church weapons which it had previously lacked.[11]

Largely through Nikephoros' efforts to justify icon veneration by Christ's hypostatic union, the Byzantine iconophiles can reaffirm the Antiochian contribution to Chalkedonian christology, and at the same time, return to the historical facts of the New Testament. The patriarch severed the doctrine of images from an iconoclastic theology, which was traceable back to monophysitism with its Origenistic accent of neoplatonic spiritualism,[12] and placed it in an uninterrupted continuation with Chalkedonian christology. This, then, should be remembered as his foremost achievement.

An appraisal of the patriarch's theological contribution must also include a critique of his methodology. As a theological polemicist, he displays unquestionable skill and the capacity for intense and sustained argumentation. Alexander summarizes:

> He is at his best where he can engage with his opponents in a duel of authoritative quotations. He takes delight in explaining what he believes to be the true meaning of a patristic text cited by his opponents, by referring to a parallel text of the same Church Father. He excels in casting doubt on the authenticity of an iconoclastic

> quotation by confronting it with another passage belonging unquestionably to the author to whom the Iconoclasts attributed the passage. Or finally, if the wording and attribution of the quotation do not permit either of these gentler approaches, he compares it with heretical passages and demonstrates its heterodox inspiration.[13]

Polemicists have not been known to represent their interlocutor's position with fairness. This is not the case with Nikephoros. Often he attempts to represent the iconoclasts' argument completely by drawing conclusions from their premises—something which perhaps they were unable to do. His sensitivity to do justice to their theses, though they are heretical, is exhibited by often including editorial corrections and securing authentic and complete manuscripts.[14]

If the patriarch's methodology can be judged positively, can the same be said of the originality of his thought? Alexander's critical remark: "on the negative side it must be admitted, however, that Nikephorus' works show little depth and originality," must be tempered.[15] Nikephoros is a polemicist. The tapestry of topics is interwoven with one thread in mind, image justification. His uniqueness lies in his ability to present theological themes in such a way as to support icon veneration.

The patriarch's attempt to insure icon veneration on a doctrinal basis is consistent with the iconophile position. He, in fact, follows the established lines of argumentation.[16] By drawing upon earlier patristic and synodal formulations, he is the direct descendant of the Church's orthodox thought, whose spring reaches back to Chalkedonian and Antiochian theology, to the Cappadocians and early Greek fathers, and finally, to the apostolic tradition. We must not suppose, however, that his achievement merely is a repetition of what had been formulated by his predecessors and no more. In important areas, the iconophile patriarch moves beyond the theses held by both John Damascene and Theodore Studites. A recovery of his theology through his writings elucidates Nikephoros' continuity, depth, and originality.

The patriarch's continuity with traditional formulations is seen in his understanding of trinitarian dogma; in his defense that the Triune God is the object of worship; in the identification of the second person as the natural and identical image of God the Father; in his anthropological formulations concerning man's unique position in creation as a divine-human relation between man and his creator, and as an image of God by adoption or by imitation; in his notion of the primordial state, Adam's sin, and the fall of man; and in his views of the eschatological reality.

Nikephoros' depth is found in his discussion of the world. The inseparable relationship between creation and creator is understood by God's divine attributes as they relate to the world. These reveal to us the work of a knowing and willing God. His discussion of the incorporeal world is an in-depth study of angelology.

The patriarch's originality can be summarized under several points within the larger context of his theological concerns. First, his appreciation for matter, not as something evil, but as part of creation through which man's salvation is worked, enables Nikephoros to see a cooperation between God the creator, man the artisan, and created matter. Together, these elements constitute the artistic product. The Cappadocian understanding of the character of the artisan, the purpose of his craft, and the finished artifact are brought together in a way which elucidates the dogmatic and philosophical distinctions between image and archetype, and the distinction between art and circumscription. Nikephoros' utilization of Aristotelian concepts in his aesthetics to describe the relation between art and circumscription is a unique addition to the iconophiles' arsenal of image justification.

Second, the patriarch's arguments for the circumscription and pictorial representation of Christ, together with his emphasis upon the mission of the savior in the world, are topics of christology and soteriology which form an original presentation directed to defending the iconographic depiction of Christ.

Third, Nikephoros does not add to what the Church teaches concerning ecclesiology. His originality consists, rather, in his ability to justify image representation on the basis of the dogmatic formula that the Church is "one, holy, catholic, and apostolic." His treatment of the Theotokos—an argument for defending the humanity of the Logos, and therefore, his iconographic representation—as well as his stirring descriptions of the martyrs and monks, exemplary members of the universal Church, are the basis for validating icon veneration.

Fourth, what is original in the patriarch's discussion of the sacraments is the distinction that he makes between image and archetype. More than either John Damascene or Theodore Studites, he emphatically asserts the categorical difference between the nature of an image and the eucharist. Whereas Christ is shown in the icons, in the eucharist he himself is the offerer and the One offered. The patriarch's unique contribution to the eucharistic doctrine during the second period of iconoclastic struggle is the reaffirmation of both the mystery of the sacrament and the 'real' presence of the archetype.

Fifth, Nikephoros' demonstration of the distinction between the cross and Christ's image is his own contribution against the iconoclasts' acceptance of 'non-anthropomorpic' symbols to replace image representations.

Sixth, the patriarch is sensitive to the historical development of Christian imagery and justifies it by ecclesiastical tradition which "the ancient Churches have given witness to and preached."[17] Beck correctly observes that Nikephoros "to a greater extent than John Damascene even, introduced this notion of tradition into the argumentation. The cult of images had to be lawful because it is the Church's tradition."[18] The historical continuity of icon veneration is validated in the patriarch's discussion of the parallelism between written and unwritten tradition. Icon veneration is derived from apostolic teaching, and therefore, from Christ. There is a continuation between the gospel of hearing and the gospel of seeing, of visual remembrance through the images.

Seventh, by recognizing that the faithful Christian is a bearer of tradition, the patriarch defends icon veneration uniquely by appealing to Christian character. The individual does not have to be told about images. Rather, the honor rendered to the prototype is derived from a Christian's instinctive desire for God and the things of God, and, finally, a burning zeal to express his piety through worship and veneration.

Eighth, Nikephoros' indictment of iconoclasm, as a heresy which lies outside of the Church, illustrates an original treatment of the problem of heresy and schism. Beck states: "For the first time there is decidedly encountered in Nicephorus the condemnation of Iconoclasm as an heretical political theology, which sought to substitute the image of the heavenly *Pantokrator*."[19] Unlike other iconophiles, he moves beyond rhetorical epithets of condemnation. His discussion of heresy and schism has the express purpose of showing the iconoclasts their heretical errors and the necessity of returning to the Church by following its orthodox teaching.

Nikephoros' originality, then, lies in his methodology as a theological polemicist, skillfully tightening, as it were, the reins of argumentation with mastery and brilliant erudition; but also, in the subject-matter which in one way or another exhibits continuity, depth, and oftentimes a unique working out of the problems faced by his predecessors.

## FUTURE INFLUENCE AND VERDICT

How influential was Nikephoros? There are two ways of approaching this question: first, through his own generation, and second, through our time. Alexander notes that the iconophile "was a tragic figure in more senses than one. This was due partly to circumstances, partly to his personality."[20] As a moderate hierarch, he was neither innovative nor dramatic in his policies; but neither was he afraid to stand resolutely when the orthodox faith was at stake. His exile bears witness to this strength of character.

Nikephoros' contemporaries measured his contribution in light of his banishment. He was a confessor (*homologetes*) of the faith by being a martyr in exile, a reconciler between iconophiles and iconoclasts, and a symbol of unity for both secular clergy and monastics.[21] But here lies the paradox. His generation overlooked, perhaps not intentionally, the patriarch's theological efforts in order to praise the sanctity of his life which reminded and inspired them for thirteen more years of persecution under Emperor Theophilos (829-42). Their devotion to him remained undiminished. When the restoration of the icons became a reality, the faithful without hesitation turned to honor their past iconophile patriarch as a saint-confessor of orthodoxy.

Nikephoros probably would have wished to be remembered more as the author whose work might have served as the basis for a future orthodox synod. He was not appraised as such by his contemporaries. As Alexander observes, this possibility, in fact, was never realized:

> From the point of view of the Council of 843 Nicephorus' literary works, learned and orthodox as they were, were unsuitable for the simple reason that they were directed against iconoclastic formulations of which one was obsolete (Constantine's writings) and the other only of ephemeral importance (the Council of St. Sophia). It is not surprising, therefore, that Nicephorus' works were but rarely copied and quoted and soon fell into oblivion.[22]

Even the modern nineteenth century editors of his works, as Turrianus, Mai, and Pitra, "destroyed the sequence of his argument by disarranging the order of some of his treatises."[23] To make matters worse, already from the tenth century some of the patriarch's works were attributed wrongly to Theodore Graptos (d. 838).[24]

Fortunately, Nikephoros' lot has changed. After centuries of literary oblivion, it is only now, in our generation, that we can begin to appreciate his contribution to the theology of the period.[25] If the patriarch's generation commended him as the confessor and martyr in exile, ours must recognize him as a father of the Church. We must reaffirm that sanctity of life and eminent erudition are inseparable characteristics of his personality. To speak of the triumph of the icons as the triumph of traditional orthodoxy, we must also acknowledge the contribution of Nikephoros, whose polemics, directed to the question of image justification, was a testing of the christological controversies of the earlier period and a reaffirmation of Chalkedonian theology. Just as important for Byzantine scholarship is the fact that he has preserved not only fragments of the lost works of Constantine V, but also the definition and *florilegium* of the iconoclastic Synod of Hagia Sophia, as well as quotations from otherwise lost Church fathers and heresiarchs.[26] This by itself constitutes an inestimable contribution toward a fuller understanding and appreciation of the relationship between the iconoclastic crisis and the earlier patristic tradition.

Patriarch Nikephoros of Constantinople received admiration and love from the faithful of his generation. Their respect continued undiminished for two decades after his death, and finally, came to fruition on 13 March 847 with the transfer of his holy relics back to Constantinople. A study of his theology as a defense of the faith, begun in our generation, has restored Nikephoros' rightful place as an important father of the Church. By seeing his influence comprehensively as patriarch, confessor and martyr in exile, and father of the Church, we may better appreciate the dual characterization presented by his hymnographer in the kontakion hymn which is chanted in Nikephoros' memory on 2 June: "As you have received from God the crown of victory from heaven today, O Nikephoros, save those who with faith honor you, as hierarch as well as teacher."[27]

## NOTES

1. Florovsky, "Origen," p. 77.

2. *Theology*, p. 51.

3. Meyendorff does not do justice to the role of the moderate iconophile patriarchs who suffered as much as their monastic brethren: "Whatever role was played in the Orthodox victory over the iconoclasts by high ecclesiastical dignitaries and such theologians as Patriarch Nicephorus, the real credit belonged to the Byzantine monks who resisted the emperors in overwhelming numbers"; ibid.

4. The assertion of imperial authority is substantiated by examining the Byzantine coins of the period. A comparison indicates a difference between the pre-iconoclastic and iconoclastic age. Under Justinian II (685-95; 705-11) the image of Christ is on the one side of the coin, whereas under Constantine V the emperor's portrait is on both sides; see W. W. Wroth, *Catalogue of the Imperial Byzantine Coins in the British Museum*, 2 (London, 1908), pls. 36 et seq.

5. *Πηγὴ γνώσεως*, PG 94.525; Frederic H. Chase, trans. *Saint John of Damascus Writings* in FC 37 (New York, 1958), p. 6.

6. *Logos* 533-36.

7. "Byzantium," p. 23.

8. "Whatever one's own theological predilections may be, it must be admitted that the iconoclasts presented the best possible case that could be made against the use of images. They omit nothing of importance that could be said on their side, and present their material with force, logic, and energy"; Anastos, "Argument," p. 188.

9. See ibid.

10. *Theology*, p. 46.

11. See Schmemann, "Byzantium," p. 26.

12. Responding to Constantia's request for a material image of Christ, Eusebios asserts that after Christ's resurrection and ascension, he could be seen in the mind only by those who were clean in the heart; *Antir. Eus.* 382-86.

13. *Nikephoros*, p. 228.

14. See *Antir. Eus.* and *Antir. Epiph.*

15. *Nikephoros*, p. 229.

16. For the iconophiles' view, see Sideris, "Position," pp. 210-26.

17. *Logos* 836.

18. "Church," p. 51.

19. Ibid.

20. *Nikephoros*, p. 225.

21. O'Connell, in contrast to Alexander, correctly underscores "the stature which Nicephorus during his period of exile acquired in the eyes of the orthodox faithful"; *Ecclesiology*, p. 52.

22. *Nikephoros*, p. 224. Alexander offers the following reason for Nikephoros' literary fate: "While the manuscript tradition of his contemporaries Theodore of Studios and Theophanes is rich and extensive, presumably because their works were tended with care and affection in their respective monasteries, the same cannot be said of the Patriarch"; p. 156. For a detailed account of the manuscript history concerning his works, see Blake, "Note," pp. 1-15; esp. pp. 4,14.

23. Alexander, *Nikephoros*, p. 229.

24. See Blake, "Note," p. 8. Both Theodore and his brother, Theophanes (d. 850), famous Palestinian hymnographers and monks, suffered under Theophilos' persecution (836) by being branded on the forehead, thus earning the name of 'inscribed' (*graptoi*); see John H. Rosser, "Theophilus 'The Unlucky' (829 to 842): A Study of the Tragic and Brilliant Reign of Byzantium's Last Iconoclastic Emperor" (Ph.D. dissertation, Rutgers University, 1972), pp. 83-85.

25. To make this assertion presupposes the pioneering efforts of the following scholars who have contributed to a revival of Nikephorian studies: Blake and Grumel in the investigation of the manuscript tradition; Alexander in the reconstruction of the historical period; and Ostrogorsky, Visser, Anastos, O'Connell, Schönborn, and Gero on some aspect of the patriarch's theology.

26. See *Epikr.*, *Antir. Eus.*, and *Antir. Epiph.*

27. *Menaion of June*, p. 8. The kontakion hymn as well as the canon was probably written by Theophanes; see G. Papadopoulos, *Symbolai*, p. 239.